~: Suitable for the Wilds

Dr Mary Percy Jackson

~: *Suitable for the Wilds*

Letters from Northern Alberta 1929–1931

EDITED WITH AN INTRODUCTION BY
Janice Dickin

UNIVERSITY OF
CALGARY
PRESS

© 2006 by Janice Dickin.

Published by the
University of Calgary Press
2500 University Drive NW
Calgary, Alberta, Canada T2N 1N4
www.uofcpress.com

We acknowledge the financial support
of the Government of Canada through
the Book Publishing Industry
Development Program (BPIDP), the
Alberta Foundation for the Arts and the
Alberta Lottery Fund—Community
Initiatives Program for our publishing
activities. We acknowledge the support
of the Canada Council for the Arts for
our publishing program.

Canada Council   Conseil des Arts
for the Arts   du Canada

Canada

ALBERTA
LOTTERY FUND

LIBRARY AND ARCHIVES OF CANADA
CATALOGUING IN PUBLICATION:

Jackson, Mary Percy
  Suitable for the wilds : letters from
Northern Alberta, 1929–1931 / Mary
Percy Jackson ; edited with introduction
by Janice Dickin. – 2nd ed.

(Legacies shared, 1498-2358 ; 17)
ISBN-10: 1-55238-169-2
ISBN-13: 978-1-55238-169-4

  1 Jackson, Mary Percy–
     Correspondence.
  2 Frontier and pioneer life–Peace
     River Region (B.C. and Alta.).
  3 Women physicians–Peace
     River Region (B.C. and Alta.)–
     Correspondence.
  4 Physicians–Peace River Region
     (B.C. and Alta.)–Correspondence.
  5 Keg River Region (Alta.)–
     Biography.
  6 Alberta, Northern–Biography.
  7 Peace River Region (B.C. and
     Alta.)–Biography.
  I Dickin, Janice
 II Title.
III Series.

FC3693.25.J33A4 2006
971.23′102′092
C2006-900190-1

Cover design, Mieka West.
Internal design & typesetting,
  Jason Dewinetz.

∞ This book is printed on Rolland Enviro
  Natural 100 PCW. Printed and bound in
  Canada by AGMV Marquis.

~: Contents

*To Jean Bartlett Dickin and Jessie Litle Heath
and to the homesteaders of the Battle River Country.*

"All my really interesting clothes – beaded moccasins and gloves, leather chaps, moose-hide coat, etc. – are only suitable for the wilds."

Dr Mary Percy
26 December 1930

❧ Preface to the Second Edition

Since the University of Toronto let the first edition of Mary Percy Jackson's letters go out of print in 2003, both her family and I have fielded frequent requests for copies. This second edition reproduces the entire text of the first edition and includes an extensive interview with her from 1994, as well as a few new photographs and an epilogue which takes her life to its end at age 95 on 6 May 2000. There is also an index, which the first edition was rightfully criticized for excluding.

I have made no attempt here to update either the scholarship or the popular material on Dr. Jackson which sprang up after the appearance of the first edition in 1995 and the National Film Board documentary, "Wanted! Doctor on Horseback" in 1996. Both scholarly and popular attention have been considerable and show every promise of increasing over time. It would no doubt please Mary to find herself written about by an Australian scholar (Maggie MacKellar, *Core of my Heart, My Country*, Melbourne University Publishing, 2004). It would no doubt please her more to find a colorful child's drawing of "DR. MARY PERCY JACKSON Alberta's Adventurous Doctor." on the internet (Calgary Board of Education, *cbe.ab.ca/ict/2learnw/jcreid/famousalbertans*). Although Mary always made it clear to me that she did not consider herself a feminist and indeed disapproved of us, I am sure the woman who relished "beating all those men" by taking top marks in medical school would have appreciated the fact that the third grade girl who crayoned the picture did not qualify her subtitle with the words "Lady" or "Woman" or "Female."

Mary also would have enjoyed learning that on 3 February 2005, she was named the first of 100 recipients of the Physician of the Century program initiated as part of Alberta's Centennial of Organized Medicine (*www.medicine100.ab.ca*). She had received many accolades and much attention at various times previously in her life but the 1995 publication of her letters by an important scholarly press and, probably more importantly, a beautifully filmed documentary by the world famous NFB the following year, made her accessible in a way she had never been before. As she complained to the director of *Wanted!*, Claire Helman, "I was living a perfectly quiet life up here until this woman came into it," gesturing to me. When I had first come to interview her in 1992, she apologized for the long pauses she took in speaking. This was not, she assured me, due to any slowness of intellect, but rather to living her life pretty much in isolation. She didn't talk to many people very much, aside of course from family and friends who kept close tabs on her.

Mary's complaint about me ruining her private life was of course disingenuous. She took pride in all this attention but this should not be mistaken as merely personal. She took considerable pride in the northern community she committed more than seven decades to. She knew the depth of her own knowledge about many things and came from a generation when doctors were expected to be active community leaders and very often were. She also had tremendous respect for the astoundingly broad array of people in her life via whom she had garnered this knowledge. She assessed everyone and everything but she was not, in the negative meaning of the word, judgmental. She took a keen interest in her life, in her surroundings and in people. I'll never forget arriving for the second film shoot for the documentary and finding her dressed in the same clothes she had worn for the first shoot. She explained that she thought that would be important in editing the two different segments of filming into one whole! I was delighted. One of the questions I had had to address when I was initiating a documentary on a 90 year old woman was whether she "still had all her marbles." I replied that she indeed did and she had a few of mine as well. It is only as I write this that I realize how much this incident told about her attention to detail, a vital part of her legendary diagnostic abilities.

The first edition of this book would not have been possible without the active participation of Dr. Mary Percy Jackson. This second edition would not have been possible without the patience and participation of Anne Vos, who welcomed me into her home in June 2004 and provided me with material on the last few years of Mary's life. Anne's daughter, Mary Lou Ng, has also been a great help, not least of all by establishing internet contact. Their one request regarding the new material added, the interview, is that patient names be omitted. I have complied with that request.

◦ Preface to the First Edition

Books require not only material but pattern. In the introduction to these letters, I have chosen to insert myself very obviously into the narrative. This is not a decision I can see myself making in other circumstances. I have done so here in order to be able to make a number of points. One of these is that the northern Peace River country is still distant and isolated, even to fellow Albertans. Another is that dealing with a subject such as this – getting access to the material, gaining the confidence of the person whose story it is – requires something beyond the basics taught in methodology courses. Yet another is that, in seeking to retell this story, I had to be constantly aware of my own status as a greenhorn in this culture, educated and sophisticated though I may be judged on other grounds. Lastly, I sought to tell the story of how I do my work. In doing so, I meant to present a parallel to Dr. Percy Jackson's descriptions of how she did hers. In short, just as her letters tell the adventures of a doctor, my Introduction tells the adventures of a historian. This strategy is meant to show continuity in women's lives. It is meant to illustrate why we choose the work we do and why we live the lives we lead and what we can find in common about those fundamental choices.

Thanks are due a number of individuals. I would like to thank most of all Dr. Mary Percy Jackson, who took me into her home as well as her life. It goes without saying that this project could not have been accomplished without her. I am also grateful to the Hannah Institute for the History of Medicine, which twice provided travel funds so that I could get to Keg River and also provided a subvention for the publication of this book. The Faculty of General Studies at the University of Calgary picked up small administrative costs.

I owe many people in terms of encouragement and audience feedback. I have read from these letters on several public occasions and have received comments which have proved very useful in terms of deciding how to proceed. I am also grateful for the comments of Jim Connor, Elspeth Cameron, and the anonymous readers of the manuscript.

Two researchers helped with the project: Lyn Landreville and Marie Rajic, both of whom evidenced considerable ferreting skills. Cliff Kadatz of the University of Calgary sketched the rough maps. From University of Toronto Press, I thank Rob Ferguson and Gerry Hallowell, who saw the manuscript through to completion, and Laura Macleod, who did much of the early work.

And for their past and future support, I thank my guys, David, Leopold, and Anatol.

Janice Dickin
Calgary, Alberta
September 1994

↶ Introduction to the First Edition

In my copy of the first published version of these letters, which came out in 1933 under the title *On the Last Frontier: Pioneering in the Peace River Block: Letters of Mary Percy Jackson*,[1] is tucked a note to my mother from her best friend, dated 24 January 1975. Jessie wrote:

> Dear Jean:
> I enjoyed these letters very much, they were so descriptive. I'd like to know what became of Dr. Jackson. There should have been a little bit added to tell where she eventually settled.

I can well imagine the relish with which these women shared this book. Both nurses, both spirited, they must have found irresistible the lively accounts by this pioneer doctor who was at once older and younger than they – born before them but preserved by her writings in a state of eternal exuberant youth.

Perhaps this volume was given to me, perhaps I simply purloined it in much the same way either Jessie or Jean laid hands on it in the first place. It is clearly stamped inside as being the property of The Synod of the Diocese of Calgary and I have no doubt it simply forgot to return itself to the tiny library in the little prairie church in which my father served. Whether as gift or loot, it does make some sense that the book should have ended up in my hands. In the mid-1970s, I was working towards a Ph.D. with the history of Canadian medicine as my focus. Doctors' letters and similar documents were my meat.

Even then, I wanted to see these letters republished. I, too, wanted to find out what had happened to Dr. Jackson. I considered briefly how to track her down and made general notes for an introduction. Then, I wrote my dissertation, taught, had two children, completed a law degree, articled, practiced, returned to academe and somehow it was 1991.

I had, in the interim, found out where Dr. Jackson had settled. I had always assumed she had returned to England, as she seems destined to do by all indications from the published letters. But in December 1983, my newspaper informed me that a Dr. Mary Percy Jackson of Keg River had been awarded the Alberta Order of Excellence. I note that I have scrawled this fact on the brown paper bag in which I keep the remnants of my *Letters*, along with the comment, "She's Alive!" Three years later, I even found out what she looked like. The Calgary *Herald* printed her picture along with the convocation address she had given in 1976 when accepting an Honorary Doctor of Laws degree from the University of Alberta.[2] I was getting closer to doing something about this project but I was not yet there.

By the time I was ready, I had absolutely resigned myself to the certainty that Dr. Jackson had surely passed on. For things to be otherwise seemed impossibly good luck. I had come home from a biography conference held in Edinburgh in May 1991 in a mood to celebrate the existence of women. I had it in mind to seek out and make available sources that allowed them to talk about their own lives. Dr. Jackson seemed the obvious place to start. I contacted the Alumni Association at the University of Alberta, which provided me with her last known address. I wrote to it in mid-July, in the hope that someone or other would answer. A few days later, I had the eerie experience of receiving a letter from a woman so many of whose letters I had already read.

Within the month, we had our first lengthy telephone conversation. During that call, I learned that the published *Letters* were not full versions and that she had copies of the originals. She also told me that since these were letters to her parents, she had left things unsaid. Clearly a trip to Keg River was in order. I sought and received funding from the Hannah Institute for the History of Medicine and arranged to travel north.

I visited Dr. Jackson in Keg River in February 1992. I flew to Peace River and landed in bitter cold. The rental agency had thoughtfully left the car running for me. I had packed a candle and some cookies and water in case I had trouble on the road. I kept my suitcase in the car with me in case I had to pile on all my clothes to keep warm.

I started up the modern highway which follows the route over which Dr. Jackson took patients out to hospital. A hundred kilometres up the road is Manning, the modern town built in the river valley where her shack once stood. I still had another hundred kilometres to drive before, according to her map, I was to turn west, go 14 kilometres up a gravel road, go past the cemetery on my left and turn down the long drive to a two storey house which even in the dead of winter I could see was set down in the midst of an English country garden.

The flat land was broken by brush and trees, the snow so cold it squeaked under my tires, the sky the weight and color of a Kurelek painting. Dr. Jackson was waiting for me. I had lost my nerve just before the turn-off out her sideroad and had gone back to reaffirm her directions at the only edifice I could recall seeing since Manning. Dr. Jackson drives this highway all the time and I had found it laughable when she expressed concern that I might find it daunting. I told her that I was a good driver, curiously offering her as evidence of my expertise the fact that I once drove alone and non-stop from Vancouver, B.C. to Schreiber, Ontario.

But I had never before been in a place at once so unpopulated and so dangerously cold. The road was excellent but if the car had broken down or I had taken it over the shoulder, I could have been in trouble. True, several lumber trucks thundered past but these offered more terror than reassurance – they kicked up snow which made it impossible to see. The white-out seemed to last an eternity. The only thing to do was to steer straight and pray. It was clear that a car passing from the other direction would never see me, nor I it. Kindly – and no doubt recognizing a tenderfoot when she saw one – the woman at the gas station at Keg River Cabins called ahead to inform Dr. Jackson that her visitor had been sighted. With Dr. Jackson's help, I abandoned my car behind her much smaller one in an out-building and went into her warm house for a welcome lunch and the beginnings of three days of work and conversation.

I could hardly complain about the cold. I had chosen to visit in February precisely in order to experience it. Cold is a major player in the *Letters*. As Dr. Jackson says at the onset of her first winter, "the cold descends on this land like a shadow." Her adaptation to that cold can be traced through the letters. She learned how to keep her shack warm at night (rising every few hours to restock the stove), to make long trips in temperatures far below zero (four to a sleigh, lying on backs, wrapped to chins, feet on communal footwarmer, eyes to the stars), to dress (moosehide, especially moccasins), to melt snow for water (warning:

put water in bottom of bucket first or it will taste burnt). And when it really was too cold to do anything, she learned to just sit back and wait the weather out.

I also had a taste of the isolation which is another major player in the *Letters*. Geographically, she was thousands of kilometres from the busy streets of Birmingham, where she had studied for many years, and from the quieter streets of nearby Dudley, where she had lived since birth. She was more than 500 kilometres from Edmonton, the closest location offering the theatre and concerts she was used to. She was about 100 kilometres from the nearest hospital, often tens of kilometres from her patients, and lived alone in a shack in a valley more than a kilometre from her nearest neighbor.

Personally, she was set apart in this new community in terms of her sex, her education, her class and her culture. On top of all that, she was largely cut off from contact with people back home: there were theoretically only eight mails a year – three in winter, five in summer – although people often found other ways of getting letters in or out. Any way you look at it, Mary Percy was on her own. None of this seemed to daunt her. As she has said in a recent interview, she felt "tremendously alone but not lonely."[3]

Dr. Jackson still lives alone. She has family and friends in the area, a dog, a cat, books, music and a satellite dish tuned to Montreal so that she can watch the news early and retire in time to listen to her favorite CBC programs. She still travels, speaks occasionally at public events, gardens and despairs whether she will ever succeed in sorting out the physical remains of a busy life – documents and photographs – which have attached themselves to her. Her house is warm and comfortable and inviting and she looked after me as I imagined in my childhood fantasies the real Granny cared for Little Red Riding Hood.

After lunch, I was installed in a large stuffed chair by the fireplace in the living room. I had a lamp, I had a footstool, I had the letters. I also had someone to tend the fire. At mysterious intervals, Dr. Jackson would come in, poke the logs, make a judgement as to what type of wood was needed at this juncture (a revelation to someone who had never needed to know that different woods burn differently), and go off to fetch the necessaries. She would also invariably urge me during these inspection tours to take a chocolate from the box on the table. "Eat this. The brain runs on glucose." I was very happy.

The *Letters* as published are very good. In the original form, they are wonderful. I was entranced and made heavy notes, still not sure whether Dr. Jackson would let me carry them away. I became terribly involved with the young woman on the pages and kept thinking how very much I would like to meet her. Then, it would dawn on me that I was about to go in and have lunch with her in a few minutes.

It is a great privilege to meet someone at the simultaneous ages of 25 and 88, especially when one is currently somewhere in the middle, wondering how much of what one is now will be useful in old age. I found this time with Dr. Jackson therapeutic. I enjoyed her company at both stages of her life tremendously. The Olympics were on T V and we would chat through them at lunch, cheerfully disagreeing with the assessments of the commentators. I would then go back to my fire and letters and chocolates, only to re-emerge at dinner for more Olympics, conversation, and one night, moose meat. I learned much – simply through chatting, no notes or tape recorder yet – and she produced other material about her life, written by herself and others. The evenings together in the dining room or the living room or the kitchen were lovely.

When I left, I took her only copy of her letters with me. I had told her I could not justify republishing the edited version, knowing that the originals were so much better and still in existence. There was no place to photocopy them nearer than Manning, possibly Peace River. She admonished me to take care of them. It would be a pity, she said, to lose them after more than 60 years. I was very grateful for her trust. Historians so often deal only with the dead or the anonymous. It is a great concession for the living to allow us to invade their reality.

It was still bitterly cold when I left. I had walked up to the cemetery the second day for air and exercise and my camera had frozen up before I could get a picture of the house. Driving back, I was much more confident on the road and ready to pay more attention to the topography. I was particularly on the look-out for a spot on the Meikle River. I had noted the beauty of this valley on my tense drive up. Dr. Jackson told me where to look to see the spot where her and her husband's garage had been. I thought at first that she meant garage, as in the place where they got their car repaired. She meant garage, as in where they stored it. There was for years no real road for cars north of the valley and no suitable way across the river. To get to their car to drive to Peace River or Edmonton or some other town to the south, they had to pack out on horses for two days. It rather put in perspective my trip from aeroport to her home in a heated rental car.

This time, I stopped to look around Manning and to find the spot where her shack had stood. I checked out the steep riverbanks which figured so largely in her efforts to get out to her patients. And I wondered at the town which had grown up to obliterate all traces of its frontier birth, really so few years before.

I spent that night in Peace River. Dr. Jackson often wrote letters from there and I wanted to get some feel for the town. In particular, I wanted to see the McNamara Hotel where she sometimes stayed. As it turned out, that hostelry – since burned to the ground – no longer seemed the sort of place a respectable matron like myself would feel safe on a Saturday night. Instead, I ate in a Greek restaurant on main street and retired to my modern motel which was noisily hosting a curling bonspiel. The next morning, it started to thaw. I spent the few hours before my flight scrambling through softening snow on sidestreets, generally exploring, and later walking over to the Peace River Centennial Museum and Archives to ask about their facilities for preserving documents.

This thaw continued as singlemindedly and rapidly as I had been led to believe from the letters. A few days after I left, ice backed up on the Peace, putting under water much of the territory I had walked. The little bridge I had crossed to get to the archives had disappeared, the museum and archives certainly inundated. But by that point I was back in Calgary, going about my safe scholarly life. First, I copied the letters and put the originals on the bus to Keg River. Then I turned to the pleasant task of editing the letters I had thought about for so long and of setting them in the sort of context, the absence of which Jessie had lamented to Jean.

It's rather a simple matter to tell "what became of Dr. Jackson." She married an expatriate Englishman like herself who had come to Alberta with his family as a boy. He had moved with his first wife to the Keg River area in 1919, set on establishing a cattle ranch. Over the years, he would learn what he could and could not do to make that type of enterprise a success in this unknown and unmapped territory. In the meantime, he worked as a fur trader.[4] Frank Jackson shows up all through Mary Percy's letters home. He was one of the men she met on the D.A. Thomas steamship on her way down the river. His wife was the Mrs.

Jackson dead from childbirth that October. And towards the end, he shows up in several seemingly unrelated guises as the man who lends Dr. Percy his car, the patient with the septic hand, the dinner companion for whom she almost fails to roast the chicken and the handyman who builds her cupboards. He also developed a habit of bringing down patients for her from the north. They married 10 March 1931 in the Mountie's House in Battle River and she moved north with him to Keg River to share his life, help raise his two older sons (the third – Frank, jr. – was raised by his mother's parents), have a daughter and son of her own, keep a practice running for which there was much need but little cash, take up a leading role in the community and live a happy life.

It is significant that these letters end in January 1931. At first, she was busy arranging for the disposition of her personal life and her practice, then she moved to a place where there really *were* only eight mails a year and precious few people coming or going to carry letters out by other means. The story of her life after making this move can be found in *The Homemade Brass Plate*, written in the first person and pulled together from the *Letters*, other documents and interviews.[5] In it, she described her life since her husband died in 1979 and was buried in the midst of his family and flowers from his own garden.

> After Frank died there didn't seem to be much point in going on. But I decided to stay in the same old log house in which we had lived for such a long time. As long as I was able to garden and keep the house moderately clean, it seemed the best place to be. A one-bedroom apartment would have been a lot less work, but it would not have had the memories that this house has.
>
> Here I am using the furniture that Frank made even before I met him, and the furniture he made after we were married. He built the house. It is very old-fashioned – it does not have any modern elegance – but I like it.
>
> I still have the little greenhouse that Frank added to the house the year of our silver wedding anniversary. I can still grow cucumbers and tomatoes in there, as well as start all the bedding plants that I need for the flower

beds and for the huge vegetable garden. It keeps me
working.

My friends and neighbours, indeed the whole
community, are all very kind to me, and when they
come to visit I enjoy talking with them to find out what
has happened to all my old friends.[6]

The question of *why* this became of her is more complicated and is embedded in the factors which brought her to the Peace in the first place.

Mary Percy Jackson was born in 1904 in Dudley, near Birmingham.[7]
Her mother was a teacher, her father a director of the same woollen
manufacturing company he started working for at 15 and retired from
at 75. Mary's parents educated their two daughters as well as their two
sons and her father early argued in favor of a legal career for her. He felt
it suited her spirit. The legal profession, however, was closed to women
at that point, while medicine – thanks to the efforts of pioneers such
as Edith Pechey-Phipson (1845–1908) and Elizabeth Garrett Anderson
(1836–1917)[8] – could offer role models. Women had also for some time
made inroads into the medical profession in North America as well.[9]

Despite the growing visibility of women doctors, Mary had never
met any by the time she formed her desire, at age 10 or 11, to follow that
path and has stated that she has no idea where she got the idea from.[10]
It is tempting, however, to imagine that the heavy casualties of the
Great War played some part in her decision. At any rate, it seems to
have been a firm resolution and one taken seriously by her family. One
consequence of this was that there was no insistence that she learn to
cook. It was expected that, as a doctor, she would always earn enough
to be able to afford domestic help. A second reason was that there was
little food to risk on amateurs during the war. As one encounters Mary's
adventures in food preparation throughout the letters, one sympathizes
with this decision.

Instead, Mary had plenty of time to practice the piano and to study.
She certainly took her schoolwork seriously. As a student in the medical program at Birmingham University, from which she graduated in
1927, she won the Queen's Prize as the best all-round student. She
told me that winning the prize was one thing, beating "all those men"
was better: it made all those mornings of getting up to study at 5 a.m.
worthwhile.

Some of "those men" had served in the Great War. Sometimes, when they were unwilling to tear themselves away from a bridge game, she would bow to their requests that she take over their shifts, gaining extra experience. She also said that some of the professors assigned the women students the most difficult tasks, on the grounds that if women wanted medical degrees, they should be forced to earn them. When I asked her whether she had any doubts about being able to do her job in the isolation of northern Alberta, she said that on the contrary, she felt that she had received excellent training, thanks to such discriminatory practices.

If Mary's confidence was increased by success in the face of adversity, it also found support in a general shift in British society brought about by the Great War. Part of that shift was due to the fact that so many men returned from that conflict damaged or not at all. She was not the only woman whose options would be changed because of the absence of men to fill the traditional roles of family supporter and paid worker. Women moved into new areas of employment and activity. En masse, this freer female earned the name "the New Woman," a designation alluding to feminism through personal acts, if not actual political consciousness.[11]

As part of its luggage, this phrase carried the idea that the world was opening up to women, offering opportunity and adventure. Mary responded to both these calls. At first, she was interested in a posting to the Women's Hospital in Calcutta. Due to both demographic and cultural reasons – women having many babies and taboos against male doctors touching them – a couple of years in Calcutta would have given Mary obstetrical experience the equivalent of several years' practice in England.[12] This appointment, however, was made only every third year and she had a year to kill. Years later, when asked by an interviewer whether her parents were not alarmed at her decision to take a posting to the Canadian frontier, Mary reminded her that she *had* been planning on going to India.

Her decision to go north, rather than south, came as the result of an advertisement in February 1929, carried in the *British Medical Journal*. It was, in effect, sending out a call for "New Women." The job offered was "country work in Western Canada." The candidates sought were "Strong energetic Medical Women with post-graduate experience in Midwifery." The contact was Dr. E.M. Johnstone, care of the Fellowship of the Maple Leaf.

Dr. Emma Mary Johnstone was a 1910 graduate of Edinburgh University. Although she served as house surgeon in a London hospital for a period, she later trained and specialized for a number of years in psychiatry.[13] Born in India, where her father had worked in an administrative position for a rajah, she decided to become a doctor at age 16 and clearly came from an adventurous family. She had a brother who had relocated to Quebec City. She claimed that, on a visit to see him, she was so charmed by the fresh air and maple trees that she vowed to come back. Her return in 1927 was sparked by a conversation with the secretary of the British Medical Association who had recently returned from Canada and told her about the great need for doctors in the remoter areas of settlement. Of particular concern to Dr. Johnstone were British war brides living in isolation.

She first tried to work in Saskatchewan but the authorities there refused to grant her a medical licence. She next tried Alberta, where she encountered no problems in obtaining registration but received no firm indication as to where she should go to be of service. All anyone seemed to be able to tell her was that there was "great need." Eventually, she was introduced by Prof. E.A. Corbett of the University of Alberta to the Honorable George Hoadley, at that time Alberta's minister in charge of health. Alberta already had a District Nursing Program, established in 1919 to send resident nurses (often World War I veterans) to remote communities.[14] Hoadley sent Johnstone to replace the nurse at Wanham (about half-way between Peace River and Grande Prairie), who was due for a vacation. Only for this one replacement period was Johnstone paid by the government. She would arrange to stay in the community on the promise of the people in the district to provide her with a house and with fuel. Sometimes she was given food. There was no money for drugs. Otherwise she subsidized herself at Wanham and later at Wandering River (about 60 km. northwest of Lac La Biche) from her small private income, saying "I was prepared to give whatever I had."

No doubt directly due to this experience with Johnstone, Hoadley conceived the idea of recruiting "medical women" for service in the rapidly developing northern part of the province. The Peace River country[15] was undergoing a new phase in its development. Its early history of exploitation by the European economic system came at the hands of fur traders. Later there would be a small spin-off of miners, some of whom had come specifically to the Peace looking for minerals, some of whom had simply given up on the difficult route from Edmonton to the Yukon gold fields. There were also Roman Catholic missionaries, intent on bringing solace to the Indian and Metis populations whose lives bore the impact of white forays into their land of forest and muskeg and prairie.[16]

None of these earlier economic mainstays required the committed input of white women. Homesteading did. What was needed was the establishment of communities and of families and homes to make up those communities: women's work. Women's work included the bearing of children, which could be dangerous. And children, particularly young ones, created their own medical emergencies – especially in an era when serious infectious diseases were still common and miracle drugs unheard of, and especially in an area where weather was harsh and conditions rough. Mary's letters make mention of women who refused to move onto the homesteads their husbands were proving up until proper medical attention was available. Fear sparked by lack of medical care was a frontier phenomenon characteristic not only of Peace River. The first two women doctors to practice on the Canadian prairies took their medical degrees precisely so that they could look after their own children.

Charlotte Whitehead Ross moved her children with her from Montreal to study medicine in Philadelphia from 1870 to 1875. Her fifth child was born three months before her graduation. For years, her husband built railroads in the west and only came home (obviously, regularly) on visits. Only after she had completed her medical training and he had settled in one place did they feel safe in bringing the family west. In 1881, she moved to Whitemouth, Manitoba where she practiced for 30 years. Despite a number of miscarriages, her own children would eventually number eight, the last born just before her fiftieth birthday. She lost one son to pneumonia. Judging that there was nothing more she could do for her own child, she was away at the time of his death, delivering another woman's baby.

Dr. Elizabeth Scott Matheson of Onion Lake, Saskatchewan already had a family in the west when she left them in the care of her missionary husband and the community in order to travel east, first to the Manitoba Medical College – which she left due to pregnancy with her third child – and later to Toronto. She received her degree from

Trinity College at the University of Toronto in 1898. Refusing to take an exam she had reason to believe was not asked of male graduates of Trinity, she was denied a licence to practice by the government of the North West Territories. She practiced anyway. After all, her patients were either her own children or people exceedingly happy to have any help at all. However, after civilization in the form of the Barr colonists began to flood into the area, Dr. Matheson decided to return to take her final year of medicine over again, this time at the University of Manitoba. By this time, she had four children. Again, she was denied registration, despite the fact that she had taken the precaution of registering in Manitoba immediately after her graduation in 1904. According to Carlotta Hacker, Dr. Matheson's famous missionary husband was so enraged by this further refusal that he wrote the cheque for the registration fee and told her to send it off. The licence came in the mail. Hacker speculates that Dr. Matheson, refused registration on the strength of her credentials, was granted it on the strength of her husband's signature. She would practice until 1918.[17]

The same problems that faced other women on other frontiers faced women moving into the Peace country. These problems find their statistical picture in high infant and maternal mortality rates for frontier areas. Canada in general was alarmed by the high death rate among the women it depended upon to repopulate the post-war, post-flu nation. This concern found expression in media ranging from government policy to public consciousness. It constituted one very strong reason for the establishment of the federal Department of Health in 1919 and the officer in charge of overseeing maternal and child health – Dr. Helen MacMurchy – would gain an international reputation as a reformer.[18] The popular press conveyed the same concerns to the general population. Maternal mortality rates, especially, were covered in regular newspapers[19] and women's magazines.[20]

Mary would come armed with the knowledge that rural areas in Canada had a maternal mortality rate three times that of Britain. To draw the figures into perspective, it was more than thirty times the Alberta rate of the 1970s.[21] In response, pressure was brought on the provincial government, especially by the Women's Institutes and the United Farm Women of Alberta, to get help into areas that had no doctors. In 1919, the Public Health Nurses Act was passed, establishing the District Nurses system and granting these women the right to deliver babies where no doctor was available.[22] Maternal mortality remained a concern of the Alberta Department of Public Health all through the 1920s.[23] But while identifying a concern was easy, finding a solution was not. Competing with forward-looking health policies meant to ameliorate conditions were aggressive population initiatives which inexorably made them worse.

In short, Alberta was moving in ways which made its health problems even more manifold by seeking to move people into frontier areas it already knew itself incapable of servicing. Following in the tradition of "boosterism" which had earlier sought to lure settlers and investment to the southern prairies, Peace River promotional material promised free land and plentiful water, favorable climate and good transportation.[24] If the literature produced was not exactly a fabric of lies it was certainly a fantasy of half-truths. By the late 1920s, some early homesteaders had already given up and moved out. The European-style house mentioned in the letters where Mary found a family of Metis living – and sitting on the floor rather than on the furniture – may very well have been one of the substantial structures illustrated in these pamphlets. This propaganda was irretrievably male in its orientation. Although there were brief mentions of churches and community halls, schools and hospitals, they were clearly not of prime concern. And, like everything else in this literature, their availability and accessibility were overblown. For women given the job of "civilizing" the frontier, such misleading propaganda was particularly harmful.

It is not surprising then that Hoadley, as Minister of Public Health, responded so promptly and so warmly to Dr. Johnstone's offer to be of service. Typically, he not only made use of her talents as a doctor but turned his fertile mind to putting her to use to attract more of her kind. The solution would involve a partnership between the provincial government and a religious organization, brought together through the person of Emma Mary Johnstone.

Dr. Johnstone came to Canada under the auspices of the Fellowship of the Maple Leaf.[25] This organization was established earlier in the century through the efforts of Reverend George Exton Lloyd, an English-born, Canadian-educated churchman who came west in 1903 as chaplain to the Barr colony to settle along the Saskatchewan/Alberta border, near what is now the city of Lloydminster. Lloyd was committed to strengthening the Anglican church in Saskatchewan but was held back in this by the unavailability of clergy. His solution was to recruit lay workers from Britain through the Maple Leaf Workers, founded in 1903 by his sister, a Mrs. Stamford. The first Sunday school teachers were sent out in 1907, followed by regular teachers. Feeling that even more was needed, Lloyd returned to England and, in 1916, established a separate church society. Under his personal care, the Fellowship began to expand; when he returned to Saskatchewan in 1922 as bishop of that diocese, the link was firmly established. He left behind as his assistant in England, the Reverend P. J. Andrews, another Englishman with Canadian connections and the man who would undertake the first edition of Mary's letters.

Lloyd's intention to recruit men as well as women was blocked by the War. He found instead a supply of women seeking, according to Marilyn Barber, "employment, adventure and service."[26] They were in fact New Women in a traditional women's field: the mission field.[27] The school teachers worked in government schools, dispensing education and anglo-acculturation. The Sunday school teachers not only taught religion but handled the sort of service work that traditionally fell to the minister's wife. Interestingly, the most complete document published pertaining to one of these women is also from the Peace River, albeit on the British Columbia side of the border. Monica Storrs was a Fellowship-paid church worker in the Fort St. John area who for ten years followed the practice of sending reports in the form of a diary home from the mission field to be circulated for use in raising recruits and funds.

The first two years of Storrs' diaries overlap the time covered by Mary's letters and have been published as *God's Galloping Girl*.[28] The temptation is to treat these two sets of letters alike but there are very real differences between them. The purposes they were written for are quite distinct. While both sought to keep contact with home and to keep a record for the writer, Monica's were meant to make a point to an audience of people unrelated to her. Mary's were meant for people who knew and cared for her on a personal basis. Her father had his secretary type each one in sextuplicate. The copies were then circulated among family and friends. This way everyone got the full story, rather than bits and pieces. In one letter, Mary expressed surprise at discovering this but the plan must have been all along to circulate them in some fashion: there is little of the repetition one would expect in letters sent to different people at close time intervals.

There are also distinct differences in emphasis between the letters of Storrs and those of Percy. Monica's emphasize the good work being done, particularly in terms of raising the standard of "civilization." It was her job to judge behavior and to change it. Mary was much more free to complain, to joke and to make honest assessments of people and how they chose to live their lives. She made mischievous remarks about moonshine and over-eager policemen, about dancing into early morning and giving up frocks for chàps. She was anything but earnest.

In his attempt to make her fit into the literary tradition useful to him, Canon Andrews edited her letters to much closer approximations of missionary tracts. Andrews learned about the existence of the letters on Mary's first trip back to England in 1931. Neither Mary nor the family seems to have been involved in the decisions regarding this first edition. They seem to have been happy to let Andrews do what he thought was needed. As they stand, the original letters are still engaging: it would take a heavier hand than Andrews' to hide Mary's light under a bushel. And to give him credit, his sins were those of omission rather than commission. He took words out of her mouth but he resisted putting them in. It is understandable though that, as they appear in this full edition, they read better and give a much sharper impression of the woman and the country.

In making his decisions about what to leave out, Andrews did not remove Mary's British nativism. Her nativism in fact fit right into the agenda of the Fellowship. In her letters, it shows up first in her hopes expressed on shipboard that she not have to practice among foreigners. Its most startling manifestation is her encounter on a train with J.J. Maloney, an Orangeman who toured Alberta for the Ku Klux Klan.[29] She not only accepted uncritically his comments on the dangerous machinations of the Roman Catholic church, she went off to dinner with him. She also bore the marks of her class in her attitudes to Lloyd George, the British Working Man ("B.W.M.") and the perceived tendency of east Europeans to accept a lower standard of living. Again, this satisfied the purposes of the Fellowship. Reverend Lloyd wanted upper middle class "girls" who would spread the word and ways of his version of the British empire.

Although the initiative and salaries ($160 per month) for the women doctors came from the Alberta government, the Fellowship lent its services for recruitment and raising of travel funds. It also provided for travel money home and could offer places such as the hostel Mary stayed at in Edmonton to give these women a sense of connection with Britain and with one another. Since it provided resources, it could also make demands. To be considered, an applicant had to be Anglican. But, whatever its limitations, the Fellowship through the years stood Dr. Jackson in good stead, continuing to make financial commitments even after Mary left her post and moved north. Among other things, it provided money for some deserted buildings she and Frank turned into a "hospital," and occasionally for drugs.

Hearing that Dr. Johnstone was returning home for a visit in 1928, Hoadley asked her to cooperate with the Alberta agent in London in finding women doctors for his new initiative. Hoadley requested recruitment of women doctors not simply – or perhaps even primarily – because most of the patients were expected to be women and children. There were, in his mind, other reasons. Women could be paid less than men because they would not have to support a wife. Women, thought Hoadley, could – by nature of their sex – be relied upon to do the nursing as well as the doctoring. And women were, in Hoadley's opinion, less likely to turn to drink. There was also the fact that male doctors had opportunities other than hard work in frontier areas: they would have been much harder to recruit. The *British Medical Journal* ads turned up several candidates and Dr. Johnstone chose three: Dr. Helen O'Brien, Dr. Elizabeth Rodger and Dr. Mary Percy. She recommended they learn some dentistry. That part of her job done, she went on a lecture tour to raise funds for their passage.

Dr. Jackson has repeatedly said that one of the things prompting her to apply for an interview was the fact that the ability to ride a horse was listed as a distinct advantage. At the time of her application she was working as Casualty House Surgeon at the Birmingham Children's Hospital and had taken up riding in the park as her only exercise on her half-day off. She thought she was becoming quite good at it. After seven years of hard study, she was eager for more air and fewer people. She also loved mountains and, upon checking an atlas to find that the Rockies were on Alberta's western border, was even more interested. All in all, it seemed to offer the double attraction of service and adventure. Both of these promises would be borne out. Her adventures were many and within months of her arrival, she wrote, "I wouldn't come back to England for 1,000 dollars just now! ... I know I'm doing the right job."

It also afforded her distinct opportunities in terms of her profession. As she would tell me later, practice in this remote area allowed her to do more "real medicine" than she ever would have been allowed to do back in England.

The English (Percy), the Scottish (Rodger) and the Irish (O'Brien) doctors sailed across the sea and railroaded across the country to join a Canadian woman doctor already with the public health service. Margaret Owens[30] had come west in March. The three newcomers were met at the railway station in Edmonton on 20 June 1929 by Kate Brighty, the Superintendent of Public Health Nursing, and one of the district nurses, Olive Watherston. The newcomers were put up in the Fellowship hostel and the next day taken to meet Hoadley. Mary was somewhat taken aback that the first comment made by the Minister of Health was that he would see they all got liquor permits before they left the office! All three, plus Dr. Owens, were soon sent out for a training period with the Travelling Clinic, another of Hoadley's ideas.

The Travelling Clinic has been described by Dr. Johnstone as being for "tonsils and teeth." It was closely tied in with the District Nurses, who would keep track of whoever needed minor surgery or dental work and do the planning necessary to get the clinic and the patients together at the same time. Mary loved it. It was completely different from anything she had experienced in England. There were different illnesses, different patients, and they all had to be dealt with without benefit of hospital or x-ray. She described it fondly in *The Homemade Brass Plate* as "a magnificent effort." The medical staff was usually comprised of two dentists, two doctors and four nurses. One big and six small tents provided housing, an operating theatre and a hospital. There were electric lights and a stove and an ice-chest, as well as the usual furniture needed for eating and sleeping. And at night, there was a camp fire and coffee and a gramophone. "It simply couldn't be beaten."[31]

Mary had originally indicated disappointment at having to spend time with the clinic rather than getting an immediate posting. As it turned out, she did not have long to wait. The District Nurse in Battle River Prairie – approximately 450 km. northwest of Edmonton – broke her arm and was recalled. Shortly thereafter, a woman died from a retained placenta. Mary was called back to Edmonton by Brighty and told to make a list of supplies. She was to go north at once. Mary ordered all the surgical instruments and medical supplies she felt she could possibly need – enough to fill 22 boxes – and started to her posting, literally off the map. She and Brighty caught the train to the town of Peace River. Mary stood at the back and watched the rails wave up and down over the muskeg. They rode the elegant D.A. Thomas steamboat down the mighty Peace to an unsettled place on the bank where they hoped to find someone waiting for them.

Although she wrote about it lightly in the letters, her new life did not start off auspiciously. When she and Brighty[32] were dropped off at Battle River Landing, Frank Jackson and Sheridan Lawrence – another famous pioneer of Alberta's north – chivalrously helped load the 1,000 pounds of belongings and supplies onto the wagon waiting for whatever cargo the boat might have. There are photographs of this trip in *The Homemade Brass Plate*.[33] Dr. Percy and Nurse Brighty are shown in frocks, calf-length coats, cloche hats, sensible shoes, clutching their clutch bags.

Apparently Frank and Sheridan had been telling them tall tales on the way down the river but had neglected to tell them that, within half an hour of the landing, all the boxes would have to be unloaded so that the wagon could get up a steep bank. When that barrier was inevitably reached, the two women had to get down and help the Metis teamster, whose language they could not speak (and who upon later examination proved tubercular), to carry the load up the bank, all the while plagued by swarms of mosquitoes thick enough to obscure the color of a horse. In all, they had to travel 18–20 miles east from the landing to the tiny settlement of Battle River Prairie.

The trip took eleven hours. The only waterhole on the route proved to be a mudhole. The ladies made tea anyway. When they arrived at Mary's new home, it was locked. When they got in, they found it filthy. ("I'd never scrubbed a floor in my life!") One could stick one's fingers through gaps in the boards. Mary discovered that the phrase "furnished house" meant something quite different in northern Alberta than it did in England. (The cutlery consisted of six 3-tined black-handled forks.) Asked years later how she felt about Frank not preparing her for the gruelling trip ahead, she replied, "there was no use telling us!" On the tape, she then laughs and says "Must talk to Brighty about that. I'll bet she still remembers."[34]

The letter announcing Mary's arrival came on the same boat she did. The morning after their arrival, Brighty sent a message to the store-keeper to call together all English-speaking settlers for a meeting that afternoon. The purpose of this was not only to introduce the new government doctor but to elect a committee to look after her wood and water supplies. This was the obligation of the district. They also were obliged to provide a horse and collected $31 in a hat for that purpose. A long debate then ensued over what type of animal to get. A stallion was out of the question. A mare would have been fine for riding but not with so many stallions running around loose. The men settled on a gelding. Mary did not know what a gelding was. She would soon have other evidence that she was not the horsewoman she thought she was. The next morning, Brighty made the return trip to the Landing to catch the D.A. Thomas on its way back upstream to Peace River and the train back to Edmonton. Mary set about having cupboards built for the supplies and a sturdy table made to drop down from the wall so that she wouldn't have to examine patients on her own bed.

She described her arrival to her family but not in full.[35] The letters report the shack as "topping," "palatial," "certainly the nicest house in Battle River Prairie." She protected her family from the truth and she continued to do this throughout the letters. Although she told them about plenty of scrapes, she rarely admitted to depression or loneliness. Asked years later if she ever thought of giving up and going home at this point, Dr. Jackson said:

> I was strongly tempted, except there was no possible
> way of getting out of the place once I got there.... By
> the end of a month's time when I *could* have got out of
> there, wild horses wouldn't have dragged me away. This
> was really quite thrilling.

The truth is, she soon came to revel in this new life. She had a freedom to be an independent woman and to be a leader that she would never have had in England. She could have her own horse (Dan) and a large dog (Brutus), both of which would have been beyond her financial means at home. She could watch 200–300 cranes overhead, live almost constantly out of doors, be moved by the Northern Lights and be surprised at her delight in seeing unsightly telegraph poles march across the landscape. (These meant quicker help for the people under her care, not only in terms of communication but in terms of transportation as the cut lines served as maps for aeroplanes and as paths for horses and sleighs.) Here, she could make a real difference in people's lives.

Mary's medical practice as described in the letters is mainly midwifery, dentistry, accidents of various kinds, frostbite, infectious diseases. Sometimes, there was something special like an appendicitis case, a stroke, a bad heart or a quinsy. But mostly, she pointed out later, people there were remarkably strong and healthy at the time. A tempting example of this is the woman she was called to treat at Jarvie, about 110 km. north of Edmonton, before she was sent to Battle River. The woman had been gored by her cow and Mary was called in to sew her breast back down. After surgery on the kitchen table, the patient rose and insisted on making tea for the doctor and nurse. She also provided good shortbread, for which Mary begged the recipe. She could never get it to turn out as well though and wondered if this had anything to do with superior cream provided by the culprit cow.

Tuberculosis, which would play such a great part when she moved farther north to live almost entirely among Natives and Metis, is also mentioned in the letters. The family of the teamster who brought her in from the landing was doomed so far as she can see. But most of her challenges came not from the difficulty of the medicine involved but from isolation and poverty.

Dr. Percy's district covered 250 square miles according to the government, upwards of 350 according to the locals. Her shack was smack in the middle to make her as accessible as possible to her patients but it also meant that on any day she could be riding to all points of the compass, covering more miles than her own horse could carry her. She not only rode her own (and borrowed) horses, she rode in automobiles, a steamboat, a leaky rowboat, wagons, sleighs, dogsleds, "cabooses" (popular northern winter conveyances consisting of a small cabin mounted on runners and equipped with benches and a stove, drawn by a horse) and once for two days behind a caterpillar tractor which drove her nearly mad with its noise. She regretted she found no emergency justifying the use of an aeroplane.

She rode across prairie, through bush, through muskeg, across rivers. She followed trails, followed telegraph lines, steered by the stars, took shortcuts, got lost. Sometimes her horse rebelled, sometimes she suffered frostbite, sometimes the mosquitoes were unbearable, sometimes she just plain got stuck – more often in mud than in snow. She admits to an "absolute genius" for hitting stream crossings at all the wrong

Mary Percy Jackson's Peace River country.

places and having to get hauled out. On one occasion, she cheerfully reported her near-drowning.

The distances involved in serving her patients also meant that she could not always get back home at night. ("I slept on the floor in so many houses, it isn't even funny.") She did not carry a bedroll with her because she had to carry everything else, including sterile sheets, on her saddle horse. Often she had to carry equipment and medicine for every possible exigency: the person coming to fetch her would not know enough English to tell her what the problem was. Staying away all night in the winter posed an additional problem. If she was not at home to stoke the stove every four hours, everything in the house would freeze, including her medicines. She finally made arrangements for neighbors to come over and stoke the stove when she was not there. She toyed with the idea of moving in with the new Mountie and his wife the second winter but rejected it on the grounds that her work life was too hectic to make her an acceptable boarder. Besides, she liked to live alone. This is obvious in her reaction to having to share her cabin for a short period with a nurse sent in to help her.

If she had a case she could not handle on site, she had to get the patient out to the nearest hospital, at Peace River. On one occasion, she took a desperately ill man down to the hospital only to find it closed and had to return with him the 100 miles back. These trips sometimes had to be made in conditions which would now be considered prohibitive. Despite the bitter cold, winter was often the easiest time to travel for the simple reason that snow is easier to glide over than mud is to plough through. When the "Sunshine Highway" (as the promotional literature cheeringly called it) was put through to replace the old trail, the route was shortened by 35 miles but lengthened by many hours in wet weather: the method of road building was to run two parallel ditches, piling the soil in the middle. The rich gumbo of the area made for a roadbed of "bottomless mud." But if she couldn't get patients out, she bore the heavy responsibility of looking after them there, without nursing support, sometimes even without family support, often in living conditions that could only be described as primitive.

There was another reason she could not take patients out to hospital and that was that, at three dollars a day, the cost of a hospital stay was beyond the means of many. She was supposed to be collecting fees for the government of fifty cents for an office call, a dollar for a house call and $10 for each maternity case. Sometimes she was paid in vegetables, sometimes in labor, sometimes not at all. Later, she would describe some of her patients as "worse than poor. I mean, some of the people who went in homesteading in those days had nothing but the clothes they stood up in and an axe." And there were more flooding in every day. There were no real numbers kept but the official estimate was that the population in her district went from 500 to 2000 during her year and a half there. She described the immigration hall in Edmonton as "absolutely full to the doorstep." In 1929, there was a particularly large influx of Poles and Ukrainians. The young woman who on shipboard hoped that she would not have to practice among non-anglos now found herself in situations where she had to communicate with patients through two interpreters translating, say, from Russian to German, from German to English.

She also found herself working in frankly unsanitary conditions. Some of the early shacks were "nothing but poplar poles and mud," with straw for a roof. There might be a partition to separate the living quarters of the family from those of the cow or horse if the family were fortunate enough to own one. Chickens and pigs were housed under the bed and remained there while she delivered babies above their heads. On other occasions, she worked on her hands and knees in tents. There were no transfusions, no electricity, no running water. Antibiotics did not yet exist. It was "only by the Grace of God if something didn't go wrong." Fortunately, she had experience working in less than desirable conditions. In Birmingham, she delivered a number of babies in the slums – dangerous as well as filthy – surrounding the hospital where she served as resident.[36]

In the north, deliveries could be difficult not only because of the unsanitary conditions but because her East European patients were not used to consulting doctors for childbirth. At home, they would have relied on "wise women" who had not in general been foolish enough or young enough to emigrate. Mary often wouldn't be called upon for help until the woman had been in labor three or four days. "It made for some pretty exciting obstetrics occasionally." She was generally successful, though. Later, in Keg River, she would mourn over the stillbirth of the first child of a Mennonite woman: Mary did not encounter this type of failure very often.

In addition to her clinical practice, she also served as the public health officer. In her letters, she frequently complained of having to write the monthly reports. Her ire was heightened by her conviction that it was the continuing boosterism of the government which was bringing more people in.[37] She considered this iniquitous, pointing out that all the medical help in the world cannot counteract problems of insufficient food, insufficient clothing and insufficient shelter. And at some point more people start to increase the problems exponentially. A good example is the fact that she had to ask people to move their out-houses away from the rivers, where they had originally been located to take advantage of good drainage. There were now simply too many people using the water to allow them to dump as they wished. She had little success in getting people to boil all drinking water. She also imposed the occasional quarantine, including one where she – with considerable amusement – effectively barred the entry of a policeman coming to arrest a family member. She was made the first female coroner she ever heard of. She also drew the only complete map of the area, making her shack a necessary stop for every new arrival looking for his homestead.

There can be no doubt that she worked very hard. One week alone, she was up for three nights running and did 78 miles on horseback in 48 hours. But she remained relentlessly good-humored under pressure. No doubt this was partly for the benefit of her parents. She had promised them a letter a week and tried very hard to meet this commitment. She must have felt the strain that comes of writing non-worrying letters when one is oneself worried to the state of exhaustion. However, it is also true that she really *was* good-humored about the challenges she faced. She now complains about the distortion represented by the heavy workweek I mention at the head of this paragraph:

> It's a pity that everybody picks out of my letters the one particularly strenuous week. It was only the combination of a busy week with atrocious road and weather conditions that made it so tough.[38]

The closest she came to complaining about her lot was when letters from England slowed down. She suspected this happened because she was unable to reply regularly due to force of work. She was used to getting bags of letters, more than anyone else in Battle River Prairie. Although she did not say it in so many words, she needed this support from her old life while learning to live her new one.

But she also enjoyed herself thoroughly. Sociable and nonjudgmental, she happily accepted invitations for a "fill-up of peas," to a dance, to a moose hunt. If there was a preacher, she went to "church." She tried her hand at shooting, at first bragging about her skills, later lamenting her lack of ability. She ordered books from the city library, she bought a gramophone and records in Edmonton, she sent home for her sheet music. She took endless photographs and traded with others, particularly the fellow alpinists she met on a mountain-climbing holiday near Jasper at the end of her first year.

It was not long before she became physically very strong, the "healthiest woman he's ever seen," according to one man's description to his wife. The new muscle, as well as the strenuous work, took a toll on her clothes and she had to deal with the vagaries of Eaton's mail order service. She learned to do without baths, except on occasional trips to Peace River and Edmonton. In warm weather, she could swim in the river below her house. In winter, the hauling and heating of water was simply too onerous a task.

Interestingly, she seems to have had no apprehensions about being a woman alone. Today, she is surprised by the question, saying "it would have been a hell of a job if I'd been afraid of my patients."[39] This attitude does not seem to have been due to either bravery or stupidity. Dr. Johnstone said that she was never nervous, that a woman could sleep in peace in any part of western Canada at that time.[40] This is in sharp contrast to the stories of other women doctors. For example, Emily Stowe (the first to practice medicine as a woman in Canada) carried a "small weighted cane," though she never once felt moved to use it.[41] And a woman doctor who worked on the American and later the Canadian frontier had at least one run-in with a patient's drunken husband and another with an unknown assailant.[42] Compare this to Mary, travelling with six men on a long trail and having to spend the night, sleeping without blankets on the floor around the stove in a cabin en route. She may have been the butt of silly jokes, such as leaving out planks in a bridge to try to get her to seek help in crossing, but she was respected.

What with all her hard work and that outgoing personality and the novelty of being a "lady doctor" in the bush, it was not possible for Mary to avoid "fame." She wrote home at the beginning of February 1930,

> It's really very funny how things have changed since I came out. I was just Dr. Percy then, now I'm `Dr. Percy of Battle River' and everyone seems to know about me! This country is a bit like America for publicity. Would you believe it, the daily paper announced on Wednesday that I was arriving that evening from the north to attend the opening of Parliament that day! I'm getting an awful swelled head.

There were other instances. On their arrival at Edmonton, she and the other two British doctors dodged photographers by leaving the hostel by another door. She was interviewed by the press at that time and later mentioned other newspaper articles on her. At a convention in 1929, Hoadley spoke of her and the other two "lady doctors" in Kinuso and Lac la Biche in glowing terms.[43] In later years, there would be occasional newspaper articles,[44] and pieces in books.[45] Alberta educational radio programs did two dramatizations at different points[46] and now my work on her letters has brought her to the microphone once again to talk about a period in her life which she has described as "really ... quite fantastic. Looking back on it, you wouldn't think it could happen."[47]

Just as Mary started to settle into this life, the letters stop. The report of the Public Health Nursing Division in the Annual Report of the Alberta Department of Public Health for 1931 announced that she had resigned to be married.[48] She in fact married Frank Jackson on 10 March 1931 in the Mountie's house at Battle River Prairie. She and Frank were late for their own wedding, held up by bad road conditions on the way back from buying the ring in Peace River. They were a good match not only in terms of background but in terms of intelligence and energy and integrity. The combination of medical knowledge on her part and northern experience on his would make them invaluable in the development of Keg River, 100 kilometres north of the area she had begun to describe by the end of her letters as "too civilized."

At the time, the Keg River area covered more than 1000 square miles and had a population of less than 400, mostly Metis. There were only a few white farmers and ranchers.[49] Frank's farm was on some of the best land north of Edmonton.[50] He had been there twelve years by the time he married a second time and had learned how to live comfortably in an area, as Mary has described it, more isolated than the Arctic is now. His first wife, Louise, had also been an intelligent and effective pioneer. Poignantly, when Mary moved in, she found herself well-provisioned in terms of the canned goods Louise had put up before her death. Used to the competence of their mother, Frank's sons Louis and Arthur were amazed at Mary's inability to perform such simple tasks as cooking and milking. At ages 11 and 12, they were already frontiersmen in their own right. They could catch fish for supper with their hands or ride out to shoot a prairie chicken, plucking and cleaning it in the saddle on the way home. Their book learning was, however, woefully deficient and she immediately took charge of their education. She turned to Department of Education correspondence courses, a challenge in a locale where there really *were* only eight mails a year. In time, she would also be able to claim their respect by learning what she, too, needed to know in her new role: cooking, baking, canning, gardening, knitting, sewing, making furniture – all the skills necessary for her to win with Frank the Master Farm Family Award from the Alberta Department of Agriculture in 1953.

Frank would be as important in helping her work as she was in helping his. Although he bragged that he had provided a doctor for Keg River by marrying her, he had in fact performed the task of doctoring in the community before she came. He covered for her again when she went back to England to have their daughter, Anne: Frank did not want to lose another wife to childbirth in the north. He delivered their second child, John Robert, a premature breech birth, in the dead cold of February 1935, when the thermometer quit registering at minus 72 degrees Fahrenheit, when circumstances prevented Mary from getting out to Peace River. Frank also served as her anaesthetist, as did a niece of his, Isobel Moulton, who came up from California to stay for a couple of years. They were not the only ones.

> Anybody who could understand English was impounded to be an anaesthetist. The things we did were justified because there was no other way. Now much of it would be criminal malpractice. But if we hadn't done it, people would have died. As it was, they survived, and they were healthy."[51]

In later years, when the highway was put through and brought an epidemic of road accidents, the Jackson car served for ambulance, the Jackson home as emergency ward and Mary always took Frank along to the scene because "he was so good at organizing the prying apart of smashed vehicles."[52]

Despite a brief comment to the contrary in *The Homemade Brass Plate*, it is unlikely that Dr. Percy meant to give up her profession. Women doctors, even at that time, tended to stay working after marriage and tended also to have happy marriages.[53] She did, however, give up her income: the cash-strapped government refused to grant the community's petition for a District Medical Officer, the same position she had held in

Battle River Prairie. Any sense of urgency the government might have had was no doubt dulled by marital customs of the time which decreed that wives accommodate their husband's careers, not vice versa. She would not get paid again for much of her work until health insurance was introduced in 1969.

In the end, the entire Jackson family made heavy accommodations to Mary's "career." Farm income sometimes had to be dipped into in order to help her patients. Gifts and inheritances also went into her medical practice, often to buy equipment for the laboratory she set up in the basement. She was simply too cut off from the nearest lab in Edmonton to rely on its services. Fortunately, she had gone through medical school at a time when it was expected that doctors would have to do at least some of their own lab work. She knew how to prepare slides and to read them. Even if she sent a patient out, she made a point of sending her diagnosis with them, taking great glee in so often being right, challenging those she thinks saw her as some "lone lorn female up in the north who wasn't expected to know anything anyway."[54]

When I commented that this sounded like a life of "immense self-sacrifice," she objected strenuously: "It wasn't self-sacrifice because I was getting such a bang out of it.... I was having an extraordinarily interesting life."[55] Her family's subsidization of the practice that she calls "an expensive hobby" wasn't simply a matter of money deflected into lab equipment. Never knowing when or how long she would be called away, all the children – but probably Anne most of all – were called upon to pick up the slack when Mary switched – on call – from farm wife to physician

Drugs were also something May finagled to provide for her patients. Once again, she turned to the Fellowship of the Maple Leaf. If the money did not come through in time to pay, she had to borrow from Frank or even from the bank. In later years, she cadged pharmaceutical samples from Edmonton doctors. One Christmas, Dr. Johnstone sent her three million units of penicillin, worth $25. Used to husbanding scarce resources, Mary decided to save the new miracle drug for "somebody who was definitely going to die otherwise."[56] She waited until a mother brought in a baby with pneumonia. Mary installed the two in the little "hospital" she and Frank had started in 1937. The Depression had helped Revillon Freres decide to close their fur trade post at Keg River and the buildings were only a quarter mile from the Jackson home. The theory was that pregnant women could come with their families just before due date to stay in the little log building. Not only could Mary be assured of being able to get to the birth in time, she would have good light to work by. If two women were due about the same time, there was a room for each family and they could share the kitchen. The money to outfit this modest operation was raised by the Fellowship and it served its purpose until 1950 when Frank also gave up trading and the family moved about a mile and a half away, making it too distant for Mary to run back and forth. In the case of the baby with pneumonia, she ran over every three hours, night and day for two days and two nights to give the child injections. After it recovered, she said she simply had to have the drug. It seemed criminal to practice without it.

She felt the same way about the new drugs developed to treat tuberculosis which became available after World War II. TB was a particular problem for her, starting in Battle River but certainly a huge factor among the overwhelmingly Native and Metis population around Keg River and north. Not eligible for admission to the only sanatorium in the province (at Calgary), Natives and Metis infected their families on the way to their own inevitable deaths. Even after the new Social Credit government changed this policy in 1935, she had problems: she could not get the people to go so far from home, even after a facility opened for them in Edmonton. One Metis trapper who had never been out of the north, sold his cow to finance his trip to the capital to bring back his son. The child's TB flared up again as soon as he returned. A brother caught it and a baby sister died of TB meningitis. Mary finally got the boy back to hospital. He stayed there three more years, came back home and died.

She tells this story in a nonjudgmental fashion. Clearly she is sympathetic to these people whose lives were being changed all around them. She respected that life. She understood completely why someone would not want to go or have their child sent south to the city, to the san. A better solution was made available by the public health campaign launched after the Second World War. From information she gleaned from fur traders and from the priest in Keg River, she figured that the death rate from TB was something in the nature of 600 per 100,000. She felt this was probably conservative, due to the fact that they would not have been able to recognize TB meningitis. Some families were completely wiped out, as many as 12 deaths in a house. The post-war diagnostic, treatment and educational campaign was successful. Deaths in the area from TB ended in 1948, from TB meningitis in 1943.[57]

She estimates that she worked about five hours a day at her practice and was called upon about every second Sunday. Christmas and other family holidays were frequently interrupted. Sometimes she had to make a round-trip of 150 miles to see a patient. She remarks that no-one in her family has followed her into medicine; she thinks they were "put off." She dealt with scurvy and goitre, an epidemic of damaged hearts in the nearby Mennonite community, axe and rifle wounds, a surprising case of Brazilian leishmaniasis, another of beriberi, one of tetany and once "delivered" a hydatiform mole (a polycystic mass in the uterus). She worked on a dislocated neck, *Gray's Anatomy* spread open before her, conscious that the wrong move could paralyse the young boy in question. All during her working life and even now, she has tried to keep up to date in medicine, going down to Edmonton for seminars, reading journals. A young woman doctor told me after a reading I gave from Mary's letters that, when she was in medical school at the University of Alberta, Mary Percy Jackson had been presented to her class as an exceptional diagnostician.

Dr. Jackson even contributed to clinical literature, not only in terms of her speech on Native and Metis health, "My Life in Keg River," given before the Federation of Medical Women in Toronto in June 1955, but in terms of letters she wrote to the *British Medical Journal*. In 1946, a letter of hers appeared describing related cases of chickenpox and herpes zoster.[58] In 1948, she sent a more detailed description regarding reduction of intussusception (telescoping of part of the gut into a lower part) on two small children by inflating with air.[59] She was forced to try this alternative to surgery – considered outmoded at the time – at first when heavy rains prevented landing of a plane to carry a child out to hospital and again when heavy snows had the same effect.

It is to this sort of thing that her reference regarding the ability to practice "real medicine" pertains. Had she remained in England, not just her lab work would have been farmed out. Back in "civilization," she would have been both able to and obliged to send her most "interesting" cases to available experts and specialists. For doctors of that time and in those isolated communities, general practice posed challenges that would now be almost incomprehensible to modern doctors trained to fit into our high-tech, high-cost health care system. Earlier doctors' practice – and their general role in the community – also offered fertile field for influence.

For example, one of the biggest challenges Mary faced had more to do with animal health than human. As a result of a forest fire in the summer of 1950 so fierce that its smoke changed the color of the moon in England, large numbers of wildlife were forced into the Keg River area. In 1952, rabies – endemic in the Northwest Territories – moved south into this large, dislocated population and blew into a full-scale epidemic. In time, the disease spread to domestic animals, affecting people from farmers who lost or were forced to sell off valuable cattle, to children who lost the pony which took them to school. In addition, if the form the disease took was that of furious rabies, people were put in danger by their own livestock and pets. Farmers hoped (in vain as it turned out) that the government would compensate their economic loss and Mary was called out to attest to the fact that the animal was indeed rabid. In addition to a number of poor animals, down and dying of dumb rabies, she saw very frightening sights, including a steer with icicles of drool, "bellowing and bellowing," eyes wild. It took three shots in the head to bring him down. Mary would comment, "You never realize how sane an animal looks until you see one that is insane."[60]

Not only did Mary take on the job of (basically) preparing death certificates for animals, she also administered the dangerous vaccine to humans possibly infected (her first patient was her new son-in-law) and, with Frank's help, all the sled dogs in the district. She also attempted to send out brains for lab analysis – to faraway Lethbridge in the southeast corner of the province – to ascertain whether the animals really died of rabies. She was very annoyed at Frank when he ruined her chance for research into infections among mice by smashing an aggressive mouse with his fist at dinner one evening, making the brain useless for analysis. Infection via rabid mice seemed to be the only logical explanation for the number of animals infected despite isolation in locked barns.

Important though her hands-on doctoring was in the face of this epidemic, of more significance was the activism she and Frank demonstrated in trying to get the government to acknowledge the extent of the epidemic and to do something about it. As far as she is concerned, there were two barriers in the way of this. One was that the government did not want to start a rabies scare. The other was that it did not want to be responsible for wide-scale compensation. Eventually, a massive poisoning campaign was carried out which, along with the rabies itself, accounted for the deaths of hundreds of thousands of animals. This did not happen until 1954, by which time there had been heavy losses, largely uncompensated, among domestic animals. Wild life was decimated, seriously disrupting the ability of hunters to gain their livelihood.

Mary's attitude to the government's slow move to action in terms of rabies mirrors her comments about government immigration and settlement policies apparent in the letters. She always evidenced a sceptical activism in terms of wresting services and attention for her community, in health but also in other matters. For example, she worked to have a school set up in Keg River and later made 250 mile round-trips (including ferry rides across the Peace) to Fort Vermilion to attend monthly school board meetings. It is significant that the Keg River school is named for her, although she thinks that, had they been polled, the people in the area might have opted to have it called something else.

She has been the recipient of other forms of recognition, some of which she seems genuinely surprised at. There was the honorary LL.D. bestowed by the University of Alberta in 1976 and the investiture into the Alberta Order of Excellence in 1983. In 1990, she was also invested into the Order of Canada. There have been other awards but she seems particularly touched by a surprise party given in her honor in 1975 by The Voice of Native Women, who named her Woman of the Year. Frank also collected his share of honors and together they were presented by the community with an unexpected celebration and tea service on the occasion of their silver wedding anniversary. In an envelope, there was a card filled with signatures and a cheque for $60, stating "Towards our doctor's medical expenses."

But perhaps the best tribute to this woman who did so much for the people she cared about is this touching piece of folk poetry written by Florence Gaucher, at the time a girl from the nearby Metis settlement at Paddle Prairie:

The Faithful Ladie Doctor

We all know a very important person
Doctor Mary Percy Jackson,
She came all the way from England
And has travelled all through this Northland.
Don't dare call her just a dame,
As she's accomplished a mighty fame.
She has saved many a life,
Without any grumbling nor strife.
Also delivered numerous babies,
And even helped to prevent rabies.
She visited her patients, rich or poor,
In fact went to the poor house much more.
Where they lived didn't matter,
In teepees, tents, cabins, or better.
And when meals we offered, she didn't care
If they were full of food or bare
Just a cup of tea you see,
Would please her anywhere.
Now I must tell you the rest,
Which is of course the best.
Years ago her only transportation
I must not forget to mention
Was in four-wheel wagons
and toboggans.
And now, oh my!
As she passes by
I sit back and just sigh.
She now travels far
in a beautiful car.
With the roads, much better!
Dear God, please abundantly bless her![61]

These then are the letters "The Faithful Ladie Doctor" sent home to her parents and her brothers Leslie and Geoff, sister Lena, cousin Winifred Frost, Auntie Lena and Uncle John Frost and Uncle Albert Percy her first year and a half in the northern Alberta. Unlike Canon Andrews,

I have made virtually no changes, other than shortening of sentences and some slight changes in punctuation. When I started the job, Dr. Jackson made only one editing request: that I remove the exclamation marks. I begged her permission to leave them in, saying they underlined her enthusiasm. She allowed them to remain, admitting that for her "Canada was one big exclamation mark!"

The letters are important as a document not just about medicine, settlement, transportation but as a document on these topics *written by a woman*. There can be no question that the perspective of this young woman is different from that of any man. For one thing, there is her fascination with the details of daily life, particularly food. No man would be likely to comment in this way on a subject usually removed from his realm of responsibility. Secondly, she moved as a single woman in a largely male world. This in itself makes her perspective an unusual one. At the same time, her background separated her from most of the women in the community. She got along very well with everyone but when she meets a "city-bred" woman with a piano in her small frame house, there can be no doubt about her enchantment at discovering a soulmate.

In response to a question in a reader's report on this manuscript asking which were my interpretations of this life and which were those of the person who had lived it, I asked Dr. Jackson whether she considered herself a "feminist" or a "new woman." She wrote back:

> As regards the freedom to be an independent woman,
> this was largely the result of the isolation in Alberta
> that I could not have had in England. I considered
> myself to be a liberated woman, lucky enough to have
> parents able to afford to send me to Medical School
> when I wanted to be a doctor. Medicine fascinated me
> then, and still does, even though it is nearly 20 years
> since I retired.[62]

The letters are also particularly valuable because of the family decision to have her write a version of the form letter. Since everyone was to get all letters eventually, there is little repetition and the story flows from one to the next. Only rarely is there an obvious break, accounted for by the fact that infrequently a letter went astray. This in itself is remarkable given the number and types of people she asked to serve as postman for her. Letters usually got to their intended recipients, though some-times they arrived late, having been forgotten in some obscure pocket. On one occasion, a letter was sent on to her parents by someone who found it lying in the street.

It is fortunate for us that these letters have survived. While there are a number of memoirs written by Canadian doctors,[63] there are few writ-ten by women. A notable exception is that of another western doctor, Phyllis K. Steele, who has given us her "story of one woman's struggle, through an era of inequality, to become successful in a male-dominated profession."[64] But memoirs are a different form of literature from letters. They are written after the fact, an older person interpreting a younger person's life. They are subject to the editing of memory and of caution. Letters are immediate; they also tend to be all over the place unless they were, as is the case with many published collections of letters from the nineteenth century, written in the first place with an eye to publication or at least to circulation on the missionary model.

While Mary's letters were not meant for either of these purposes, they were meant for circulation among her family. We therefore have the advantage of continuity combined with intimacy. The only compa-rable text in Canadian medical historiography is that of the diaries of Elizabeth Smith, edited by Veronica Strong-Boag.[65] But again, there are differences between diaries and letters, the former tending to introspec-tion, the latter to description. These letters from Peace River provide us with a cross-over document for a number of fields: the histories of medicine and settlement, the west and women. In addition, the quality of the writing elevates them into the realm of literature.

Certainly this has for me been an unusually engaging project. While I have basically been working with letters written by a woman much younger than I, I have been able to hear her voice taped at age 65 and to correspond and meet with her in her 80s. I have been able to ask her for information as I go along, to ask her to respond to interpretations. I travelled a second time to Keg River – this time to make my own tapes to fill gaps in the record, this time in April, the snow gone from the fields and the sun still up at 10 p.m.

While I am convinced that this has been the proper method to fol-low with this subject, I am certain that it would be the wrong one to follow in other circumstances. Were I producing a "life," for instance, I would never have sought to work in such close co-operation. I see this introduction instead as an extension, an elucidation, of the original letters, meant to provide the perspective of later life and to identify my own participation in the process, to identify my own needs as an historian dealing with a subject and as a woman dealing with a foremother.

Mary's responses to my demands have been generous but almost detached. A good example of this is her general response to one reader's report, which she found

> ... most interesting. You can have no idea how weird it
> is to read about myself, and my life, and my motives!
> It has started me off on some very heavy thinking, and
> I'm sure I could argue with her [the reader] for hours.[66]

She then answered the main questions in a straightforward fashion and even took sides with the reader – and against me! – on the matter of repetition in the letters themselves. While I would not characterize this volume as a collaboration, there is about it something in the nature of a dialogue, a correspondence.

I want to end with my favorite scene in the whole book. A blizzard has blown in and the busy Dr. Percy can't get out to do anything for anyone. She does not fret; she rejoices in her solitude. This is 20 September 1929 and the shadow of winter has already descended on this land.

> It apparently snowed most of the night – it was 3 or 4
> inches thick this morning. The wind is still howling
> fiercely and threatening to lift my house off its feet.
> It's alternately sleeting and raining. The snow is half
> melted in some places, altogether a typically English
> sort of day. You wait till I see some of these dozens
> of people who told me that it was always *dry* cold
> in Canada, nice crisp snow and no slush! I got up
> and made breakfast for the pup at 10 a.m. and then
> went back to bed. Didn't get up myself till just after
> 12!! Since then, I've made a fire, cooked and eaten
> an enormous meal (tomato soup, ham and potatoes
> mashed with milk and butter, stewed apples, hot
> cakes with butter and honey, and coffee) and cleared
> up, made my bed, fetched in lots of soaking wet wood,
> fetched in all the water I'll need till tomorrow and

– attired in boots and puttees, a blazer, a mac and a
groundsheet on top of all my clothes – I sallied out
and fed poor old Dan.... And now I'm sitting in my big
easy chair with 3 cushions, and my feet on the stove,
coffee, cigarettes, chocolate, butterscotch, oranges, the
gramophone and an unread Punch all within reaching
distance. I'm not entirely without the comforts of
civilisation you see!!

This is what I felt like sitting by her fire on those cold February days.
May anyone who reads these letters have a similar sense of engagement
with the simple act of living a life well.

Notes

1 Mary Percy Jackson, *On the Last Frontier. Pioneering in the Peace River Block. Letters of Mary Percy Jackson* (London: The Sheldon Press, and Toronto: General Board of Education, 1933). Edited by Canon P.J. Andrews of the Fellowship of the Maple Leaf.

2 "Outside forces remain chief source of abuse for Natives," *Calgary Herald*, 11 December 1986, p. A5. Reprinted as a background piece to a discussion of contemporary native issues.

3 Interview with David Gell, "Saturday Side Up," CBC-AM, Calgary, 6 February 1993.

4 There are two books of memoirs by Frank Jackson, both told to Sheila Douglass: *A Candle in the Grub Box. A Struggle for Survival in the Northern Wilderness* (Victoria: Shires Books, 1977) and *Jam in the Bed Roll* (Nanaimo: Shires Books, 1979).

5 Cornelia Lehn, *The Homemade Brass Plate. The Story of a Pioneer Doctor in northern Alberta as told to Cornelia Lehn* (Sardis, B.C.: Cedar-Cott Enterprise, 1988).

6 Ibid., p. 205.

7 The main sources for the biographical material here are *The Homemade Brass Plate*, and my personal conversations with Dr. Jackson. Where other sources are used, they will be noted.

8 For material pertaining to these two women specifically, see Edythe Lutzker, *Edith Pechey-Phipson, M.D. The Story of England's Foremost Pioneering Woman Doctor* (New York: Exposition Press, 1973) and Jo Manton, *Elizabeth Garrett Anderson* (New York: E.P. Dutton, 1965). For an impassioned review of the early fight by women to enter medicine, see Mary L. G. Petrie (Mrs. Ashley Carus-Wilson), *The Medical Education of Women* (Montreal: John Lovell & Son, 1895).

9 In fact, in the United States, the number of women in medical school began to *decline* after the turn of the century. Historians have attributed this to closing of some of the medical schools solely for women. On the topic generally, see Mary Roth Walsh, *"Doctors Wanted: No Women Need Apply." Sexual Barriers in the Medical Profession, 1835–1975* (New Haven: Yale University Press, 1977) and Virginia G. Drachman, *Hospital with a Heart. Women Doctors and the Paradox of Separation at the New England Hospital, 1862–1969* (Ithaca: Cornell University Press, 1984). Canada was later in allowing women into medical school. For the problems of early applicants and students, see Veronica Strong-Boag, "Canada's Women Doctors: Feminism Constrained," in *A Not Unreasonable Claim. Women and Reform in Canada, 1880s-1920s*, edited by Linda Kealey (Toronto: The Women's Press, 1979), pp. 109–129. Some Canadian women chose the option of going to American schools for training.

10 Gell interview.

11 This term seems to have been coined in the 1890s. Among other things, the New Woman was seen as a woman who had availed herself of "freedom to work, to educate herself, to be healthy, to remain single without stigma as she chooses." See the definition and quotes in Cheris Kramarae and Paula A. Treichler, *Amazons, Bluestockings and Crones. A Feminist Dictionary* (London: Pandora, 1992), p. 300–301.

12 Mary Percy Jackson, interviewed by Janice Dickin McGinnis, Keg River, 18–19 April 1994. Provincial Archives of Alberta [PAA], Acc. # 94-149.

13 The main source of information on Dr. Johnstone is an interview with her made by Naomi Radford in Victoria on 18 August 1969. PAA, Acc. #69.259.

14 A collection of the experiences of the early district nurses has been compiled and edited by Irene Stewart in *These Were Our Yesterdays. A History of District Nursing in Alberta* (Calgary: Friesen Printers, 1979).

15 Due to federal administrative decisions having to do with settlement coming earlier from the west rather than the east, the British Columbia-Alberta border veers east of the Great Divide as it proceeds north. As a consequence, the Peace River flows from British Columbia into Alberta. The term Peace River country refers to the land drained by that river on both sides of the border. The term Peace River Block, strictly speaking, refers specifically to a block of land that British Columbia ceded to the federal government in payment for a deal made with the Canadian Pacific Railway. In order to have the railroad go through, B.C. was required to repay the CPR with provincial farm land. Since there is little good farm land in B.C., the federal government instead gave the CPR land in the prairies and B.C. in turn paid back the federal government with a large tract of land in the Dawson Creek/Fort St. John area, called the Peace River Block.

The use of the term is therefore erroneous in the title of the first edition of these letters, the explanation being that it seems to have grown in colloquial use to mean the entire settlement area in the rough vicinity of the Peace River. David Leonard of the Provincial Archives of Alberta to J D M, 14 March 1994.

16 There is an extensive literature on the Peace River country. Various communities have put together their own local histories. For a recent and very fine volume directly on the question of settlement, see David W. Leonard and Victoria L. Lemieux, *A Fostered Dream. The Lure of the Peace River Country* (Calgary: Detselig Enterprises Ltd., 1992).

17 Both Drs. Ross and Matheson can be found in Carlotta Hacker, *The Indomitable Lady Doctors* (Toronto: Clarke, Irwin & Co., 1974). In addition, Dr. Matheson is the subject of a biography by her daughter, Ruth Matheson Buck, *The Doctor Rode Side-Saddle* (Toronto: McClelland & Stewart, 1974) and Dr. Ross has been subjected to a fictional treatment by Fred Edge, *The Iron Rose. The Extraordinary Life of Charlotte Ross, M.D.* (Winnipeg: University of Manitoba Press, 1992).

18 Among other honors, she would be awarded the Elizabeth Blackwell Centennial Citation as one of the twelve leading woman physicians in Canada, the United States, Britain and France, by Hobart and William Smith College in 1949. See *One Hundred Years of Medicine, 1849–1949*, a booklet produced by the Federation of Medical Women of Canada in 1949 to celebrate the 100th anniversary of the first degree of medicine conferred on a woman (Blackwell), p. 6. MacMurchy would produce a series of advice books on maternal and child health, as well as reports such as *Infant Mortality* (Toronto: King's Printer, 1911) and *Maternal Mortality in Canada* (Ottawa: King's Printer, 1928). She has in recent years become the focus for feminist scholarship on women reformers. See for example, Dianne Dodd, "Advice to Parents: The Blue Books, Helen MacMurchy, M.D., and the Federal Department of Health, 1920–34," 8 *Canadian Bulletin of Medical History* (1991), 203–30.

19 For example, "Canada's Maternal Mortality Rate Far From Satisfactory," *Edmonton Journal*, 26 November 1929.

20 *Chatelaine* in particular took an interest in health issues. See, on the topic of maternal mortality, Bertha E. Hall, "Must 1,532 Mothers Die?," *The Chatelaine* (July 1928), 6–7, 57, 60 and John W. S. McCullough, "The Prevention of Maternal Mortality," *The Chatelaine* (October 1930), 28, 48.

21 Zonia Keywan, "Mary Percy Jackson: Pioneer Doctor," *Beaver* (Winter 1977), 41–47 at 44.

22 The Public Health Nurses Act, S A 1919, c. 7, s. 49.

23 Alberta's activities in this area repeatedly got coverage in *The Canadian Annual Review* (Toronto: Canadian Review, 1901–38) from 1920 on and the annual reports of the Alberta Department of Health record specific statistics and initiatives. Alberta. Department of Health. *Annual Report*, 1922-.

24 For example, see Peace River Chamber of Commerce, *The Peace River Country* (Peace River: Record Printing Company, 1926), 32 pp. and Peace River & Western Development Co., Limited, *Grimshaw District, Peace Municipality and the Battle River Prairie* (Peace River: The Record, 1927?), 16 pp.

25 The best source for material on the Fellowship is the work of Marilyn Barber. See Marilyn Barber, "The Fellowship of the Maple Leaf Teachers" in Barry Ferguson, ed., *The Anglican Church and the World of Western Canada, 1920–1970* (Regina: Canadian Plains Research Centre, 1991), 154–66.

26 Ibid., p. 154

27 There is now a considerable body of work appearing on women in the mission field. For ones pertaining to Canadian women, see Rosemary R. Gagan, *A Sensitive Independence: Canadian Women Missionaries in Canada and the Orient, 1881–1925* (Montreal and Kingston: McGill-Queen's University Press, 1992) and Ruth Compton Brouwer, *New Women for God. Canadian Presbyterian Women and Indian Missions, 1896–1914* (Toronto: University of Toronto Press, 1990).

28 W.L. Morton, ed., *God's Galloping Girl. The Peace River Diaries of Monica Storrs, 1929–1931* (Vancouver: University of British Columbia Press, 1979).

29 See the brief reference to him in James H. Gray, *The Roar of the Twenties* (Toronto: Macmillan, 1975), p. 281.

30 Dr. Margaret Owens has left us a short memoir in Leona McGregor Hellstedt, *Women Physicians of the World. Autobiographies of medical pioneers* (Washington: Hemisphere Publishing Corps., 1978), 79–84.

31 *Brass Plate*, p. 20.

32 Nurse Brighty has left her own memoir. See Kate Brighty Colley, *While Rivers Flow. Stories of Early Alberta* (Saskatoon: Prairie Books, 1970).

33 *Brass Plate*, p. 27, 30–31.

34 Mary Percy Jackson, interviewed by Naomi Radford, Victoria, B.C., 11 March 1970. PAA, Acc. #70.166.

35 For the other side of the story, see ibid. The following quotes also come from this source.

36 MPJ/JDM interview, 18–19 April 1994.

37 The rush to the Peace mirrored the stock market mania of the same time. The bubble was close to bursting in October 1929 when the land offices at both Peace River and Grande Prairie reported themselves swamped with work. Edmonton *Journal*, 4 Nov. 1929.

38 Letter, Mary Percy Jackson to Janice Dickin McGinnis, 30 Sept. 1993.

39 Mary Percy Jackson, interviewed by Janice Dickin McGinnis, Keg River, 19–23 February 1994.

40 Johnstone/Radford interview, 18 August 1969.

41 *100 Years of Medicine*, p. 37.

42 Alfred M. Rehwinkel, *Dr. Bessie* (St. Louis: Concordia Publishing House, 1963), p. 41 and 47.

43 Hon. George Hoadley, "Address at Fairs Convention, 1929," PAA, Dept. of Agriculture Collection, Acc. #73.307/35.

44 See for example, "Dr. Mary Jackson, Pioneer," *Edmonton Journal*, 25 November 1961.

45 See Hacker, p. 214–7; Henri Chatenay, *The Country Doctors* (Red Deer: Mattrix Press, 1980), p. 61–72; Heber C. Jamieson, *Early Medicine in Alberta. The First Seventy-Five Years* (Edmonton: Canadian Medical Association, Alberta Division, 1947), p. 139–40; and Donald Jack, *Rogues, Rebels and Geniuses. The Story of Canadian Medicine* (Toronto: Doubleday, 1981), p. 131.

46 See tapes at the PAA. " Mary Percy Jackson," in the series, *Men and Women of Achievement* 1965, Acc #83.288/49 and "Pardon me, Ma'am. Is the Doctor in?" in the series, *For Albertans All*, 27 November 1978, Acc. #83.288/301.

47 "Pioneer Doctor," p. 44.

48 Alberta. Department of Public Health, *Annual Report*, p. 40.

49 Mary Percy Jackson, "My Life in Keg River," 38 *Medical Women's Federation (G.B.) Journal* (1956), 40–56 at 41.

50 E. C. Stacey, *Peace Country Heritage* (Saskatoon: Western Producer Prairie Books, 1974), p. 142.

51 "Pioneer Doctor," p. 46.

52 *Brass Plate*, p. 190.

53 Regina Markell Morantz-Sanchez. *Sympathy and Science. Women Physicians in American Medicine* (New York: Oxford University Press, 1985), p. 137. There is no comparable source for Canada.

54 MPJ/JDM interview, 18–19 April 1994.

55 Ibid.

56 *Brass Plate*, p. 126.

57 "My Life," p. 50.

58 Mary Percy Jackson, "Varicella Herpetiformis," 2 *British Medical Journal* (27 July 1946), 138.

59 Mary Percy Jackson, "Acute Intussusception," 2 *British Medical Journal* (24 July 1948), 224–5.

60 *Brass Plate*, p. 174.

61 Quoted in ibid., p. 207–8.

62 Letter, MPJ to JDM, 24 March 1994.

63 For reference to some of the most interesting ones, see S.E.D. Shortt, "'Before the Age of Miracles': The Rise, Fall, and Rebirth of General Practice in Canada, 1890–1940" in Charles G. Roland, ed., *Health, Disease and Medicine. Essays in Canadian Medical History* (Toronto: Hannah Institute for the History of Medicine, 1982), 123–152.

64 Phyllis L. Steele, *The Woman Doctor of Balcarres* (Hamilton: Pathway Publications, 1984). The quote is from the front cover.

65 Elizabeth Smith, *'A Woman with a Purpose.' The Diaries of Elizabeth Smith, 1872–1884* (Toronto: University of Toronto Press, 1980).

66 Letter, Mary Percy Jackson to Janice Dickin McGinnis, 24 March 1994.

~: The Letters

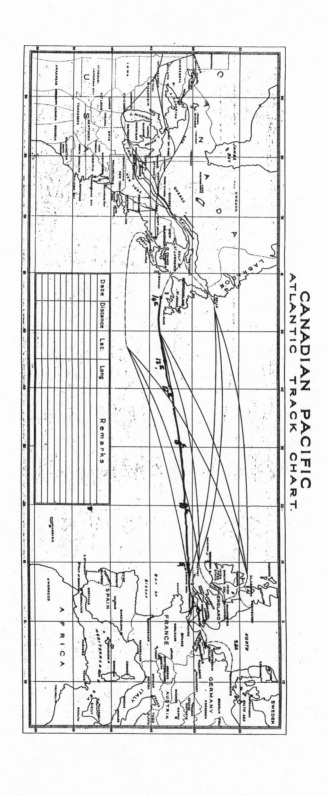

CANADIAN PACIFIC
ATLANTIC TRACK CHART.

Date	Distance	Lat.	Long.	Remarks

~ S.S. Empress of Scotland
About 50 N. 40 W.
Wednesday, 12 June 1929

It seems an enormously long time since I sent off that note from Cherbourg.

Well, we've got over the worst of it now I think and I'm really enjoying life. But Monday was *awful* – very cold, very wet and *very* rough. The sea was washing over the promenade deck and even came over the top deck once and soaked my rug! Every now and then as we went down into a trough the propeller was right out of water and raced – a horrible sensation. At one time I really felt that I'd like the wretched ship to sink!

You'll gather from this that I'm not quite as good a sailor as I'd thought! However I wasn't very bad, and I only missed two meals. Most people were ill for 36 hours. I thought of sending you a wireless to tell you I was all right – it seemed a pretty bad storm to me – but a sailor told me it's always pretty rough there. It's called the devil's hole. Seven currents meet there and the weather we had was nothing very unusual. We only did 375 miles though, as compared with Sunday's 435. We shall not get to Quebec till Saturday evening now.

Dr. O'Brien moved to another cabin, so Dr. Rodger and I have lots of room. The beds are extraordinarily comfortable and I've slept 12 hours each night so far! The food is excellent and the variety astonishing. I manage a 5 course breakfast, 5 course lunch and a 7 or 8 course dinner without turning a hair! And I'm hungry for Bovril and biscuits by 11 a.m. too!!!

We get a newspaper each day at lunch time, printed on board, with all the latest news from the wireless. There's a good orchestra too for meals and dancing and they gave quite a good concert on Sunday evening.

My luggage has been put in the baggage room and not in the hold so I have been able to get at my big leather coat. With that, my thick scarf and a rug and my thick fur gloves, on top of my costume with a woolly jumper, I manage to keep warm sitting on deck! Before we land, I shall be able to put all my oddments from my suitcase into my trunk, and my rug as well, which will save me carrying it on the train.

We're in some difficulty about our rail tickets at present. They won't book our sleepers from Quebec to Montreal on the boat train as we may get held up for some time at Quebec. Being emigrants, we have to see sundry officials that the visitors escape. Also Mr. Andrews booked us C.P.R. to Edmonton which means going to Calgary and changing, as only the C.N.R. goes direct to Edmonton. Calgary is about a day's journey out of our way!

Ramon Navarro is on board.* I haven't seen him yet and doubt if I should recognise him if I did. Still, it's something to have crossed in the same boat!

We expect to see land tomorrow sometime. We go round Cape Race. There are usually icebergs about. I do hope we see some. The Stewardess is a cheering woman. She says they nearly ran on to one last trip and had to stop and go astern!

This letter will be put off on the pilot boat at Rimouski and will come on to you by the next eastbound boat.

~ *Friday, 14 June 1929*

Well, we got held up for over 12 hours by fog and icebergs and shan't get in till Sunday, but I saw a beautiful white and pale green iceberg less than a ¼ mile away yesterday so I'm quite happy! I unfortunately missed seeing a whale this morning but I still live in hopes.

We've passed Cape Race and are now between Newfoundland and Cape Breton Isle. (We can't see either of them, of course. They're too far away). I'm sending you my little map with the course marked. You'll see how little we did on the 12th–13th. It was intensely cold and there was a thick mist – icebergs near but we couldn't see them – so we just had to stop. It seemed extraordinarily quiet without the engines going or the noise of the sea alongside; and the feeling that any moment the mist might lift and show an iceberg close to was most alarming.

There's a man from Edmonton on board who has told us quite a lot about Alberta. It has a very large non-British population apparently. I hope I don't have to practice among Poles or Russians!

I'm enjoying this life immensely, though I'm an awful dud at deck games and seem to be drawn with a French man I've never

* American film idol.

met for the deck tennis tournament today! The fact that there is no swimming bath on board doesn't worry me as much as I thought it would. It's been much too cold. Yesterday when we watched the iceberg, I was wearing all the warm things I possess on top of each other, and with my rug round my shoulders too, and even then my nose nearly froze.

The latest information is that we shall get in very early on Sunday. So, if we manage to get a train to Montreal in time to catch the 6:45 p.m. Trans Canadian Express, we may still get to Edmonton on Thursday evening.

I'm getting awfully lazy. I know I ought to write lots of letters but I've only written 8 so far and I'm going to send postcards for the rest! One seems to spend an enormous long time over meals. The rest of the day just rushes past.

The customs men are coming on board at Rimouski tomorrow. I get my luggage examined on board and checked through to Edmonton and never see it any more till I get there, which is delightfully simple. I'm going up to change the rest of my money soon. The other two have changed theirs. Dollars and cents are much more complicated than they seem – 5 cent pieces (= 2½) can be about half a dozen different sizes!

There are quite a lot of Canadians on board. Their accent is quite as bad as American. I can't always understand what they say. But one thing I have learnt, "My, it's fine" in an excessively nasal voice is the height of praise! I hope I shan't be talking Canadian in 2 years time.

The other two seem to know just as little about the job as I do. I think we must all be a little bit mad. But at any rate, from all I hear of Alberta, we *are* going to see Life!!

I'll cable from Quebec.

S.S. Empress of Scotland.
Saturday, 15 June 1929

My letter to you went off this afternoon and I've written a cable which will be sent off as soon as we get in (4 a.m. tomorrow) so you'll soon know I'm safe. We are later getting in than any trip this year. We've had fog and mist nearly all day today as well. It's cleared up now and there's been a lovely sunset over the mountains to the N.W. The St. Lawrence is an enormous river. We've been sailing up it for 2 days now and even yet can only see one bank clearly. The country is very much more mountainous than I had ever imagined, almost like the Lake District.

Well, there's nothing like travelling under Government protection!! The number of strings that have been pulled on our behalf is quite surprising. The customs men knew about us. I didn't even have to open the lid of my trunks. The baggage men knew about us. All my luggage is checked through to Edmonton and they had instructions not to charge for excess weight!! The railway ticket man had a long note about us and our tickets have been specially marked so that we can stop at Ottawa and interview the chief of Maternity and Child Welfare, Department of Public Health.

Altogether, we're getting on rather well! We've been able to get all this done on board, which will save an awful lot of muddle tomorrow. Our seats and berths are booked to Edmonton. We hope to reach Ottawa tomorrow at 9 p.m., see Dr. MacMurchy on Monday morning and go on by the Trans Canadian Express at 1.15 *a.m.* on Tuesday, getting to Edmonton at 6.50 a.m. on Friday! 6.50 a.m. is a ghastly hour to arrive after a fortnight's journey, isn't it?

It's only 9.45 p.m but I think I must go to bed as we have to get up at 5 a.m. tomorrow and be off the boat by 7 a.m. They sail again on Tuesday. It doesn't leave much time, does it?

Apparently we are going to the Peace River District – the railway people seem to know more about it than we do – but it seems almost too good to be true, so I'm not going to count on it.

~ *Sunday, 16 June 1929, 3.30 p.m.*

Well, here we are in the train on our way to Montreal and Ottawa. It's a brilliantly fine day and very hot. We continue to be marvellously looked after. We were met as we came off the boat by the Rev. La Touche Thompson, the port Chaplain, who put us into a taxi and sent us off for two hours to see Quebec. Meanwhile, he collected our luggage and had it passed through the Customs without even being unlocked!! When we got back, it was in his room waiting! Then he introduced us to Miss Tremaine, head of the Red Cross, who gave us tea and biscuits and showed us the Red Cross Nursery for the immigrants. Then he saw us safely into the right train and here we are. We have since been hunted up by a C.P.R. conductress who also seemed to know all about us!

Quebec is a wonderful city – but quite French. The buildings are French, the people talk French and all the notices and advertisements are in French, sometimes with an English translation underneath. We went right up the hill and round the Chateau Frontenac. There's a lovely view up and down the river. It was very early in the morning (8 a.m.) and beautifully cool and clear.

We were dying to go into the Chateau Frontenac (which is an enormous hotel) and demand ice cream just to see what the inside was like but we felt that 8 a.m. on a Sunday morning was not quite the hour to ask for ice cream! The old castle itself is at the top of the hill, very strongly fortified. We went all round it. Was it the heights of Quebec Wolfe scaled? If so, it must have been jolly hard work.

We have just had tea made in my picnic kettle. (The case was never even unlocked at the Customs so there was no trouble.) It really is exceedingly handy. I'll write to Bert Adshead and thank him again during the next day or two.

This is a shockingly dirty train. I don't mean the carriage – we're travelling 1st and that is beautiful – but the smuts! Some of them are small chunks of coal. I shall post this to you in Montreal when we change. We are due in about an hour's time.

~ *Wednesday, 19 June 1929*
In the train

We have just left Port Arthur and Fort William and expect to reach Winnipeg in about 9 hours' time. The heat yesterday was simply terrific but I'm enjoying the journey immensely. Living on a train is most amusing. Everything is done by black porters and at intervals all the day black men come along selling cigarettes, chocolates, fizzy drinks, magazines, bread, milk, ice cream and fruit – all at about 3 times their proper price. The dining car is really excellent, but the *expense*! Pot of tea for one = 25 cents = 1/-!, etc. My lunch yesterday – cold beef and salad, brown bread, half a grapefruit and tea – cost me $1.80 = 7/6! Needless to say I'm only having one meal a day in the dining car.

We have been passing through forest now for 36 hours! It's almost unbelievable till you see it. Even the towns are only little clearings in it. We passed through Sudbury yesterday, where 95% of the world's nickel comes from. Even that only took about ½ hour to pass through.

There are lots and lots of lakes in the woods, and some beautiful rivers and waterfalls. There are tree trunks floating down all the rivers and some of the rivers are solid from side to side with wood. When we were in Ottawa we were shown how the big booms are made and saw several big paper and pulp factories. But, in spite of the millions of tree trunks we've seen about, they don't seem to have made any impression on the forests.

We came right along the edge of Lake Superior early this morning. It was rather chilly and misty and I was very sleepy, so I didn't take as much notice as I might have done. I didn't realise that the track was hewn out of the rock *overhanging* the lake.

I wish I'd inoculated myself against typhoid before coming out. I was told that it wasn't necessary farther west than Winnipeg. But I haven't passed Winnipeg yet and I keep on drinking water and eating ice cream and I'm awfully doubtful about them. They had 650,000 cases of typhoid in Canada last year. And that was a very good year, without any typhoid epidemic!

The drinking water supplied is ice water and tastes very nice. But I saw them putting in the ice yesterday. It is brought to the side of the train on an open barrow, chopped up with a dirty iron thing, carried up to the top of the train by a nigger with dirty hands, put into a hole and, if too big to slip down, is stamped with his dirty boot!! And we drink it! And this is what is described in their advertisement as "the effortless perfection of the C.P.R."!!!

I can't help this paper getting filthy. The train gets abominably dirty in spite of the windows being shielded with a fine-meshed wire netting. You know, I'm awfully sorry for the colonists travelling 3rd. It must take away their last scraps of energy and courage. First, they're seasick and nearly frozen to death on the boat. Then, they're herded together in pens and chivvied about by officials in Quebec. Then, herded into the train and, in the same clothes they nearly froze to death in on the boat, they have to stand a temperature of about 110°. None of them have less than two children apparently and some of them seem to have six. The heat makes them all miserable and some of the people are train sick. And the C.P.R. doesn't seem to provide any bedding for 3rd class. What a start! I walked through one 3rd carriage yesterday and the smell nearly made me sick.

I am tremendously impressed by the Canadian cities. They're clean and well built and beautifully shady. The women are exceedingly well dressed. Ottawa puts Paris in the shade. It isn't just a few beautiful frocks; every single girl was well-dressed. I was astonished at their white skins, though. I am much more sunburnt than most of them were.

~: Thursday, 20 June 1929

We are well on the last stage of our journey now and are crossing the prairies towards Saskatoon. It is not nearly as flat as I expected and in this part, at any rate, there are lots of trees. The land does not look particularly fertile and the wheat we've passed seems very short to me.

We've just had a little mild excitement. The train stopped at a station and the conductor said there was a 10 minute stop. We walked out into the village and nearly got left. The train, being late, didn't wait its full time!!!

These small towns and villages are most amusing. All the inhabitants turn out to see the train. The girls in these Western Towns wear the same sort of clothes as the men – shirts, cotton trousers and braces ,a nice cool-looking get up. It is another very hot day but I'm getting used to it now. It's funny to think that we saw an iceberg just a week ago.

We get to Edmonton tomorrow morning; I'll send a cable from there. I hope you'll notice what time it arrives because we've put our watches back 7 hours so far, which will make it appear to take an enormously long time. It's an awful game altering our watches. It was simple enough to put them back on the boat – they always gave us the extra hour during the night – but on the train they don't. Yesterday our watches had to go back two hours before lunch, one hour because we'd changed from Eastern to Central time and the other because we crossed from Ontario which has daylight saving to Manitoba which hasn't. Quite simple, of course, only we weren't expecting it and were getting abominably hungry by lunch time at 3.30 p.m.

I had grilled salmon trout for lunch. It had been caught in Lake Superior and brought on to the train in the morning. It was quite the most delicious fish I have ever tasted.

Winnipeg is a funny city, growing very rapidly. The main street
has 7 or 8 storey banks and insurance offices, etc., etc. next door to
wood and corrugated iron single storey eating houses and shops. The
barbers' shops in all the towns are funny and they have big glass
windows. You can stand in the street and watch all the men being
shaved! Then there are shoe shine parlors where you have to go if you
want your shoes cleaned. They don't do them in the hotels apparently.
And, of course, beauty parlors! Do you know I walked about a mile
along the main street of Ottawa looking for a hairdresser's (I wanted
a shampoo) before I realised that the beauty parlor was the place I
wanted! I'm already getting so used to things that I can hardly realise
how funny they seemed four days ago.

We wired the Minister last night to tell him when we were arriving.
We hope to get sent on to our districts by this time next week,
possibly sooner.

~ *Edmonton*
20 June 1929

We arrived here at 7 a.m. and interviewed the Deputy Minister at 11.
We go to see the Minister himself at 2:30. We have already been
interviewed by a reporter and have escaped the press photographer
twice, once by sending him a message that we were all in our baths
and then, when he waited outside, by walking past very rapidly. If he
took us, it will be back view going through a doorway!

I am just going out to send your cable. We are settled in Edmonton
for two or three weeks apparently and then are going round the
districts before we settle down finally. But I'll tell you more when
we've seen the Minister. Please address letters to c/o The Public
Health Department, Edmonton until further notice.

~ *Clyde*
26 June 1929

Thanks ever so much for your letter. It arrived two days ago, so that
was only 13 days on the way.

If I told you all I'd seen and done since my last letter I should
have to send this by parcel post. We saw Mr. Hoadley (the Minister

Clyde: doctors and nurses of the travelling clinic, June 1929.
Doctors O'Brien, Percy, and Rodger are sixth, fifth, and fourth from the right, respectively.

of Health) Friday afternoon and had a long talk to him. He was awfully nice and will be a ripping man to work under. He said they had decided that it was not fair to us – and would not give the best results – if they dumped us straight into our districts and left us to sink or swim. So, for a month or more we're to move round and see all the different parts of the work – and one or two different districts – so that when we eventually settle we shall know something of the conditions and difficulties, etc.

A very good idea, of course, but at the same time we were rather fed up. After a fortnight's travelling, we were only too anxious to settle down and get unpacked. However, we're much more resigned now and I'm on the Travelling Clinic this week and am enjoying myself immensely. We have been at Clyde, 50 miles N of Edmonton, since Monday and today are moving 25 miles further N to Jarvie.

This clinic is a magnificent effort. There are two dentists, two doctors (I'm an extra for this week) and four nurses. They carry round with them a complete operating theatre and hospital. No makeshifts, they've even some gadgets we never rose to in the Children's.) And they have 6 small tents & a big one, with buckets, stove, tables, chairs, beds, an *ice chest*, a really good gramophone, electric light, etc., etc.

They came out here Sunday afternoon and set up. Monday, they examined children all day. Over a hundred came and that was not a big clinic. Yesterday, they did all the teeth, tonsils, and minor operations required, 35 I think the total was.

Of course, this isn't an extremely isolated district. There's a doctor 10 miles away and Edmonton is only 50 miles. And there are two trains a week at any rate, maybe more. The children seemed a particularly healthy looking crowd to me. Of those ops, some were only teeth extractions, some circumcisions, a quinsy and the rest were tonsils and adenoids. They were most of them picked cases, too. A nurse came out here a week or so before, examined all the school children (200–300) in the district and referred in those she thought needed treatment.

The school arrangements are amusing. Children are supposed to start at 6 or 7 years old but some of them live 15 miles away and can't start till they're older. So you get girls of 17 or 18 in the same class as children of 10, working for some farmer in their spare time so as to pay for their keep.

The camping out part is simply topping, everything most luxurious, and I've never been better fed in my life. This camp is in a clearing amongst little silver birch trees. There are lots and lots of wild roses and some honeysuckle & little blue lilies. It's a most delightful spot. Sitting round a huge camp fire with the gramophone on – and good coffee to drink – simply can't be beaten.

Central Alberta has suffered from a 3 month drought till today. It has been frightfully serious, ruined the wheat for miles round. Some of the farmers have already begun to plough the wheat in as manure, all it was good for. However, it started to rain last night about midnight and is pouring still. All the people in the streets are going round with a grin from ear to ear. The wheat round here was not quite done for and is now saved. But the roads have to be seen to be believed. They're feet deep in mud and water. Whether we shall ever get to Jarvie tonight is doubtful. They've put chains on the wheels and of course every car has a spade and pick axe to dig it out of the ditch and cut trees for it to start again.

~: Jarvie
    27 June 1929

Well, we got to Jarvie all right but not till 6 a.m. this morning after travelling all night. Fourteen hours for 30 miles is not bad, is it?

Jarvie: travelling clinic camp, June 1929.

Everyone is awfully bucked at getting here. The roads were said to
be impassable. At 5 p.m., having done 18 miles in 3 hours, the lorry
got stuck in the mud. The other cars were ahead of it. The Ford went
back to help but couldn't pull it out. Meanwhile, the Studebaker got
stuck. We managed to get that out after half an hour's hard work and
Miss Watherston and I went on in the Essex to get horses from the
nearest farm. When we'd gone about a mile, we go stuck in the mud
– right up over the running board – and so we walked on. It took us
half an hour to walk half a mile. However, we got a team and some
men. In the meantime, we were so long that Dr. Washburn came after
us in the Studebaker, found the Essex abandoned in the road, tried to
pull it out and only succeeded in getting the Studebaker stuck.

So, when we got back with the team, there were two cars to dig out
and a mile back a lorry *completely* stuck. Well, to cut a very long story
short, they pulled the cars out and then went back to the lorry. Seven
horses and eight men had failed to shift that lorry by 10 p.m., so we
had to send for a tractor. And, at 11 p.m., see us starting off for Jarvie,
only 12 miles but, oh the roads! (I may say that all this took place on
the main road to the north – the "Peace River Highway".) Anyway,
all went well till 3 a.m. when the lorry got stuck again. We managed
to get it out ourselves eventually, with the aid of two telegraph poles
mercifully found abandoned by the roadside a mile or two away.

There were lots more excitements but I don't want to bore you. I
took some photos but the light wasn't too good.

I go back to Edmonton on Saturday. I'm going to buy myself a gun when I get there. Dr. Washburn has taught me to shoot (he's done a lot of big game shooting) and, though I says it as shouldn't, I'm rather a good shot for a beginner.

~: 28 June 1929

Jarvie is a lovely place. The camp is just above the river. I was too lazy to bathe this morning but it's an ideal place. There are lots and lots of wild strawberries about here and the raspberries will be ripe soon.

Miss Conlin, the District Nurse here, was the pioneer nurse of Alberta. Dr. Johnstone did a locum for her here and this is one of the places she told you about. Miss Conlin has a ripping shack, 3 rooms and a wide balcony, built on the river bank. I wish there was a chance of getting sent here. It's an ideal place and the district is quite big, 30 to 40 miles across. Dr. Rodger went through on the train last night on her way to the Peace River district. I wonder where I shall get sent after tomorrow?

We do get funny meals in Canada. My breakfast was (1) porridge and cream, (2) bacon & fried eggs & bread, (3) a pancake and syrup, (4) stewed rhubarb, (5) a doughnut and (6) coffee.

I hope you won't get worried at not getting this letter till over a week after the last. I was expecting to write to you Monday or Tuesday from Edmonton but on Monday morning was snatched away to Clyde at ½ hour's notice. It's no use trying to post this here. I shall get to Edmonton before it. I will send it on by air-mail if possible tomorrow. You mustn't get worried if my letters don't arrive regularly once a week. If the Government send me off again at a moment's notice to a place where the mail only goes once a week it may easily be a fortnight late getting to you. But I'll write as often as I can.

I am enjoying myself immensely. I've had more excitement since I came out last week than in all the rest of my life together.

My Dear Lena,

I certainly meant to write to you sooner than this but I really haven't had much time since I got here. You see, all my clothes were awfully creased after being packed for 3 weeks and, between ironing those and washing and ironing things as I got them dirty, I seem to have spent most of my spare time in the laundry! This house has an awfully nice laundry we can use – with an electric washing machine, a mangle, an electric iron and an ironing board – so I get on fairly quickly once I get started.

Oh, Canada is a funny place! You expect it to be just like England and at first most of it does seem English. And then you find the weirdest differences. Just up this street is a big house standing back from the road, with a big lawn in front and a notice sticking up out of the grass saying "Funeral Home." Well I couldn't think why an undertaker should label his house Funeral Home so I asked about it last night. Apparently, when anyone dies they are taken to this place and embalmed and then dressed in their best evening frocks. Their hair is marcelled and their faces rouged and they're made altogether better looking than ever they were when alive!!! Isn't it a priceless idea? And no one dreams of wearing black.

The girls out here are amusing. From the time they're 14, they seem to spend all their time collecting "boy friends." They get these boys to autograph their mackintoshes (their oil-silk affairs) which they call "slickers." So, you see girls going round with signatures all over their macs!! I've even seen some tennis pumps covered with signatures! Most of the girls are well dressed but their frocks are inches above their knees – and they don't wear anything underneath but a brassiere and a pair of knickers!

Oh, it's a funny place, I assure you. Food is much the same but they've some exciting extras. Hot dog, waffles and syrup, and squash pie seem to be favourites. I haven't tasted hot dog yet. It seems to be a sausage between two biscuits. They serve tea with every meal, not after it as we do. I don't like drinking tea when I'm eating hot meat much. And they eat pickles with everything, hot or cold. And they've all got ice chests or refrigerators. Even in villages where the water isn't fit to drink and the sanitary arrangements are appalling, you still find electric refrigerators and beautiful ice cream! I've never eaten so many ices before.

There are lots more funny things. This house is number 9707, 107th Street. That doesn't mean that there are 9707 houses in the street, only that we're north of 97th Avenue on 107th St. There are about 4 more houses, then the next number is 9801. You see, that's N of 98th Ave. Horribly complicated till you get used to it.

I bought myself a dog yesterday, a pedigreed Great Dane!!! Yes, quite mad I know but he's a lovely little pup, 6 weeks old. He's being taken to a construction camp 60 miles away to be kept till I am settled down and can take him. His father is an enormous dog, about the size of a tiger. He could knock me down with one paw! When I was sitting in a chair he was standing near, he wagged his tail & nearly knocked my glasses off! So you can guess how tall he is.

I haven't tried any cooking yet, so I haven't anything very interesting to tell you.

Do please write to me.

~ *Edmonton*
4 July 1929

Glory Hallelujah and likewise Hooroosh.

By the time you get this I hope to be on my way to Battle River Prairie on the Notikewin River which is to be my permanent district. It's the newest and much the most exciting district in Alberta, 100 miles from the nearest town or railway, no telegraph, no telephone. Mail is delivered occasionally by boat up the river. It throws the mail bags out on the bank and there they lie till someone finds them!!! You must admit it sounds exciting. I think it's going to prove primitive enough even for me. I don't know whether you'll be able to find it on the Times Atlas. It lies to the West of the Peace River about 18 miles and 100 miles N of the town called Peace River. Fort Vermilion is NNE of it, about 100 miles away. On second thoughts I've traced a rough map of it.

This afternoon I'm off to Jarvie to stay with Miss Conlin for a week or 10 days. I was at Jarvie with the clinic last week and am very much in love with the place, though of course it's moderately civilised. It has a train going N through it twice a week, Monday and Thursday, and a train coming S on Wednesday and Saturday!!! It also has a telephone and two shops!

I am now busily rearranging my luggage. I shall want gum boots, riding kit, bathing togs and clothes for a fortnight – and most of my instruments. So that has meant delving down to the bottom of both trunks. I've got all I want now and my room is full of clothes, etc. When I've packed my suitcase I've got to find room for the rest somewhere. This hostel is awfully convenient. I can leave all my luggage here while I'm at Jarvie and pick it up when I go to Battle River.

I have had an interesting few days since I came back to Edmonton and have met some awfully nice people. I've got standing invitations to go to four different houses whenever I'm in Edmonton, which is awfully nice. Canadians are very hospitable people and much less formal in their entertaining than we are in England. I certainly could never imagine myself getting friendly as quickly at home. I played bridge with the Johnsons again last night till midnight. We had a very good game but I must have been nearly 1,000 down. (We didn't count.) They all use the new method of scoring in Canada, 125 for game instead of 250 for rubber, 10 for each honour but double for 4 or 5 in your own hand (i.e. 30 for simple honours, but 100 for 5 in one hand), no chicane and the same scoring for tricks.

I went all over the University Hospital and the Children's Hospital yesterday. By Jove, they can give us points in hospital building. And they keep two qualified dieticians (B.Sc. in Dietetics) in a hospital of 180 beds! Why, we haven't got one in Birmingham anywhere. They're very keen on sunlight treatment. All the children were lying outside without any clothes, beautifully brown.

The University Hospital is next to the University, the University hostels and the University Farm. All together they occupy an enormous area, so the hospital is beautifully quiet.

I'll post this before I go this afternoon, then it will catch tomorrow's mail.

~ Jarvie
6 July 1929

The mail leaves here today so I'm sending you a note so that you won't be worried.

I had a most exciting ride yesterday evening, *bareback* at a gallop! Then they found a saddle for me and I went for a long ride. It was really great. I've never ridden so fast in my life but, as I was being taken by a boy of about 14, I didn't dare to slow down! I'm hoping to get some riding during the next week. It will certainly be useful to get hardened again before I go to Battle River, though I'm not so stiff today as I expected to be.

I haven't been for a swim in the river yet. It looks too cold and there's been a good wind blowing. The wild strawberries round here are perfectly marvellous. We have bowls of them for tea and supper! The wild raspberries will be ripe in a week or so and the wild gooseberries and currants are getting on. I ate dewberries yesterday for the first time. They are most delicious. I'm going to cultivate strawberries and raspberries in my garden at Battle River next year, in my spare time of course.

I've already seen a number of most interesting cases. I begin to feel the difference in working away from a hospital with X-rays and a lab. I saw a case yesterday I'd have given anything to get X-rayed. I'm afraid it is hopeless anyway. The man will die whichever it is but I'd have loved to settle the diagnosis.

People are awfully nice out here and everyone calls me Doc, which amuses me immensely. I only hope the people are as nice out at Battle River.

I'll be sending you some photos soon I hope.

~ Jarvie
7 July 1929

I am sitting outside watching the sun set across the river. It's about 9:45 p.m. and I've just come back from chapel. I feel I must write and tell you all about it before I forget. There is no church in Jarvie (though they've started to build one this week) so the Methodists hold a service once a fortnight in the schoolhouse at 8 p.m. There were 42 people there, including children, which is pretty good considering that the total population, including infants and the bedridden, is 75, isn't it? It was just as I imagine early Methodism was in England. Moody & Sankey at their best & brightest! I wish I could have kept a hymn book to look through. I noticed several that I've heard you two quote. And at intervals quartets got up & "sang." My hat! I've never heard such an inspired lack of tune in my life.

And yet I wouldn't have missed going for anything. It didn't seem a bit out of place here. The way they're building the church is interesting. You see, there are no building contractors and bricklayers out here, so they just appeal to everyone to go and help when they can. They expect to get it done in a week!!

I was in Mrs. Helverson's this afternoon, being treated to ice-cream (they keep the ice-cream store), when two homesteaders came in. They'd neither of them any idea what day of the week it was, sort of hoped it might be Saturday!

There is a wonderful sunset. I've never seen anything like these sunsets in England. From where I'm sitting, I see a line of spruce trees silhouetted against a flaming gold and the shadows of trees and the reflected light in the river. It is getting too dark to write.

~: 9 July 1929

The mail leaves tomorrow so I must finish this tonight. Thanks ever so much for mother's letter of June 23rd. It arrived by last night's mail. We're having quite an exciting week of it and were out all night on Sunday to see a baby with whooping cough and bronchopneumonia 16 miles away.

I've seen a collection of cases out here that wouldn't have disgraced a teaching hospital and, by Jove, I was glad to know there was a cottage hospital 27 miles away. What I'll do when I am 90 miles from any help I don't quite know. I shall need a truck load of outfit to be adequately equipped for emergencies.

I've been taking photos of a little bear this afternoon. (There are moose and bear and deer in moderate numbers round here.) He was captured in a man's garden two days ago. A big bear and 3 cubs were rooting round in the garden. The man took a shot at the bear and missed. The bear went off and the cubs ran up trees. He managed to

Full English riding habit, summer 1929.

coax them down eventually and put dog collars and chains on them. The one he brought to show us was awfully friendly and simply loved strawberries! Half a dozen children were kept busy picking them for him! He also likes honey, condensed milk and chocolates. I do hope my photos come out.

It has been very hot these last two days. The river has been beautiful for swimming in but is very low. I could walk across it in most places.

Arrived at Peace River this morning after travelling all night. I'm just off to my shack in the wilderness. It's right off the map, 100 miles up the river by boat, then 20 miles by wagon, two miles from the nearest house; I have to drink the river water and have to ford the river to see patients the other side. Mail only leaves once a fortnight so don't be worried if you don't hear for over a fortnight.

~ *21 July 1929*

I haven't time to write a long letter but there's a chance of getting a note out to you by some people who are going down to Peace River, 100 miles by car, this morning.

I arrived here at my shack on Wednesday night about 10 p.m. and have been frightfully busy getting straight. My shack is really topping. I've a big living-room/kitchen, a biggish bedroom and a dispensary/consulting room. It is on the bank of the First Battle River, about 50 feet above the stream, and I've got lovely views from each window.

It is just set down in the middle of the bush (mainly rose bushes), no paths or fences round it. A few yards in front runs an old narrow trail which is going to be the main road north. The river is very stony and rapid. There is a ford across it not far from my house. The water comes above the hubs of wagon wheels and I haven't seen a car get across without horses to help it yet.

They have just started to build a bridge over the river above the ford. So far they've only got a wooden framework up but it is possible to get across. It is rather a nightmare in one place as there are only two planks along 20 feet of it, 50 feet above the water and very springy. That's the way I have to cross. It's quite impossible in a wind. They've put a third plank now, though, so it won't look quite so bad. The bridge engineer informed me at the dance yesterday that they'd put two planks only so that they'd have a chance to help me across but as I'd managed without help they might as well add the other planks!!

There is a gang of 14 living in tents and working on the bridge. They are my nearest neighbours and of course only temporary. They bathe in the river just above the place where I get my water! Thank heaven the stream flows quickly. The river water is the colour of weak tea and is my only water supply but I've got used to it now and it tastes quite nice.

My district is extremely scattered, spread over an area of 25 miles by 10 or more. I'm roughly in the middle of it but my nearest house is across the river about a mile away. The store-post office is there too.

My horse is being bought for me. Mr. Tyson (the blacksmith) is my guardian angel and is bringing it over for me to try this morning. He is really awfully nice to me. He has done everything from putting a lock on my house (there wasn't one) to chopping wood, carrying water, mending the hammer and rescuing me from the most drunken men at the dance!! I'm in the midst of the moonshine industry (you know Alberta has government control of the liquor trade – you can't even get beer without a permit) and this home-made whisky, etc. is pretty powerful.

I haven't time to write any more. I shall be sending you a 30 page letter by the next mail, I expect. I shall have more time when I've unpacked and straightened up completely. By the way, I didn't get a single thing broken.

ᕦ 23 July 1929

I can't remember how long it was since I wrote a proper letter. The last one was written in a great hurry, standing up.

By the way – before I forget – if you should want to get through to me very urgently, if you cable the Minister of Health, Edmonton, he could get at me in an hour or so – by aeroplane if necessary, as they use aeroplanes quite a lot north of the telephone system.

I believe I sent you a post card from Peace River last Tuesday. That was while we waited for the boat. The train got in at 11 a.m. and the boat was due out at 5 p.m. but Mr. Lawrence, who met us on the station, said the boat was unloading grain and might not leave till next morning. Well, about 2 p.m., we went to see the Captain and he said he thought he'd be able to get away by 5. So, at 5 o'clock we all went down to the boat and went on board and waited and waited and waited. Nothing happened and we found that they were all having dinner! So at about 6 o'clock the mayor of Peace River (ahem?) took me for a motor ride. (I may say I met him over the counter of his shop. I bought 30 cents worth of tin tacks and he introduced himself.) Anyway, the boat eventually sailed just after 7 p.m.

Well, it's over 100 miles to Battle River Prairie Landing and we expected it to take 5 hours, so we were a bit worried at leaving so late. But about 9:30 p.m. the boat tied up by the bank and proceeded to load wood (used as fuel for the boilers). The Captain came and sat down and talked to us. He hadn't the vaguest idea when we should get there but eventually decided to tie up till dawn! So we took berths and went to bed. We got up at 6 a.m., as he said we should get in at 6:30 a.m., and we eventually landed at 8:30 a.m. Did you ever hear anything so delightfully vague in your life? The half-breed who came to fetch us had camped out all night on the bank.

You should have seen me and my luggage, 29 pieces weighing over 1000 lbs. in all, and only one small wagon to take the lot and Miss Brighty (from the Department) and me. However, with the aid of the Captain, the Purser, Mr. Lawrence (of whom more anon), a parson on his way to Fort Vermilion, two traders on their way north and some of the crew, we got the wagon loaded and set off, cheered on our way by the entire ship's company who all got off the boat to wave Goodbye!!!

All went well for about ½ hour, then we came to the hill. A section across the river would be something like this.

where we landed

Miss Brighty and I got off and the horses managed to get about ¼ of the way up and then stuck. So there was nothing for it but to unload and carry the trunks etc. up the steep bit they'd stuck on. 95° in the shade, mosquitoes by the millions – and you remember the weight of my baggage?? Well, we had to do that twice. We managed 4 miles in the first 4½ hours but that was all the hill.

The man told us it was two miles further to the water. So we plodded on, only to find when we got there that the "water" was a filthy little puddle perhaps 2 feet × 3 feet, black with mosquito larvae! However, he assured us that was the only water between Peace River & Battle River, so we made tea!! You just don't know how I thanked heaven for that kettle & spirit stove Bert Adshead gave me. I didn't feel quite so bad about drinking that water well boiled. It was a jolly good job we made tea there too. It took us till 10 p.m. to get here!! (i.e. 11 hours to do 18 to 20 miles). Miss. B and I walked a good deal of the way – 95 in the shade, remember, and there wasn't any shade most of the time.

I must say I liked the idea of going into a new country with all my goods on a wagon and me walking behind in true homesteader style but there are more comfortable ways of travelling. When we got here, there was no sign of a key and the house was safely locked. My house is out of sight of any other and the nearest man lives ¾ mile away. I thought I should collapse on the doorstep but the mosquitoes were eating me alive, so I didn't. However, we went down to the camp and the cook gave us tea while a man went to get a key for us. We got in eventually, fell into bed and slept till 11 a.m. next day!

Since then I've been frightfully busy unpacking the 22 boxes and crates of drugs and instruments, cleaning up the house, etc. Friday night there was a dance in the schoolhouse 4 miles away. Mr. Bissette, the storekeeper, took me in his car. It was a shriek. It was supposed to begin at 8 p.m. but no one dreamt of arriving till 10 or 11 and I left very early, 3 a.m.! There was just the one big room. You hung your coat and hat on a nail somewhere and powdered your nose in full view of the world. There were crowds more men than women and more than half the women were half-breeds. The men wore their ordinary clothes, pretty grubby most of them. Their boots were assorted, from heavy hobnailed clogs to high riding boots and galoshes and moccasins, and you can imagine what my feet felt like by morning.

There were no programmes, of course. In fact, you didn't even have one dance with one man. Every now and then another man would come up behind the one you were dancing with, tap him on the shoulder and then go off with you!! As there were lots more men than women this happened pretty frequently! The "music" was one violin and one mandolin, played by Mr. and Mrs. Fife. But as she could only play in one key the tunes were a bit limited!

Supper was priceless, too. We all sat down on the benches round the wall – women one side and men the other – and they brought round a cup for each one in a big 3 inch wash-tub, then a tub full of sandwiches and then a huge kettle full of coffee. The cake was in huge slabs in the tins it had been cooked in and they just cut it into hunks & carried it round. However, as my partner remarked, "It sure was a dandy supper!!"

The bridge engineer is going down to Peace River tomorrow so I'm getting him to post this. The mail is due in here tomorrow. It will be nice to get some letters. It's 10 days since I had one.

I've bought a gun and am practising whenever I get time and I also bought an H.M.V. portable gramophone, so I have breakfast to the strains of the Moonlight Sonata.

I've got to go out to see if I can get some eggs, now, so I can't write any more. I shall be sending you some photos next week but I want to mount them first.

~ 26 July 1929
My Dear Uncle and Auntie,

Your letter of July 2nd arrived here two days ago and gave me very great joy. The thrill of getting letters is increased about 200% now they only arrive twice a month, and uncle John's letters were always very welcome.

Oh! this is a great life! I've certainly got all I asked for. My district was estimated by the Department of Public Health as about 250 sq. miles but people here say it's certainly *upwards* of 350 sq. miles!! There are no roads. There are three rivers running across it. All of them have to be forded at present, though a bridge is being built across this one. (My shack is on the bank of the First Battle River. Notikewin is Indian for Battle.)

I live in a most palatial shack, 14 × 20 feet, divided into three rooms: (1) a living room, which is also a kitchen, scullery, and waiting room for patients, (2) a bedroom, and (3) a dispensary which is also a consulting room and in which there is just about room for me and a patient! However, I'm not joking when I say palatial. It's certainly the nicest house in Battle River Prairie, considering that it is for one person only. I'm having lots of cupboards built for me and in a week or two shall be extremely comfortable. It is extremely well screened, which is another great thing as the mosquitoes are fairly numerous here by the river.

It is just 9 days since I arrived. I haven't been frightfully busy, medically, but I've done quite a lot of dentistry. Oh! I must tell you. While I was having lunch yesterday, in walked a Red Indian – Mr. Bottle by name! – who informed me that he hadn't slept for 3 nights for toothache and demanded that I should remove the tooth. He also added that he'd twice before had teeth removed and each time the dentists had said how awfully difficult his teeth were to extract.

Well, I looked at it, an upper *wisdom* tooth, half way down his throat nearly! However, there's not a dentist nearer than Peace River, 100 miles away, so I went for it. Bared my right brawny arm and gave a colossal pull – and nearly went backwards through the window. It came out as easily as any other tooth!! I was awfully bucked, of course, and he could hardly believe his eyes. My reputation as a dentist will certainly spread. So then I went back to my lunch and finished it to the strains of the Moonlight Sonata on my H.M.V. portable! I've had awfully good luck with all my dentistry so far and I've raked in more cash in a week than the nurse who preceded me did in a month!

A horse is being bought for me. I hope to get him on Sunday. There has been a good deal of argument as to which of the three horses I was to have. I didn't want a horse that stood on his hind legs at the slightest provocation, as lots of them do out here. Neither did I want a horse that was too dead to gallop. The one they're thinking of getting sounds all right and I shall be able to try him out before he's bought.

It's awfully nice living on the *main* road north. Of course, if you didn't know it was the main road you might miss it and walk straight across it without noticing it. But it goes just in front of my front door, so I see all the traffic. Seven vehicles today!! Three of them were for me, and one car belonging to the engineer working on the bridge. Still, it's quite a lot of traffic for these parts! Last night about 1:00 a.m. there was a banging on my door and I cursed bitterly and got up, expecting to have to go to a case. But it was only a man and a little girl of four who wanted shelter for the night, as he couldn't get his car across the river in the dark. So they slept in my kitchen-living room all night! He got across this morning quite safely.

It's a very tricky crossing. There's only one safe way and the water a few feet this side of it is 10–12 feet deep! Even the ford is often too deep for cars. They usually have to get horses to pull them out. I've crossed on horseback quite safely but I always take my feet out of the stirrups in case I have to swim! So you see life is providing me with plenty of excitements.

There are quite a number of wild animals about. I saw a young moose standing in the river drinking last week and there were fresh bear tracks by the river the other morning, I am told. And there are two sweet little chipmunks living in my woodpile. They are like tiny squirrels and very bright and attractive. I have great hopes of taming them.

My garden (about 50 acres of bush) is full of prairie chicken. There are a few grouse and any number of ducks in the slough a quarter mile away. I haven't been out after any yet. I'm spending my spare time shooting at tin lids. When I can hit them with moderate certainty I'm off after duck.

I don't know when you'll get this. The next mail doesn't leave for 10 days yet but I shall try to send it down to Peace River when someone goes down there.

⌁ 31 July 1929

Letters of July 8th & 14th have just arrived. It's not the proper mail day. In the ordinary way, they'd have had to wait at Peace River for the boat and would have got here a week tomorrow. But Mr. Bissette was down in Peace River and brought everyone's letters, a small box full, nearly half of it mine! So I've just spent an hour reading it all and it's made me want to write back to everyone immediately.

It's a fortnight all but two hours since I arrived at this shack and no one would know it for the same place. Cupboards, shelves, a bookcase, curtains at the windows, curtains at the doors, cushions, pictures and the windows mended are the most obvious differences. My horse Dan'l (I suppose it's spelt Daniel but that's how everyone pronounces it) is fastened about 100 yards from the window. May he remain there. It's the first time I've had to do the tying up myself!

He's a very nice horse, well broken and very comfortable. He ran away with me this evening but that was my fault for letting him trot down a steep hill. Please don't get worried. I don't mean that I couldn't have pulled him up with an awful effort. I think I could have but he merely went off on a gallop without any stimulation from me. People are awfully funny about my riding. Of course, everyone here rides. Children can ride as soon as they can walk. So, I carefully didn't say more than that I "could ride after a fashion" when I was asked. One man looked at me the first time I went out on a horse here. "Oh yes – you can ride – but you'll know a whole lot more about it in 6 months!" He was about right, too.

This is a great place. Life is extraordinarily interesting, from scrubbing floors and cleaning windows to removing teeth for Red Indians. I'm enjoying every minute of it. I really do seem to fall on my feet.

The food question is solving itself very satisfactorily, too. Did I tell you that I couldn't get any fresh food whatever? Neither milk nor eggs nor vegetables nor meat nor fruit – only canned and dried sorts!!! The reason, of course, is that this is an absolutely new district. Only a very few acres have been broken more than a year and homesteaders need all the land they've broken up for crops and feed for their animals. They cannot spare either land or time for much gardening. Such gardens as they have are all too small to supply their own and their families' needs. So, in the whole lot of Battle River Prairie, there is not a potato to be bought.

However, I'm writing this while I'm eating my supper – fresh milk, fresh eggs, lettuce, new potatoes and delicious young carrots – all gifts!! I expect I'll be getting some fresh meat before long too because, although deer may not be shot at this time officially, I saw some very good deer steaks hanging outside the shack of a half-breed whose baby is a patient of mine.

Work has been quite slack since I came here. Two or three cases a day, that's all. It has taken as long as 6 hours hard travelling to see two cases sometimes but most of the patients have been to see me, thank goodness. It has given me the opportunity to get the house arranged and show the carpenter just what I wanted done. (Did I tell you that all the cupboards, etc., etc., etc. are being put in for me? I'm not paying a sou.) The horse and saddle are also being provided, of course, and I'm to have a big barn built and a well dug and a cellar made, also without cost to myself!

The weather is simply glorious, blazing hot but always a good breeze. I'm very brown and very fit and only 4 pounds overweight now!

We're going to have a skating rink on the bend of the river just below my house this winter, I hope. So I ought to be able to skate well before I leave Canada. The mosquitoes are not nearly so bad now as last week and I have become almost immune anyway. They bite me, of course, but the bites don't worry me for long. The shack is extremely well screened, too. The screen door is the best fitting one I've seen in Canada, so I don't get a mosquito or a fly indoors.

There's another thing about Canada. There are no wasps – and no nettles! Also the wild raspberries, which are just getting ripe, are equal in size to our cultivated ones and much finer in flavour. Oh, it's a great country!

The bridge is getting on rapidly. It should be finished by September. The telegraph will be in before the fall and tenders are out for carrying the mail once a week. They've got hundreds of men making the road from here to Grimshaw. When finished, it'll be 65 miles, as compared with the present trail's 90 miles. The old trail has to go round a lot of muskeg, hence the difference in length. Also no trail ever goes straight, even across prairie as flat as a billiard table.

They are all trails round here. There are no roads at all yet. I'm getting to know one or two trails quite well and I begin to see why they are all so winding. We had a big storm here last week, quite the most terrific storm I've ever been in. It blew down a number of trees and branches across the trail through a little wood I go through every few days to see a patient. Do you think anyone bothered even to lift a branch up? No. They just made another trail round it!

So from being like this *it has just become this* *tree* *tree*

My district, I believe I told you, was estimated by the Department of Public Health as about 250 sq. miles. Well, it's a good deal more, probably about 350 is nearer the mark. But mercifully, the only people who are ill at present are within twelve miles.

I haven't found looking after myself a bit tiring yet, and cooking is a huge joke. These wood stoves do take some managing. They burn out in about twenty minutes unless you keep stoking. They get so hot that everything on top boils furiously, however far from the fire you put it. They require the most complicated cleaning out, above and below the oven, and if you clear out the top too effectively things in the oven get red hot on top while still stone cold at bottom. And, after having a good fire for half an hour, the whole shack becomes unbearably hot in this weather. I use my primus stove when I only want to boil a kettle or fry bacon and eggs for breakfast. I'm going to get a sheet of asbestos to put on the wall behind the stove. I shall have to get it from Edmonton. Bissette doesn't stock it.

Oh, I was awfully amused. Miss Brighty (I think I told you she came up with me?) told some of the men we thought I ought to have a fire guard as my shack was so isolated and I was so often out. I couldn't make out why she thought it necessary. The stove is entirely closed. Even sparks couldn't fly out. Then it suddenly dawned. She meant a ploughed fire guard round my shack to prevent any fire creeping across the prairie to it! This entire prairie, as far as I've seen (8–10 miles), was forest only a year or two ago. There are old half burnt stumps about and the grass is full of half burnt branches lying about, rather tricky for horses when you get off the trail.

I suppose Geoff will have finished his exam now. I'd like to see the papers sometime if he can spare them. As far as I remember, results don't come out till about the beginning of September. Let me know as soon as you hear.

I am afraid Daddy's birthday will be passed when this arrives. I'm sorry to be so late wishing him many happy returns. I'm afraid Joe Bissette doesn't rise to anything suitable in the way of birthday presents and his is the only store within 90 miles, so it will have to wait till I can get something in town. Unless he'd like a moose-hide coat, wonderfully fringed and beaded by Indians? They really require a wide hat and fringed leather chaps, though, to look most effective! When I've learned to ride properly, I'm going to get some leather chaps, coloured leather preferably, then I shall look the real thing!

Dorothy Round* has done brilliantly. I'm really bucked to think I know her! I'd have liked to have seen that game.

* Ranked tenth place woman player by British Tennis Association, November 1929.

Glad the Anniversary went off well. I wonder how long it will be till I get to Church again. There isn't one here. Services are held in the schoolhouse during the Summer by a student.

This letter is long enough!

~ *4 August 1929*

My last letter to you only left yesterday and here I am writing again. I hope you won't get tired of my effusions. Really, if I wrote all I wanted, you'd be getting about 20 pages a day! I hope you'll keep my letters. I should rather like to have them myself in my old age. They take the place of a diary! I meant to keep a diary but soon discovered that life was too short to write down all interesting things that happened. I am trying to tell you about things as soon as they happen because I'm already getting so used to things that I can hardly realise how different they will seem to you.

And it certainly is a great life. I can hardly believe that I'd never been on a horse 6 months ago. And I suppose in another 6 months I shan't even be able to believe that I didn't know all about feeding, watering and saddling a horse. I'm getting much quicker at saddling already. It only took me 20 minutes this morning to go and untie him (he is tethered by a rope about 30 feet long and gets it tied round and round everything within reach), water him, saddle him and get him off to Church. I may say I was ¼ hour late, the service began ½ hour late and lots of people arrive an hour late!!

It was the only C. of E. service to be held here this year. It was held in the schoolhouse by a C. of E. parson who has a church in Montreal but is only out here on holiday, camping. After the service I went out to dinner at the Schamehorns'. I was awfully tickled at the invitation. He said after church, "You'd better come over and get a fill-up of peas at my place." So I went and helped wash the breakfast dishes and shell the peas.

By about 1:30 p.m., there were 14 of us there, 7 visitors collected casually like myself and the family. Do you wonder Mrs. S. got a bit hot and bothered? Remember we *all* sat round in the living-room/kitchen watching her cook the dinner! Still it was really a good dinner: *fresh meat*!, peas, potatoes, raspberries. Nothing canned. And I came away with a small sack of peas that they picked for me! Then

Settlers arriving at their homestead.

I managed to get some fresh meat at the store up there (4 miles from here) and also some oranges, so I'm going to live on the fat of the land for a bit.

You see, fresh vegetables are not to be bought within 90 miles. I'm absolutely dependent on gifts. But I may say I'm doing really well at present. The veal will be an enormous treat. I haven't had any meat but bacon since I came out. This veal is the remains of 60 lbs. which was got for the lunch for the Powers that Be yesterday.

Oh, I had a real day out yesterday. The Premier and two M.P.s and the Principal of Alberta University and several other big bugs came out to view the land. They made sundry speeches, just here by the bridge, and were all most frightfully complimentary about me in their speeches. Most of them called on me (thank heaven I'd just finished scrubbing the floor when the first one arrived!) and I trotted round with and generally behaved as though I was used to the society of Prime Ministers!! The natives looked *most* impressed! I must get hold of an Edmonton Journal with the reports in if I can.

From all that was said, I gather that this district has the finest wheat crop in Alberta this year and it's certainly lovely to look on. Mr. Schamehorn (at whose shack I had my dinner today) is the owner of the finest crop round here, and of course this crop means *everything* to him financially. That is the snag about homesteading. You can't get a sou out of the land in less than two years and if anything happens to that crop you go broke.

'All the world goes past my door.'

This is a lovely place to live. Sitting in my living room here, I can hear the noise of the river, though I can only get a glimpse of it down at the bend. This room faces NE and later on I shall be able to see the northern lights from my doorway.

I'm right on the main road and all the world goes past my door, sometimes a dozen vehicles in a day! And lots of horses, of course. I see the land seekers – going north and further north. Keg River will probably be the next settlement. That's about 70 miles north. I see the homesteaders coming in, all nationalities except British. I've only met two British homesteaders out here! It's rather thrilling to see them. The men and their wives and families. Their stove, bedsteads, and pots and pans, and sometimes children's toys and violins and weird oddments on the wagon. An odd cow or two and an odd dog or two running behind, the whole procession moving at about 3 miles an hour. There's something astounding about their courage when they arrive, miles from anywhere. They've just got to camp out as best they can till the man has built a house to live in. Do you wonder they're mainly one roomed shacks?

Did I tell you about the family I found in a tent – man, woman and 11 children? The tent about 12 ft. × 10 ft., and the whole thing about 2 inches under water after the heavy rain? The baby had whooping cough and why in the name of wonder it hadn't also got pneumonia beat me. They'd only been there 10 days but the man had got his house as far as the roof. Pretty good work when his timber was 4 miles away. I'm sorry there are so few British out here. But perhaps it's as well. They don't make the best of settlers, unfortunately. Our 8 hour day seems to have ruined the men. They won't realise that the work has got to be done while the weather is good, even to 16 hours a day.

Winter hangs over this country like a shadow. Everyone mentions it before they've been talking to me for long. The absolute necessity for getting anything I want from town by the middle of September (as the boat stops coming up the river then), weatherboarding and banking my shack, storm doors, sufficient fuel etc., etc. But I'm not nearly so afraid of the winter as I was before I came out.

It's just 10 p.m. and I've been writing till now without a light. I hope you will be able to come out for a holiday next year. It's well worth seeing. It will be less interesting as it gets more civilised!

I wouldn't come back to England for 1,000 dollars just now! That doesn't mean that I don't miss you all most frightfully. I do. But I'm not homesick enough to want to come back. And I know I'm doing the right job. The women out here are so awfully glad to have a doctor. You see, the 100 miles from here to Peace River is a three or four day journey in bad weather and that was the nearest doctor. Several women (not ill) have told me that it makes just all the difference to this place to have a doctor available if necessary. It seems so much more worthwhile to me to be looking after these people too, for they're a fine type. There are Norwegians, Germans, Hungarians, Ukrainians and Americans, but they're all of them decent hardworking people.

I think I'll get to bed. I want to try my hand at cake-making tomorrow. This is the first time I've had any eggs to spare.

~: *Monday August 12th.*

Am sending this to Grimshaw by wagon.

A settler's log cabin.

~ *13 August 1929*

I wish you could see me now. It's 10:30 p.m. and I'm energetically
making raspberry jam by lamplight, to the strains of the Moonlight
Sonata on my gramophone!!

You see, it's *much* too hot in the daytime to have my stove on. It
gets the whole shack to furnace heat after about half an hour. Also,
patients wander in at all hours from 8 a.m. to 10:30 p.m. so I have to
do these things when I can. The cookery book is awfully helpful up to
a point but it doesn't tell you what to do when you haven't got – and
cannot get – half the ingredients. Oh, and do write and tell me how
to make drop scones again. Mine don't happen like yours. They're
much too thick. Also how to make potato cakes. The good book
doesn't say.

Long pause while I put the jam in jars and clear up.

I'm still enjoying every minute of this life. The weather alone
would be enough to make me happy. Day after day is brilliantly fine
and hot. I can only remember one dull day in the last month! We get
a thunderstorm every day practically but you can usually watch them
moving up the valley in time to get home before the rain.

The wild raspberries are marvellous. I picked just over 2 lbs. in an
hour this afternoon and could have picked 10 lbs in the same place

had I wanted them. I'm almost living in my shirt and breeches. Even if I do put a frock on I usually get a call and have to change.

Food supplies are almost as difficult now as they were before but the difficulty now is to keep up with the enormous quantities given to me. I've got 25 lbs. of new potatoes waiting to be eaten!! (That's the gospel. I've just weighed them.)

Carrots, turnips, beets, rhubarb, lettuce, peas, bottles of wild strawberries, spiced bread (Norwegian) are just some of the things I'm given. I calculate that I'm some dollars to the good on last month's salary, even though I bought a gun and 500 cartridges, a gramophone and some records, a dog, and had to pay $65 (£13) registration fee to the Alberta College of Surgeons! And if things go on at this rate I shan't be spending more than 10% of my salary. However, I expect I shall find ways of spending money!

~: *Wednesday Aug 14th*

My mail is rapidly becoming the joke of Battle River Prairie. Mail came in this morning and I had to borrow a sack to bring mine home in!! I had seven large parcels, nine newspapers, etc. (B.M.J.,* Punch, Observer) and 14 letters. Sorry I bothered you about not getting letters. They arrived eventually, except one week's that seems to have gone astray. Your letters of July 21st arrived by this mail. I'm glad Daddy reminded me of Hiawatha. I've a little suede-covered copy of it somewhere at home. You might send it out if you can find it, will you? It would be awfully interesting to read now.

Haunch of deer I've eaten now. It's simply delicious. I saw some deer being dried for pemmican by some half-breeds yesterday. And deerskin leggings worked with hedgehog quills and beads are the common riding kits out here. I'm going to have some made when I can ride well enough. There's a half-breed woman who owes me five dollars (her baby had a big abscess in his neck which I opened and treated) who is said to make beautiful deerskin gloves etc., etc. so I expect I shall have to get her to pay me that way. I shall want some moose-hide moccasins for the winter, too. It will be funny going round in moccasins in the snow. Most of the breeds wear moccasins all the year.

* *British Medical Journal.*

There are lots of breeds in this district. More than white people, I should think. They vary considerably. Some look like pure Indians. Some I couldn't tell were not white people. Most of them are obviously half and half. They talk a language called Cree but most of them can talk some English too. They are extraordinarily difficult to deal with. They come into my house and sit down and say nothing. I talk to them politely for about half an hour. Then they say something and I think I've grasped what they've come for. But no, they stay for about another half hour and then sometimes just as they are going away they say what they really want!

That's not one case only. I've had half a dozen who've taken from ½ to an hour to come to the point! It's rather annoying, when you've got ready to have a meal and have everything cooked, to have to leave it and talk to a woman for *an hour* before she'll ask you to pull out a tooth! They don't pay either.

The kiddie I went out to see yesterday was living in a tent about 10 ft. × 6 ft. and about 5 ft. in the middle (i.e. you had to stoop to get in and crawl round on hands and knees inside). I know that three other children and the father and mother are living in it. And there may be more children that I haven't seen. There were four or five dogs there, too. Just outside the tent was a wonderful erection of branches over a fire and strips of deer meat hung on it to smoke dry. (Some of it is afterwards pounded to a powder – pemmican – and the rest looks hard and brown, like leather that's been wet and dried quickly. But they told me it made good broth when boiled.) I took a photo of it and part of the family. I hope it will come out but, as the strap of my camera broke and it fell off my horse and jerked the front open afterwards, I fear it won't.

Inside the tent sundry bits of suet were hanging up and the bladder was *stuffed with clothes* and put in one corner to dry. Need I say that the flies were rather troublesome? You see the seriousness of it when I add that I've a suspicion that the kid may have typhoid. It's too early yet to say and I've nothing definite to go on, only a sort of feeling that there's something funny about it. I hope to heaven he hasn't. They're living right by the river and I've told you already I think that the river is *the* water supply of the district.

Lots of people drive in from 1 to 2 miles every day to get water. (That's how I get my milk. Mr. Bekker comes in every other day for water and brings me a quart of milk.) I'm urging everyone to boil their drinking water but, because they've never had typhoid up here, they won't bother. Also, it's a rapid stony stream and they imagine it's therefore less likely to be contaminated than a slow sluggish one.

Thank heaven I'm going to have a well dug after harvest. It's such a nuisance, this boiling and cooling of water. I didn't bother for a few days but then it struck me how horribly risky it was. There are not many people higher up the river than me but Mrs. Thompson washes her husband's dirtiest shirts in the river *above* me, and there's the bridge gang who swim in it, and the horses who are watered just below the bridge, and the ford – all within half a mile above where I get my drinking water!! Of course, I can't say anything about Mrs. Thompson washing her husband's shirts in my drinking water. After all, I wash myself in Slim Jackson's drinking water!!

There's a beautiful sandy-bottomed stretch just beyond my path down to the river. It's not deep enough to swim much but I go and splash about in a bathing costume and then sit on a rock in the middle of the river and proceed to wash myself, with soap. After all where else can I bath? I've not got a wash tub – nothing bigger than the bowls we use for washing up at home – and anyway, I can't haul water up from the river just to bath in! Even washing my clothes is a job. I've got a breed woman to wash my sheets, tablecloths, towels and tea towels. I wouldn't trust her with anything else, but that makes a difference.

~: Thursday Aug 15th

I'm having this taken down to Grimshaw for me tonight so I can't write much more. I've lots and lots to tell you but I really have been busy just lately.

I went out to Mr. Maclean's last night to get my hair cut. (He lives 6 miles away. He's homesteading but knows something about haircutting, having worked in a barber shop once.) He wasn't in but his wife is a most attractive woman. And joy of joys, she's got a piano!!!! It's the only piano within 50 miles certainly, and possibly within 100 miles, and it's really good and in good tune. I'm going out there to supper on Sunday (D.V.) and I've a standing invitation to go and play whenever I can. Hurrah! She is a city-bred woman and has heard Pachmann and Paderewski and knows a lot of music I know, a great joy of course. So will you please send my music out? I want particularly:

1 Schumann Album
2 Chopin's Nocturnes
3 Brahms Album
4 Moonlight Sonata
5 All the Beethoven Sonatas you can find. There are the First, Fifth, Twelfth and Pathetique in more or less complete condition, I think.
6 Sibelius – Valse Triste
7 " Romance
8 Rachmaninoff's Melodie
9 The Island Spell, if you can find it. I couldn't the last time I looked.
10 Anything of Balfour Gardiner's
11 " " Grieg
12 Anything else you come across that you know I'm keen on!

If you can get these off soon I should be glad as we don't get any mail at all from the end of September till sometime in November. I don't know whether I can get letters out then either. You see the mail comes up the river by boat till towards the end of September. Then the boat stops, but until the Peace River is solid enough the Indian who brings our mail in once a month during the winter can't get his dog team up the river. It's rather thrilling getting mail by sledge, but I do wish it was a bit oftener than once a month.

You might imagine from the piano that they had a house but it's only a one-roomed shack, about 12 × 10 ft. Arranged like this:

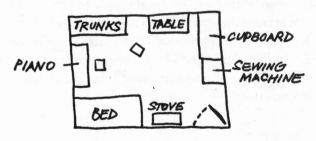

Not much room to spare! There are four people, 5 dogs and 2 kittens!

Well I must stop. I've several more letters to write and I've only another hour. I hope Sandy won't get too tight to remember to post these. He tends to get a little the worse for wear when he goes down to town.

~: *29 August 1929*

It must be nearly a fortnight since I sent a letter to you but I've been really busy. I did start a letter to you the other evening but I'd been riding all day and was very sleepy and the result was both incoherent and illegible, so I tore it up. Now I've got so much to tell you that I hardly know where to start.

First and foremost, I've got my dog. He arrived just a week ago. He's simply enormous now. When I bought him he was a little puppy about half the size of our dog at home. Now he's about as big as a Collie and only four months old!!!

You can imagine the amount of destruction a playful young elephant could do at 7 Ednam Rd.* Well, I assure you it's *nothing* to what my dog did in half an hour here! He has to live outside. There simply isn't room for both of us in my shack. He's got an enormous appetite, too. I have to cook about six times as much as I used to. He eats five times as much as me and even then looks at me hungrily!

I'm sitting on my front doorstep writing this and cooking 6 or 7 lbs. of moose meat for him on my Primus! I don't like the smell of moose at all but there'll be no other meat to eat during the winter. I'm going moose hunting with the Butlers in a few weeks time. (The season begins in November officially but up here where people only kill to eat, we don't take very much notice of "seasons").

I'm hoping to go bear hunting during the winter too. There are lots of bears about within a few miles of here. I heard tales of an enormous bear track about 18 inches long in a wood not far from a patient's house but I didn't believe it. I'd been told that there weren't any grizzlies in this district and I knew brown bear tracks were never that big. However, Mr. Napper (the patient) shot the grizzly on Sunday, so that's that!!

* Address of Percy home in Dudley.

I assure you it adds no end of a thrill to riding through a wood at 2 a.m. to know that it's frequented by bears! It makes it even more exciting when your horse shies violently and can't be persuaded to keep on the trail!! Horses hate the scent of moose as well as bears and there are moose in all the woods.

There is still a great deal of trapping done up here. In fact, it's the only occupation of most of the breeds. They get moose and deer and beaver, skunk, ermine and bear. Further north than the third Battle River there is no settlement at all and lots of it is unexplored. (That's only 20 miles from here.)

But we're frightfully civilized. The bridge was finished yesterday. The road is through to North Star, i.e. the store six miles south of here. It's only been through for about 10 days and I had the results of the first motor accident 6 days ago!! What ho!! Many are the advantages of civilization!! No one would have possibly had an accident on the old trail. You couldn't do more than about 15 miles per hour in a car on it. Now the new road is made you can get to Grimshaw (65 miles away) in about 2½ to 3 hours.

The telegraph will be through before winter too. I'd heard rumours about that and had hardly believed them but yesterday a man came and dumped an enormous pile of boxes and sacks in my "front garden", and told me they were for the telegraph gang who would be through in 2 weeks. And a day or so ago I was at Schamehorns' to supper and he told me that he thought he'd got the tender for carrying the mail, *once a week*!! Just think of it!

You ought to try this mail every two or three weeks business before you realize what a difference a regular weekly mail would make. We had a mail last week. It wasn't due then but someone went down to the Peace River hunting and saw the mail sacks lying on the bank. So Bissette sent a wagon down to fetch it. Now the mail is due this week and may be lying there at the landing but Bissette only has a contract for carrying mail twice a month so he won't send down to see!

My mail last week was a little larger than the time before, 34 letters and parcels! It included your letter of July 29th which had reached Edmonton on August 12th (14 days) and got here August 24th (12 days). Rather amusing, isn't it? Edmonton is only 400 miles or so. When we get a weekly mail I shall be able to get letters from you fairly regularly in 17–19 days.

Of course it won't be so "wild and woolly" as having mail brought up by an Indian with a dog team, once a month or so, but I don't think I shall mind that much!! Anyway, I expect I shall see all I want to of dog teams. I gather that they'll be my chief means of transport this winter!

I can't imagine what a temperature of 30–50 below zero will feel like but that's what we shall have. The first snow will probably fall in about a month's time. (We've had a slight frost already.) That melts but then in October everything freezes up and from then until May, everything is frozen. In mid-winter, we shall get 5–6 hours daylight.

They say I shall be able to hear the timber wolves but, again, I shall believe that when I hear them. Of course, I know there are lots down the Peace River but that's 18 miles away and much less inhabited. They also tell me that I ought to be able to hear the coyotes (little prairie wolves, the size of small collies) barking at night now but I haven't done yet, though I was out all night once last week and till after midnight several other nights. So you see, in spite of bridge and road and telegraph, it's still sufficiently uncivilized to be interesting.

I'm browner and stronger than I've ever been in my life before. (I'm almost the colour of an Italian now.) And although I've been doing my own cooking for six weeks, I'm not starving yet! As a matter of fact, I'm rather a good cook. You should just see my pastry! Mother herself couldn't beat it. And my cookies positively melt in the mouth. But I can't make drop scones. They're eatable but that's all. Waste of eggs, I call them.

Of course, I'm having to manage without lots of utensils that are really rather necessary. For instance, I haven't any scales to weigh quantities. My dispensary scales weigh up to 2 teaspoonsful and the scales for weighing people from 7 to 240 lbs. Neither have I a decent sized basin for mixing or a pastry board or a rolling pin or small cake tins, but it's surprising what you learn to do without in this country.

I've really been pretty busy this last two or three weeks. I did over 150 miles on horseback last week! Really, one needs the strength of an Amazon for this job. If ever there is much sickness about I shall need help. There's hardly any illness about just now. I've been seeing mainly accidents and oddments. I've seen five fractures in five weeks!

The one that has taken up so much time is a little girl of 7 who lives 10 miles north of here. She broke her arm, also dislocated her elbow – a beastly mess. Her little brother aged 12 came to fetch me. I think he's the bravest kid I've ever met. He had to ride over 15 miles, *after dark*, and ford two rivers and came through a wood in which he'd seen bear tracks, to get me. He arrived here at 1 a.m.! We started back at 2 a.m. and didn't get there till 5:45 a.m., as his horse went lame. She'd done over 40 miles that day. And the fatherly way he looked after me was delightful. But it was bitterly cold (we had our first frost that night) and he wasn't very warmly clad and he must have been nearly done in when we got there. He insisted that he wasn't tired, though. There are 4 children, all of them particularly attractive. I took some photos of them last time I was there. I hope they'll come out.

Later

At that point I had to stop to see a patient and then I went out to try and shoot a chicken for supper and was very unsuccessful. The dog seems to think it his business to run ahead and rouse every bird for half a mile. The idea is to shoot 'em before they see you. You see, it's a question of shooting to eat, not sport. Fried prairie chicken is really delicious, very tender and a lovely flavour. The birds themselves are about the size of pheasants but rather a dingy brownish grey colour.

By the way, how much tea do you use per month at home? I seem to be using it at the rate of 1 lb. per month which seems excessive to me. Oh, and I've just remembered. I told you how many potatoes I'd been given when I wrote you last time? Well, please add 12 lbs.! I'd put them up in the corner because I hadn't any room in the cupboard. I've had a few more given me since then but mercifully most people have given me peas, beans, carrots, onions and rhubarb lately. These things are literally without price in this district. I couldn't buy potatoes if I tried.

I get asked out to a lot of meals, too, but of course I can't be away too far or too often. I had dinner with the Butlers when I was north of the Second Battle last week. Mrs. Butler is the most blandly Middle West American I've ever met but she *can* cook. She has a really beautiful log house in the woods and two big moose-hides for floor coverings. I must have a moose-hide for my house. I hope I can manage to shoot one this winter.

I'm going out to dinner on Sunday to the Surveyors' camp again. They've just got back. I told you about the bachelor's party I went to at their camp before, didn't I? I can't remember. Anyway, that was when I first discovered that I was a "bachelor". Anybody who is living alone and doing his or her own cooking, etc. is said to be a "bachelor" in this country. Of course, women don't often do it.

The surveyors have been up north to Keg River and back. It took them 8 days to do 25 miles coming back!! There's no trail through the woods, you see, and it's very slow going because of all the fallen timber. They took from 9 a.m. to 5 p.m. to do just over a mile one day!! And this is only 20 miles NW of here!! I should love to go up in to the unmapped country sometime. I know it wouldn't look very different from the mapped variety but it would be topping to be really "off the map"!

I was hoping to get down to Vermilion Falls, north of Fort Vermilion, this fall but I don't think I can make it. The boat will only be going for another three weeks, you see, and then it will stop till June. Mr. Lawrence invited me up there for a weekend and I should have loved to see his place.

I suppose you wouldn't like to start and save up now to come out here next summer and go down the Peace River to Vermilion and then on to Great Slave Lake and down the Mackenzie River to Aklavik, would you? You'd see the midnight sun, Alaska and Red Indians and Esquimaux and the Arctic and the great forests of the North West Territory. And there aren't so many people who've done it. Of course, it would be rather expensive but I hope to do it myself before I leave Canada. I've met two people who have.

But anyway, even if not for Aklavik, I hope you'll start and save now to come out next summer. I'd love you to see this place. It's extraordinarily interesting to see the very beginning of settlement. I was a bit late getting here but anyway I got in before the bridge and the road and the telegraph and the school, and most of the land is still unbroken.

There's a big fire burning on Big Prairie just now but it's not exciting. There's nothing to see but half a mile of thick smoke and at night a red glow like the furnace lights at home. My fire guard was ploughed two weeks ago so I ought to be all right even if we get a fire on Little Prairie.

It's awful the way my letters meander on but it seems such a pity not to tell you everything because it's all so utterly different from England.

By the way, Mac says something about my letters being typed. What's the bright idea? Is Daddy having extracts typed because he doesn't think them suitable for circulation or what?

I suppose I'd better clear up and get to bed. I sleep awfully long hours here, 10 or 11 p.m. till 8 a.m. usually! You see, I never know when I shall have to go out in the night so I go to bed early. And I never seem to manage to get up before 8 unless I have a patient. I've had them as early as 6:45 a.m.!!

The bridge is going to be opened officially on Sunday, so I'm hoping I can get someone to take this out then to post.

Sunday's programme is rather amusing. Bridge opening 1 p.m., followed by picnic, then a baseball match 4 miles away at Schamehorns' at 3 p.m. Then a church service in the schoolhouse, followed by a dance for the bridge crew also in the schoolhouse! I wish they'd had it some other night. I like the bridge crew. They've been my next door neighbours for 6 weeks but I can't go to a dance on Sunday. Most people don't mind but there are a few people who disapprove and I don't really like it myself.

It's raining!!! Apart from thunderstorms, this is the first rain we've had since I came here.

Copy of letter written on 7 picture postcards of Peace River.

~: *Royal Hotel*
Peace River
6 September 1929

I came down to the hospital last night with a patient, arrived at 2 a.m. I had a most exciting evening chasing a "criminal" with a policeman "mounted" in a motor car. (The NW Mounted Police no longer gallop round on horses when a car will do.) I'll tell you the whole history when I next write.

Now I'm sitting on a big rock on the banks of the river in brilliant sunshine. The wooded high hills and the wide river look extraordinarily like Switzerland. I could imagine myself near Lake Lucerne just now. I marked the hotel with a cross on the first p.c. It's quite nice – one bathroom to 20 bedrooms. Still, there is a bathroom! Of course, you're not allowed to bath in it – but that's too much to hope for!! This p.c. joins on at the end of the first, overlaps about ⅛". So you see what a large town Peace River really is? I'm feeling I'm almost back into civilisation again, in a town where you can buy clothes and vegetables and post cards.

I don't know how I'm going to get back to Notikewin. Hiring a car would cost $30–$50 (£6–£10) and I doubt if the Government would like it!! I think I shall have to go to Grimshaw (only there isn't a train till Tuesday!!) and go up with the truck. I may be able to get taken in on Sunday. I hope so.

I had three letters from you by the mail on Tuesday. I believe the date of the last one was August 18th. I'm sorry you're not thrilled by the sound of Notikewin. After all, it's just what I wanted. I'm absolutely in love with it. It's a hard life, certainly, but awfully interesting. Perhaps you'll like the look of it better when you see my snaps. I've just had a lot up from Edmonton. I'll mount them and send them by the next mail. I've been waiting for Miss Brighty to send some she took but she hasn't sent them. (Miss Brighty is the Provincial Department of Health's Inspector of Hospitals. She came up with me for three days to see me settled in.)

I certainly would have sent you p.c.s of places had any been obtainable but they were very amused at Jarvie when I enquired if they had any.

I suppose you'll have heard by this time about Mac going to South Africa. I'm awfully glad but I *should* have been envious if I'd been still stuck in England. I am seeing life, you know. Sometimes I can hardly believe that this is me! But goodness, don't I just appreciate electric light and having my bed made and my meals cooked!! The Hotel is priceless. I arrived at 2 a.m. It was all lit up downstairs and the door on the latch. I went in. Nobody about but on the desk a list of rooms vacant. I went up and had a look at 3 or 4, chose one, went down and crossed it off, put my number down under the time I wanted to be called and went to bed! Hot water arrived to time. I got up, nobody about, went out and have been in again since but still haven't seen the proprietress!! This is a funny country!!!

Thank you so much for Britannia. I read it from cover to cover, advertisements and all. I had to keep it hidden till I'd finished it, otherwise it would have been borrowed! I shall be awfully glad to have it. I get Punch & The Observer but that's all and we can't even get a newspaper at Battle River. I should be glad if you'd forward any magazine you may happen to buy on railway journeys, etc.

This bit of the river is called Hell's Mouth. I don't know why. I'm being taken out for a motor ride shortly. Also the mail goes out soon so I won't write any more. I haven't any more p.c.s. anyway.

~ 10 September 1929

I got back here Saturday evening, came back in Joe Rousseau's car. I was having lunch in a cafe in Peace River when I caught sight of him. (He's the owner of the store 4 miles N of here). I dropped my knife and fork and rushed out and caught him and arranged to come back with him. So that was that. While I was walking along the main street of Peace River, Mrs. McArthy saw me and recognised me. I went there Friday evening to supper and to hear their most wonderful gramophone. (I don't know if I mentioned her before. Her name was Middleton. She stayed at 9707 Edmonton for a few days while I was there and we came up in the train together as far as Jarvie. She was on her way to marry Rev. McArthy then.) So I've now got three houses to visit when I go down to Peace River again.

I enjoyed being there very much but it was nice to get back home and into breeches and a jumper again! Dan was so pleased to see me and came running up to rub his nose against my shoulder and the pup did Mick's stunt of running round me in circles jumping up. (Don't forget he's already a big dog. I can't lift him!)

I spent lots more money than I could afford down in Peace River, 37/6 in a fruit shop!!! I got grapefruit, greengages, apples, pears, tomatoes and cucumbers and some tinned things. The grapefruit and the greengages are certainly the only ones there have ever been in this district. I had a swell dinner on Sunday for I went out and shot a nice plump chicken too. My shooting is certainly improving.

I've been very busy since I got back, have been at it steadily. Yesterday I went out immediately after breakfast, saw a man 7 miles away, came back and found another patient waiting to see me, saw her, had a meal, then went off and saw three more. Luckily I had supper at the Schamehorns' when I went to see her. Then on to

Lafoys' again 7 miles N, got back at midnight. Was fetched to go to Lafoys' this morning before I'd got breakfast but the man was dead when I got there (that's 2 deaths in a week), got back about 11:30 a.m. to find Mr. Lien waiting with a truck to take me to his brother (10 miles S) who had split his foot open with an axe. Sewed that up and had a meal there (the first bite since 6 p.m. the night before), got back here at 4 p.m.

Had just been down and watered the horse and was thinking of making the bed when Mr. Sexsmith arrived with his little girl, the one with the broken arm. So I redressed that, then saw a man with some bad teeth, then cleared up a bit and decided to have a meal before going off to see another child I meant to see today, had supper, went to get the horse and the blighter has disappeared!

He is a nuisance. You see, I'm still having to picket him as I've neither corral nor barn. But Bill Asmussen told me yesterday he thought they could start on my barn at the end of this week. However, it's no use building a barn after the horse has gone! I suppose I shall have to borrow one of Joe Bissette's horses in the morning and go after mine, bother him! I've got three patients I know of to see tomorrow, 14 miles riding at least, without having to do another 10 miles looking for my horse.

It's a great life, I assure you. But this business of housekeeping in my spare time is no joke. I worked out the most beautiful plan of which days I'd clean out the stove and scrub the floor and wash and iron, etc, but it's no use trying to plan anything. It's all I can do to keep the place moderately clean and tidy. I've got mother's photo over my "kitchen" table and she always looks at me so reproachfully if I go out without doing the washing up! I did some washing about 10 days ago. The things are still rolled up, waiting for ironing! And I've the material for more curtains and things still not made up. And as for letter writing, the heap of unanswered letters grows higher with every mail. I shall be simply snowed under if I can't get at them soon.

The weather is changing rapidly. We still get brilliantly fine hot days but it freezes every night and gets dark quite early (8–9 p.m.). Last night, I rode 7 miles by the light of the northern lights. They are getting more and more beautiful. They are not just in the north, they spread over half the sky. I was riding due south last night and the edge of them was in front of me and right over head was a wonderful sweep of coloured lights, pink and green. I got an awful crick in my neck from looking up all the time.

The telegraph line is only 20 miles away now and they will be up to here next week. I'll send you a cable perhaps for Xmas, right from here! Oh, we are getting civilised. We're even going to have a cemetery! NB. They'll need one if I go on at this rate, 3 deaths in 2 months! Not that I could have prevented any of them – or anyone else either – but it looks bad.

It is now 10:30 p.m. I'm going to bed. I get sleepy awfully early out here. No 1–2 a.m.'s for me.

~ Monday Sept 16th 10 p.m.

This is absolutely the first minute I've had to write to you since I started this letter last Tuesday. I've covered over 160 miles in the last six days! Of course, that doesn't sound very much to you people used to cars and trains and good roads but anything over 20 miles is a good day's riding out here.

Since the man who split his foot open, I've had two more accidents to go and see – in different directions, of course – and a baby aged 14 days who had been convulsing for about 12 hours when I got there – and who strangely enough seems to be recovering. But 4 patients can keep me really busy when one of them is living 11 miles in one direction and another one 7 miles in the opposite direction. However, it's been lovely weather for riding. There's a nip in the air now that is very exhilarating and the autumn colouring out here is infinitely more beautiful than any I've ever seen in England.

I've lots and lots to tell you but it is now 11 p.m. (I stopped to have supper; I started this while I was waiting for things to cook) and I think I can get this posted tomorrow morning. Even that will be more than a week since the last but I can't manage letters regularly once a week when I'm dependent on odd passers-by to post them 70 miles away.

You need never worry if there is a longer pause than usual between my letters. Because, if anything happened to me, you'd get a cable from the Powers That Be about three weeks before my letters stopped arriving. The mail is due in on Wednesday night. You can't think how I look forward to it.

Your letters of Aug 25th and Sept 1st came up by last night's mail. It was a great joy to have them and hear all about everybody. I am glad you've enjoyed my letters. Sometimes I feel that they're hopelessly feeble and, for all the idea of Canada they give you, might as well have been written from Dudley Port. However here are some photos. They'll help you to visualise it a bit. I hope you haven't been expecting anything too "wild and woolly". I did take two of bucking broncos but neither of them were any good. They were taken in a hurry and I hadn't time to adjust my camera for $1/50$ sec. exposure and so the result was a blur.

I find it absolutely impossible to keep my letters up to date. In fact, I'm writing very few letters other than to you. I have extraordinarily little free time. Alas for my ideas of sitting outside in a deck chair, reading and sunbathing! The flow of cases continues to be all that I can manage – and occasionally a little too much for comfort. I've had another outbreak of dentistry this week too. However, I'm beginning to enjoy tooth pulling. Of course, pride cometh before a fall and I suppose sooner or later I shall break one.

My shooting is abominable. It's worse than that. I only know of one worse shot in Canada and that's Dubé, the garage-keeper. He's a priceless youth. Every time I go past (it's 5 miles south of here and on the way to the Russian baby, and also to the man who chopped his foot with an axe), he makes rude remarks about my horse and my rate of travel. He wants to sell me a coop (i.e. coupé)! I believe he's an even worse shot than I am. Anyway, it is rumoured that he took 50 shots to get 4 chickens the other evening! But I've been out for an hour this evening and achieved *nothing* – not a feather. And I did nearly tread on two. I have to leave the pup at home when I go shooting. He believes in fair play for the chickens and goes ahead and warns them all! Also he's difficult to see in the bush, being dark brown and striped, and I should hate to shoot him.

It's lovely weather again. (It was rather chilly last week.) I've gone back to a sleeveless shirt and breeks for riding, no coat or hat. I saw a big flock of cranes going south this morning – 200–300 of them, I should say. It usually means bad weather when they fly in big flocks and the wind, such as it is, is from the north so we shall get it if it does. The geese and cranes have been going south steadily for the last week or more. They fly very very high and only come down on the lakes and rivers at night. The shooting season for geese began in Peace River about 10 days ago. They're difficult to get.

~ *Saturday evening 9:30 p.m.*

What ho! What about the last page for weather prophecy? It was pouring in torrents when I wakened this morning and had obviously been raining most of the night. I've been indoors all day – had no visits to do, praise be – and a little while ago suddenly realised that the noise of the rain had stopped. Looked out through the window and thought the moon must be shining. Then suddenly realised that it was *snow!* Thick snow already – and still snowing steadily!! No wonder I've had to keep stoking. Drying the wood is a darned nuisance. It takes a tremendous lot, you know, when you use nothing else.

Snow – Sept 20th. Well, that's about when they said we should have it. I'm feeling rather thrilled in a way. It's the beginning of the really exciting part of this adventure. So far I've only been playing with it. You know, one gets so used to conditions up here that they become hardly noticed. It's only when people come along and gush over me that I feel that there is anything particularly out of the ordinary. It's usually parsons and such like who come and spout about "pioneer" and "our great Empire" and take photos of me. I'm tickled to death to discover that the theological students I've met in different places, all of whom have taken photos of me, all belong to the same college in Toronto!!!

But I'm a very late comer. Most of the white women up here only came in this year certainly but Mrs. Robertson has been up here over 3 years. She and her daughter (now Mrs. Slim Jackson) were the only white women here for two years – and they came up in the days when there wasn't even a trail and they had to cut their way through the bush. And there are women who came up in 1922 when you couldn't even make it on a saddle horse. The only way was on foot, 100 miles. Of course, men still walk in from Peace River, with all their worldly goods on their backs, but there is so much traffic on the roads now that they can usually get a lift part of the way.

I told you we'd got a cemetery? It's become the stock joke; everyone tells it to me. "Oh, we're getting on awful fast. First we got a doctor

and now we've got a cemetery"!!! I must say I'm a little tired of it!
The old chap (aged 67) had had his trouble for 12 years, after all. You
notice that the breeds don't count. They've an old burial ground 3
miles down the river (built on a hill by the river so that drainage shall
be good!!) but there's no white man died up here before and of course
Mr. Luxford couldn't be buried amongst the "breeds". You get the
attitude? Someone remarked to me that Mr. Luxford must be the
first death I'd had up here. I told him there'd been two others, both
breeds, and he said "oh well", as though the deaths of two half breeds
didn't count – though *they* were aged 5 and 21 and both died of TB.

I'm very sleepy. I think I'll go to bed and finish this tomorrow. The
roads will be impassable for a day or so anyway so I can't get this out.

~ *Sunday 2:30 p.m.*

It apparently snowed most of the night – it was 3 or 4 inches thick
this morning. The wind is still howling fiercely and threatening to lift
my house off its feet. It's alternately sleeting and raining. The snow is
half melted in some places, altogether a typically English sort of day.
You wait till I see some of these dozens of people who told me that
it was always *dry* cold in Canada, nice crisp snow and no slush! I got
up and made breakfast for the pup at 10 a.m. and then went back to
bed. Didn't get up myself till just after 12!! Since then, I've made a fire,
cooked and eaten an enormous meal (tomato soup, ham and potatoes
mashed with milk and butter, stewed apples, hot cakes with butter
and honey, and coffee) and cleared up, made my bed, fetched in lots
of soaking wet wood, fetched in all the water I'll need till tomorrow
and – attired in boots and puttees, a blazer, a mac and a groundsheet
on top of all my clothes – I sallied out and fed poor old Dan (who is
a shivering wet misery, poor beast). I haven't a barn for him, yet I've
got an awfully elegant corral, complete with a haystack and lots of
green oats. Bill Asmussen put it up for me last Monday. And now I'm
sitting in my big easy chair, with 3 cushions and my feet on the stove,
coffee, cigarettes, chocolate, butterscotch, oranges, the gramophone
and an unread Punch all within reaching distance. I'm not entirely
without the comforts of civilisation you see!!

Unless the ink supply fails, this letter will probably be about 30
pages – maybe even longer, if this weather continues! Thank heaven,

the Russian baby chose to convulse last weekend and not this. 22 miles per day to see it would have been no joke. The infant has made the most dramatic recovery I have ever seen. It's only a week ago since I stayed there 7 hours expecting it to die at any moment and now all that's wrong with it apparently is that it cries too much for comfort.

I can't remember which day I wrote to you last – and if I told you all about these people. I don't think I did somehow. Mrs. Spivak is a young, nice-looking and exceedingly well-educated Russian woman. She doesn't talk English much but is picking it up quickly. The baby is 3 weeks old. There are 3 other children, aged 4½, 3, and 1½ – called Dorees (Doris), Veeliam (William), and Antonina, and they're the best brought up children I have ever seen. I wish you could see Antonina, aged 1½, washing her hands and face and drying them herself, without even being reminded, before meals!! They're not goody-good children, either. They can be little monkeys, but they're awfully happy jolly children. I do wish I could talk Russian to them. Their baby Russian sounds delightful. Anyway, all six of them are living in a little shack about the size and shape of the cycle shed at home. It is possibly a foot bigger each way, no more. Their nearest neighbour (until 3 days ago) was a mile away. The shack is right in the middle of the bush, not on any trail. And you can't see another house from it.

They only came in the Spring and have very little money – like everyone else. But the man must be a good workman. The house is well built and banked and has a big deep cellar – and he's got about 15 acres broken and disced and harrowed (and that bush is pretty heavy clearing) and they've a wonderful garden. Mr. Spivak went off to Grimshaw hunting horses about 10 days ago, leaving his wife and 10 day old baby quite well. The baby began to be ill and for 3 days was getting worse. Mrs. Spivak was alone, with a sick baby and 3 small children, and absolutely no help till Mrs. Simpson, a mile away, happened to send some of her children round for some eggs and they went back and told her.

Mrs. Simpson went over and found the baby in convulsions. Mercifully, she's one of those intelligent people who know what to do for most emergencies. She looked after the baby and sent one of her children for Mrs. Gutan, 3 miles away. By the time Mrs. Gutan got there it was pitch dark, so she stayed till dawn and then set off walking, to Downies', which was the nearest neighbour with a horse. The Downie boy rode over (11 miles) to fetch me. I didn't get there till 9 a.m. and by that time the infant had been in an almost continuous convulsion for 12 hours and was absolutely at its last gasp. That's what pioneering involves for women with children.

Do you wonder I'm glad I came out?

Sometimes I get a bit scared, I must admit. There are several families in here now who would have remained in towns but their husbands told them they might as well come up, now they could get a doctor as easily as at home and a lot cheaper. (They only have to pay me for drugs and dressings, you see.) I feel most frightfully responsible.

What ho! A man has just ridden past. That's the first soul I've seen for 2½ days!! I suppose it will be like this in the winter. It's been quite nice to have this rest from patients. It's the longest gap I've had since I came in. I've managed to get lots of oddments done, from cleaning out the dispensary and washing about 60 bottles to finishing repapering my bedroom, making the curtain to hang in the front of my clothes, staining the wood box etc. To say nothing of ironing some clothes I washed about 3 weeks ago.

I've found a washerwoman, praise be! A Hungarian who lives about 2 miles away. She really can wash – and even believes in ironing sheets and towels! That is absolutely unique. In future I shall only wash stockings and silk things. I'm going to get her to come in and scrub the floor and clean the stove once a week, too, if she will. It's quite worth 12/- a week to me to get most of my washing and cleaning done. You see, it isn't only the actual work of washing and cleaning. It's carrying in the necessary wood and water, too – and then getting called out to an accident just when I've got the water boiling! It will reduce my year's savings by £25–£30, of course. Still, I can't help that.

You know Dr. Johnstone lived in a very different way, much more cheaply than I intend to. Porridge, potatoes, bread, coffee are the diet that lots of people here do live on – and she did too, apparently. But I'm not going to. If I can't get fresh meat, I'll buy it tinned. And when I can't get fresh fruit, I'll get dried or canned fruit. It may be extravagant but, hang it all, there's nothing else to spend money on. I think I must be getting more work to do than Dr. Johnstone did, too. I certainly didn't gather that she saw so many cases.

You've probably wondered at my constant references to horses getting away, and people going off to Grimshaw (70 miles) hunting for horses etc., and I don't think I've ever explained. You see, this is a very new district and we've still got what is called Open Herd Law. In other words, you don't have to keep your own horses and cattle on your own land and you're not responsible for any damage they may do on anyone else's land. It's up to the man with an oat field to keep it fenced so that horses can't get in. If my horse gets into Slim Jackson's oat field (he did one night) then Slim has no redress and my horse gets a free feed.

So there are enormous numbers of horses wandering round. There's a bunch of about 70 who wander over a big patch of bush to the SE of here. Dan usually makes for them when he breaks loose. There are probably 500 or more between here and Grimshaw and, since all horses seem to like to get together in bunches, when your horse runs off you set out on another horse to hunt these bunches and see if you can find yours. It may take a day or a week or a month. Sometimes well-known horses are recognised 100 miles from their home. Then a message is sent, may take a week or so to arrive, the man goes after it. Only to find when he gets there that it's (a) the wrong horse or (b) has moved on in the meanwhile! My horse is a very well known one. He won in the races at Waterhole for 4 years running. Also, he is shod on all four feet. Very few horses are shod in this part of the country and, as far as I know, he is the only one who has more than two shoes. This makes him easy to track. People remark sometimes when they meet me coming back from a case miles away, "oh, I saw you were out this way today". The dust is inches thick on the roads (or was before this rain) and shows tracks beautifully.

I've been writing this, reading, sucking oranges, playing with the dog and making butterscotch all afternoon. It's 6:20 p.m. now, still blowing and raining. I'm going to have another meal shortly and then go to bed. That's what Canadians do in the winter, you know, get up at 10 and go to bed at 8 and have only 2 meals a day instead of 3. At least, that's what they do up here, I'm told. I was invited out to supper tonight but I shan't go. They're two nice Germans.

By the way, did I tell you that one day this week I had breakfast with some Norwegians, dinner with the Russians and supper with some Germans?!! You've no idea how interesting it is to meet all these people. The Norwegian is going to teach me to ski this winter if we can find a suitable slope. They're all either too flat or too steep that I've seen.

Mrs. Spivak is teaching me some Russian. I can already ask for boiling water, cold boiled water, water to wash my hands, milk, sugar, soup. She taught me some more words but I've forgotten them. She has also explained how the Bolsheviks are modifying Russian grammar and making it easier because, as she explains, even the rulers can't read or write and existing Russian is too difficult for them to learn.

I should love to know who she is and where she comes from. She's absolutely silent on the point but she's evidently of much better class than most white women up here. Her shack is exquisitely clean. Her clothes are hand-made and beautifully cut. (She makes her own patterns on tracing paper first, lovely things.) She boils and cools every drop of drinking water; she and I are the only ones who do. She looks after her baby awfully well – feeds it by the clock, etc. I'm very curious about her.

I've just had supper and been out and fed the horse again. It's still raining and sleeting. There's one thing about Canadian weather: it is thorough. When it's fine, it's gloriously hot and sunny and when it rains, it's equally definite about it. I've only wanted my mac about 6 days in 3 months and on each occasion it has been absolutely inadequate, though it stood hours and hours of steady rain one day in the Lake District and never let a spot through.

It's a funny feeling being shut away here in my little shack, not a sign of life or a habitation to be seen, nothing but a lonely river valley and snow-covered banks, no sound but the crackling of the wood in the stove and the rain coming with gusts of wind. That's another thing I don't think I've ever told you: how extremely silent Canada is. The birds make very little noise. There are none of the comfortable farm noises – cocks and hens and cattle and wagons – and no church bells. And no traffic worth speaking of, just silence. I ride sometimes for hours with no sound but Dan's hoofs thudding on the ground and the creak of my saddle, seeing nobody for 10 miles at a stretch. It gives you a sensation of being absolutely *alone*, quite a different sensation from loneliness. I wonder if you get my meaning?

(Page 28! I told you to prepare for 30.)

I love it. And these weeks of hard riding, in the open air from morning till night, have made me browner and fitter than ever I've been. That Krushen feeling* is a feeble description of the sensation of unlimited energy I get when I go galloping across big prairie and Dan is full of oats.

I had a most exciting gallop the other day. I'd fastened my lamp oilcan on to the saddle, was going to Bissettes to get it filled. Dan was feeling perky and started to canter. Of course, the can rattled against him. He didn't like it and went faster. By the time I managed to get it unfastened, we were going up the hill absolutely hell for leather. We must have covered the mile in about 3½ minutes!! As an imitation of John Gilpin, it must have been rather good! But if I'd ridden at that speed in England I should have fallen off and broken my neck.

I shall ride in the races next year if I can get a decent horse. Dan is too old for racing now and I'm working him too hard and steadily for it to be fair to demand any great speed. Most times I go round at a steady trot, when I'm out for pleasure and not visiting patients. I occasionally gallop for a mile but the dog can't keep up with a gallop for long, so I don't often.

I take the pup whenever I'm doing less than 10 miles but he's been unlucky lately. I've been doing 20–30, most times. Then, he has to stay chained up at home. He's not at all a bad watch dog and has a most ferocious growl. He came out suddenly from under the house and growled fiercely when I arrived, on Dan, at 1 a.m. the other night. Dan nearly had a fit, stood on his hind legs and went off at great speed!! One day the pup will do that to someone arriving on a half-broken bronc and there'll be trouble.

Well, I said 30 pages. I could go on meandering for hours but perhaps this is a long enough instalment. They'll probably all be this length in the winter when I'm not so busy. The photos will arrive in a separate parcel. I shall send them out with this but they may take longer.

* According to its well-known advertisement, a rush achieved by taking Krushen mineral salts.

~ 1 October 1929

Dear Mother,

I haven't had a minute all the week to write to you. I wrote a long letter last week end. I hope you got it. A half breed was going to post it for me – *if* he ever got to Grimshaw – and the roads were impassable to anything but a horse.

We had 9 inches of rainfall last weekend! And I've had a heavy week and two confinements to attend since then, and the roads knee deep in water.

This would have been posted in time to reach you before your birthday but for the impossible weather. Very many happy returns anyway.

Goodness knows when I shall be able to send this out. I've just missed one car, but I don't suppose it will get through. One man got in yesterday – but he walked the last 25 miles! I wish you could see these roads.

I'll write a long letter as soon as ever work slacks off a bit.
Mary.

~ 17 October 1929

Your letters of Sept 23rd and 30th came up by last night's mail, together with the parcels of books and music. Thanks ever so much for them. The parcel of magazines has not yet come, but the magazine post does not leave England as often as letter post. I shall be delighted to have them. Sooner or later, things may quieten down enough for me to have time to do some reading. At present, I haven't even finished the Punches of the mail before last!!! But I think this last three weeks has been a record. Ever so many other people read the mags I get. In fact, I never see them again once they leave here. I expect they drop to pieces.

I'd have liked to have seen Elizabeth Harper on Peace River. I couldn't believe when I got your letter that I hadn't told you all about her. I met her just in that hectic week end in Edmonton before I came up here, so I suppose that's how I came to miss her out. "Elizabeth Harper (Lady Harper's daughter you know)" – that is how she always introduces herself!! She is a large woman with a *very* large voice, on an infinite number of committees, who came out to Canada to investigate the conditions of emigrants. A job that certainly needs doing – but oh dear! – she is the last on earth to do it.

Heaven knows this emigration business is a tragic muddle for a good many families and there are lots of criminal mistakes being made. But Elizabeth Harper, with the best intentions in the world, will only make things worse. She believes all that the emigrants tell her against the authorities and nothing the authorities tell her against the emigrants. And the Canadians dislike her. However, perhaps she won't do much damage. When I left her she was going back to England to make things hot for the Prime Minister and this wicked Labour Government! If you can get a copy of the article I'd very much like it.*

That reminds me, too. There must have been several articles in the Times on the Peace River Country. A Times correspondent was up in Peace River with the C. of C. delegates on Sept 7th. Of course they didn't come up to this part as the roads were too bad. Still, they were within 60 miles of here. You might be able to find the articles in files of the Times in the Library.

This district is growing at an unbelievable speed. My district is now over 40 miles long!! It is becoming quite unworkable from my point of view. Next year I shall have to have a car or two horses. Poor old Dan can't do 20 miles a day steady and then be expected to do an odd 35 or 40 in a hurry. I got back one night after a 38 mile ride to find another call to a place 5 miles away and couldn't do it. Dan was nearly all in and 10 miles more would have been the last straw. Of course, I'm not supposed to answer messages but I would have gone because I was afraid it might be something really bad. However, they brought the man to me instead. He almost severed his big toe with an axe and had had a string tourniquet on his leg for 16 hours when I got him. However, I sewed the toe on again and prayed hard and it's healed up perfectly!

Since our 9 inch rain the roads have been simply *frightful* – miles and miles under water. The rivers have been flooded. I very nearly had to swim my horse across the 2nd Battle last week and, but for the bridge over the river here, I should have been absolutely cut off.

* This refers to an article in the *Morning Post* in which "ᴇ ʜ" says she had the honour of meeting Dr. Mary Percy.

It must have been at least 5 feet deeper than usual and very swift. It was very muddy, too – thick greyish-white coloured, like the glacier streams in Switzerland. I had to filter every spot I used. I couldn't even wash dishes in the unfiltered water. You couldn't see the bottom of a cupful of it, so you can guess what it was like!!

I'm more in love with this country than ever. You can't imagine how fascinating it is – and I can't describe it. It's just like living in a book or on the films. The whole district is just bubbling with excitement now. All the trappers are off for the "Bush." Wherever I go, the women are washing shirts and patching pants and the men are like schoolboys off for a holiday. And what they are really going to is 5 months' absolute isolation in uninhabited forest, deep snow, intense cold, bears (grizzly and brown), wolves, wolverines, foxes, silver foxes, beaver, ermine, moose and deer – but no human beings. They are all off this week; some have gone already.

Lots of them will be 2 weeks on the trail. After the first 20 miles, there is no visible trail in lots of places and the divide is already covered with snow. They take up food, traps, guns, etc. on pack horses, leave them up there and then bring the horses back and walk back to their trap lines. Some are about 50 miles away but most of them 100 to 200. Most of them have 6–10 cabins built on their lines. They go from cabin to cabin, spending a night in each. But the breeds often live outside all winter, sleeping on the snow with a couple of blankets and a fire to keep them warm – when the temperature may be 65 *below zero*! I am hoping to get up to the nearest trapper's cabin this winter – in a sleigh with a team of huskies! I hope I shan't have to go to anyone sick up there, though. It's still my district, I suppose.

There was a woman very ill at Keg River on Saturday. Doctor from Fort Vermilion couldn't get there and so a man rode down here and got Bissette to go down to Peace River in his car and they sent an aeroplane and a Dr. out from Edmonton. I haven't heard whether she was alive when they got there. She is a Mrs. Jackson, the wife of a man I met on the boat on my way up here. I was very glad I didn't have to go up to Keg River – 100 miles over a pack trail in a hurry would be no joke – but failing the aeroplane I suppose I should have had to.

By the way, have you a copy of Canada West, a highly coloured emigration pamphlet? If you haven't, get Leslie to get one from the

C.P.R. in Birmingham. It has a very good map of Alberta in it and you'll be able to find all these places.

I had one patient from Carcajou (on Peace River) last week, an Indian woman with some of the most appalling stumps of teeth to be pulled out. My reputation as a dentist seems to have travelled even through 100 miles of forest! I am treating a trapper who came down from Fontas River (140 miles NW). The journey took him 11 days to do!

I had my longest journey last week, up to the 3rd Battle, 22 miles N of here. A man working on the telegraph line was sick. The man who came to fetch me was almost sure the man had diphtheria – said it started with a sore throat 5 days before and now he was awfully ill, couldn't swallow and could hardly breathe. So I had to take up serum, etc. in case it was diph. and all the things I might need for almost any emergency.

When I got there (we did 22 miles, which included several through muskeg and bush without much trail, in 4 hours), I found the man had a huge quinsy. He really was jolly bad, too. And lying in a sleeping bag laid on spruce boughs is none too comfortable for a sick man. It's pretty cold at night under canvas, too. I had to stay there for the night – the men emptied a tent for me, which was awfully decent of them – and next morning we brought the man down as far as Rousseau's in a wagon and I commandeered their store room and turned it into a hospital! The man is better now and has gone back to work, just a week after I saw him!

Thanks ever so much for the weights and measures and the recipe. They're just what I wanted. My cooking is getting more ambitious but the time is getting less and less. And I've been so unlucky in getting called to something urgent whenever I've started doing anything lately that I'm getting a bit fed up. However there are some people just come into the district (they're camping by the bridge) who are going to build a log house on my 100 acres and start a bakery, cake shop, etc. What ho! What could be more convenient for me? And Jim Robertson is going to build on his quarter, which adjoins mine, and they're going to have dances once a week in the winter. So I'll have a great time.

This is going down to Peace River today, I hope. I've got two visits to do now so I'll send this and write again tonight or tomorrow if I don't get anything urgent. I was awfully sorry not to be able to get a letter to you for such a long time. I do hope you weren't too worried. It may happen again like that, so please don't get worried. I'm just as safe up here as in New Street, Birmingham, if not safer, and I'm amazingly fit and well. A woman I met a while ago introduced herself and told me that she knew who I was because her husband had told her she couldn't mistake me – I was the healthiest looking woman he'd ever seen!

~: 22 October 1929

This is the first free minute I've had since the last letter I wrote to you!! I'm afraid my sackful of letters on mail day will begin to get smaller. I must owe somewhere between 50 and 60 letters now and I know lots of my correspondents won't write again till they've heard from me. But if I don't write to you now, goodness knows when I'll get the next chance and I believe there's a man going out to Grimshaw tomorrow too.

We are still getting marvellous weather – Indian Summer, they call it. It's brilliantly fine and really hot in the daytime, though at night it gets very cold. It's usually below freezing point by 8 p.m. Every morning I have to chip the ice out of my water butt (it's been ½" thick once or twice lately) and one morning at 11 a.m., finding the ice thicker than usual, I looked at the thermometer and it was then 22° F!! And mind you, I was going in and out of the house, getting in wood and water, in a sleeveless silk jumper and not feeling cold.

I've had my cellar dug and boarded and the house moved over it. I had the house moved about 100 yards. It's nearer the river and farther from the bridge, close to the Spruce trees. It's slightly off the hill now and does not catch the wind so badly. I've also had it faced south (so that its back is to the river – dispensary faces east and living room south). It's on a nice flat patch with a sort of natural lawn in front and all surrounded by bush. Next year I shall get ½ acre broken and have a garden. I'm also going to have a verandah built round the south and east sides next year. I'm hoping to get a well dug this week or next, if the weather holds, but once the wind changes I suppose the winter will be upon us. However, I'm not grumbling. You can't expect much after October even in England and at any rate we shan't have rain and fog.

Unfortunately, it will soon be too cold for riding and I shall have to be fetched to all my cases. It will make it awfully difficult. But even if I bought a cutter (they cost about £15–£20), I'm told I should probably get frozen while hitching up the horse. And looking after a horse in the winter is no joke. You have to melt snow to water them and even when I had no visits I should have to go out twice a day to feed the horse, so it's hardly worth it. I shall get someone to take him and look after him for the winter.

I'm leading an absolute cat and dog life at present. In other words, I've added a cat to the menagerie temporarily. You see, I've been overrun by mice this last two weeks. The first one I saw, about 2 or 3 weeks ago when I was having supper one night, didn't worry me much. I thought it was just a stray one from outside. And anyway I didn't know quite how to deal with it. My gun was loaded, certainly, but I doubted very much whether I could hit a mouse and my attempts wouldn't have improved the furniture. And the only other thing I could think of, the carving knife, seemed altogether too much like "Three Blind Mice"! So I left it and by the middle of last week there wasn't a corner of the house they hadn't got into. They'd even made a nest in the cotton wool in my instrument cupboard!

So I got a trap. Every time I set it I caught a mouse (I got three per 24 hours) but they seemed to get more instead of less. I was warned that they'd get into my clothes. I looked at my clothes one night and they were all right, wakened in the morning and found the mice had pulled my beautiful rabbit wool jumper to the floor and eaten great holes in it. I swore vengeance, so I looked round for a cat. That night the mice were so bad they wakened me about a dozen times. They were eating great holes in the walls. So next day (Saturday last) I borrowed one of Mrs. Olsen's cats and brought her home.

I wish you could have seen me. Olsen's is 3 miles away and I came back on horseback, the cat, tied up in an apron, clutched firmly in my right arm. Suddenly she let out a simply heart-rendering howl. Needless to say, Dan shied violently, right across the road into the bush, and if you'd seen me trying to control a scared horse with one hand and a struggling and highly indignant cat with the other you'd have shrieked with mirth! However, we got home eventually. And then the fun began. This cat does *not* like dogs. The pup doesn't mind her much. In fact, he ignores her as far as possible. But if he gets within a yard of her she spits and swears at him. She won't even let him sleep in peace. She's a wretched little thief, too. I have to shut everything up. I daren't leave anything on the table and go out of the room for a second.

However, she's killed the mice. She appears to have killed the last one on my pyjamas yesterday morning!! Nasty little beast. I do *hate* cats. And my beautiful little bear skin rug out of my bedroom simply reeks of *cat*. I hung it up outside this morning to get rid of the smell and of course the pup thought it a fine thing to play with and was growling and worrying it when I rescued it! What a life!

However, I'm surviving. And I weigh just a pound more now than I did when I came out. But it must be muscle. I only get two meals most days and ride from 15 to 40 miles a day. Of course, I get 9 or 10 hours sleep nearly every night which makes a difference.

ᴧ 22 October 1929

My dear Uncle & Auntie,
I love hearing all about your garden. It sounds so delightfully English & peaceful. Western Canadians are all too busy rushing after the Almighty Dollar to have time for gardens, books, music or beauty in any form. They don't even notice the beauty round them. They think I'm quite mad to prefer living between the river and that old slough to living on the corner opposite the store and the schoolhouse where the town is going to be. It's no use telling them that I don't like absolutely flat treeless prairie and that having come 8,000 miles to get out of living in a town I don't want to live in another. They just wouldn't understand. However, I'm going to have a garden next year and at least half of it will be flowers.

ᴧ Sunday – October 26th

I have had another busy few days but am hoping for a peaceful afternoon. I've seen two patients today and I only reckon to see accidents and emergencies on a Sunday, so I'm hoping that the rest of the day is my own.

October 26th – the "Frozen Northland" – and here I am, sitting out of doors in a thin linen frock wondering whether I hadn't better fetch a hat because the sun is so bright!! Since our big rain the weather has been marvellous, day after day of cloudless beauty with a tinge of frost that makes the air deliciously fresh and sparkling. We occasionally get a day or two like this in October in England.

My dog is an enormous joy. He's awfully intelligent and easy to train. I wish I had more time for training him. It took me just one day to teach him to shake hands. I wish you could have seen him the next day following me round on three legs, sitting down and holding a paw out every time I stopped to look at him! I can't get him to sit up properly, though. He's awfully big and unwieldy and falls over. He follows the horse beautifully. I hardly ever have to call him. I take him on all journeys less than 20 miles and I think I can increase it to 25 miles soon. When I go into houses he lies down beside the horse and waits for me.

Our weekly mail service is due to start tomorrow and it is hoped that it will be pretty regular right through the winter, as they are going to put road gangs on to try and keep our new road open all through the winter. Of course, it remains to be seen whether they can manage that. The road goes through several belts of very heavy timber and there were half a dozen trees blown across it in the last storm.

I've been buying things for the winter just lately. I wish you could see me setting out on horseback attired in moose-hide moccasins, a marvellously fringed moose-hide coat and moose-hide mitts (also fringed), over my ordinary English shirt and breeches. I must get myself some leather chaps and then I shall look the real thing! I'm wearing a frock today, the first time since the beginning of August that I can remember!! It's the first Sunday (except the one when it rained) for 10 weeks that I haven't had to go out to see patients! I certainly have been hard worked lately but mercifully everybody is recovering now. I'm hoping to polish off a dozen or two of the 70 letters I owe and mount some more photos to send home. I believe I've about another 40! Photography is an expensive hobby but it is a joy to be able to send actual pictures of these places home.

I heard all about Mac's weekend in Dudley and how she enjoyed you and Auntie Angie telling the tale! Lord, it did make me homesick for a few minutes. Sometimes I wonder how long I can stick living out here away from everyone. Most times I wonder how on earth I could possibly bear to go back to England to live.

Here's a tale that may amuse you. It is gospel truth. I went out 3 days ago to see a man with pneumonia, camping out in the bush, and while I was in the tent another homesteader came in, a Yankee who arrived two weeks ago. He also was living in a tent and had caught a bad cold. Oh, a frightful cold, he said. He thought it might turn to pneumonia, too, but was quite sure that a drink of gin would cure him. But when he discovered that (A) I did not stock gin and (B) though I was a government Doctor, he had to pay for my services, he decided that it was only a slight cold and was already getting better!!

~: 27 October 1929

It seems months since I wrote a proper letter. I've got dozens of things accumulated to tell you about and about 30 more photos to mount and send you and I don't know which to do first. Perhaps you'd sooner have photos than a letter? I hope you got the others safely. They had to be trusted to a car going down and I didn't know the driver. The mail service petered out for a time because the "Weenusk" got stuck on a sand bank in the river, otherwise I should have registered them.

Life continues to be full of thrills. I spent another interesting night out with a policeman on Friday!! He was taking me to the Thresher's dance at the schoolhouse here and we got stuck in a mud hole!! I got to the dance at 1:30 and stayed till 5 a.m.!! He's a priceless young policeman aged 25, known in Peace River as Baby-face and dead nuts on clapping folks in jail!! He came up here to keep an eye on the dance, as $200 worth of alcohol had been shipped in here for the event! In Canada, it's an offence merely to be intoxicated in a public place. It isn't necessary also to be disorderly and driving to the public danger or anything like that. Needless to say, the news that there was a policeman in the district was all over the place before he got here. So not only was there no moonshine about but they didn't seem to have consumed much of the $200's worth. They're probably making a day of it today somewhere! There's quite a lot of trouble up here lately – thefts and wife beating and moonshine in large quantities – so we're probably going to have a resident policeman in the district next spring.

The telegraph line arrived in my back garden last night. I greeted them with a loud cheer and took photos of the last pole this side of the river being erected.

Heavens! Did I ever consider a telegraph line a blot on the landscape? That row of poles, cutting right across the slough and along behind my shack, spoiling the group of spruce trees by the river, is a sight I thank heaven for every time I see it. It may mean life or death to people up here whether I can get into touch with town quickly. Do you know how Peace River had to communicate with this district last winter? Telephone to Edmonton to get the Broadcasting Station to send out the message half a dozen times on the off chance that someone up here would hear it!! Two of the telegraph gang, one of them the man I had to go north to see two weeks ago, were down here today with a little telephone attachment, talking to their friends in Peace River over the line!

I'm living in great hopes of seeing a bear any day now. There was one seen just the other side of the river last week. Three men were camping in a tent there and he came in and took all their bread and cleared out a lard pail and never touched the men. And they hadn't a gun between them!!!!! The idea of three men camping out here without a gun is as funny as three men in a smoking compartment without a match in England! I didn't believe the tale because I'd been riding past their tent that night and again next morning and I didn't believe I could get my horse past the smell of bear. However, other people also saw him. Bissette says that if he was about here so late in the fall he will probably den up quite close for the winter. So I live in hopes! I admit that I felt a bit worried when I heard some trappers talking about the hungry bear who leaned up against the door of their trapping cabin and came in to get food, because the door of my shack opens inwards and I can't lock it! However, I hope he won't get that hungry!! I look round hopefully for tracks whenever I go out.

I think Daddy's idea of a "Trade Directory" to the district is an awfully good one. When I've got time I'll write one for you, but I'm trying to clear off a whole lot of letters today so I can't stop. I thought I'd described most of the people I'd mentioned so far? However, I'll start at the beginning and write you a sort of history, geography, and directory of the district when I can.

Now I'll mount those photos!

The first three of these pages of photos were taken by Miss Gilmour and Miss Chadwick, the two American friends of Miss Brighty's who were making the trip up to Fort Vermilion. Miss Gilmour sent me these photos from New York last week. They should be filed in with mine of the same dates in the album.

The next page, of various people passing my front door, goes in after the photos of two families coming in that I sent you before. I'm trying to get a whole series of the people who pass by, but they will go past when I'm dressing or washing or otherwise unable to dash out and take a snap.

There are only 18 here. I've about another 15 and a dozen more being developed but I haven't time to mount any more just now.

By the way, if I have to queue up I'm determined to send the first telegraph when this line is opened. It will probably be about 10 days hence. So, I'll send you a cable, if not too expensive. I don't know how they'll charge.

~ *27 October 1929*

Dear Winifred,
I suppose you're getting a bit fed up with me as a correspondent. But my goodness, these last 6 weeks have been the hardest I've ever done in my life. I've been riding day and night – serious cases in all directions – and between that and trying to keep house I've not had 10 minutes for letter writing. Thank heaven things are quieting down a bit now and everyone recovering, thank God!

I've been really panicky about one or two patients. It's an awful responsibility to keep a bad case up here instead of shooting it into hospital. But when the cost of getting there and the doctors' and hospital fees are so enormous ($100–$150, i.e. £20–£30 for a straightforward midwifery case), one simply has to try and keep everything possible up here. And the roads have been almost impassable for weeks, so that my worst case I couldn't get into hospital for a week. Had to ride 32 miles a day to see him and then had to get him in as soon as the roads were fit.

~ *Tuesday 12:30 p.m.*

The Royal Hotel
Peace River

I arrived here at 1 a.m., found the hotel almost full. All the Travelling
Clinic were here on their way from Slave Lake to Spirit River. Gee,
it was good to see them all again. To have someone to talk shop to
– and someone to rag with. Dr. Gilchrist was just as delightful as ever.
I only had breakfast with them, of course, but it *was* a joy.

Later

At that point I went to keep my appointment with the dentist,
talked to him, went out and met Dr. Sutherland who took me up
to the hospital and showed me the X-rays of my patient and all the
other interesting cases in the hospital. Then I had tea there with
the Matron and Dr. Sutherland and Dr. Agnew and we all talked
shop till 5 o'clock. Then I went to see Homer Johnson (the Road
Surveyor) and he's going to take me back to Battle River tomorrow.
Now I've had supper and have just got an hour before I go out to Dr.
Robinson's for the evening!

People are friendly in Canada. Almost everyone I meet asks me to
their house.

It does amuse me to try and see Peace River as I saw it just 15 weeks
ago. I thought it was a priceless little one-eyed town. It might almost
be the model for "Main Street." Now, it has become the centre of the
universe, the metropolis. I feel as though I am really in the centre of
civilisation again!! And it feels simply priceless to be wearing a skirt. I
keep looking down to see if something is coming unstuck. I can't get
used to the feel of flapping things around my knees.

It was very very cold motoring last night. Although there were 4
of us in a closed car and I was wearing a big coat over my costume
coat, I still felt cold. Today, I see that the edges of the river have been
frozen all day. So, another week or so will see us frozen in. Oh, you'd
love Peace River. It combines the beauty of the lake district and bits
of Switzerland with an atmosphere absolutely its own – the feeling of
being in the great North West, with unlimited big game and all sorts
of adventures only just round the corner!

I shall never come back to settle in England. The thought of being
shut in by houses and deafened by traffic makes my head ache. I may
not stay in Canada. I may move off to some other part of the world

but I shan't come back to a town. My tastes would be altogether too expensive in England, too. Dogs, horses, shooting all cost too much in England.

My patients are so interesting too – every nationality except Chinese, all sorts of men – and the half breeds just fascinate me. Of course, I haven't got Mrs. Blue any longer. She was the greatest joy. Did I ever tell you about her? She came twice to scrub my floor for me and also did some rough washing. She's gone to Grouard now. She talked English pretty well for a breed and her favourite expression was "Gee-whiz." She came out with it about once per sentence. She gave me an enormous hunk of moose meat once. She'd killed the moose; she did quite a lot of hunting. As she said once "I no frightened him bear gee-whiz! I got gun, I shoot um bear, I shoot um moose, gee whiz!" Oh, she was a delightful charlady. Unfortunately, she had no notion of honesty. I think her attitude was that anything left about was hers for the taking!

I wish you could see the half breeds travelling, the man riding a horse and the woman walking behind and carrying the baby! That's the way to keep women in their place!

I'm sorry for the breeds, though. They've neither the rights nor protection the Indians have, nor the rights of white men. No matter how white they are – and some of them have blue eyes and medium brown hair – yet they still can't live like white people. They try sometimes but they just can't do it. There's a family whose house I was in one day who are trying to live like whites. Their house – complete with a gramophone, big clock, photographs of the most Victorian type, curtains, chairs – looks "white" but you've only got to go in, as I did one evening, and find the family sitting on the floor round the stove while the chairs remain arranged round the wall, to realize how far from white they really are. There's something awfully pathetic about it.

I'm gradually going "squaw." I'm getting more and more moose-hide clothing. It's delightfully warm and yet fairly lightweight. See me going out attired in wonderfully beaded moose-hide moccasins coming high up my legs, a fringed moose-hide coat, moose-hide gloves. I shall have to wear moccasins all the winter. Seems a bit mad, doesn't it, but one gets frost-bitten in shoes. My greatest winter difficulty is going to be keeping my house warm. I've a heater and a cooking stove and 10 cords of wood (i.e. 2,800 cubic feet) is being cut and split for me. But it seems to me that I'm going to have to put on my alarm clock and wake in the middle of every night to stoke up because wood goes down so quickly.

The other night the outside temperature went down to about 20° F. I went to bed at 11:30 p.m. The temperature in my shack was then just over 70° F and I left a good fire burning and all windows and door shut. I got up at 8 a.m. and the temperature inside the house was then 33° F. Well now, if the temperature drops 40° in 8½ hours when it is not particularly cold outside, what on earth will it do at a temperature of 50° or 60° below zero??? I feel there should be some way of calculating this out but can't do it. However, it means that the house would be a little too chilly to get out of bed in the morning! Of course, I shouldn't know anything about this if I hadn't just acquired a thermometer. I'm wondering if I shouldn't keep warmer this winter if I got rid of that thermometer!!

Have they sent on the photos I sent home yet? I've just sent home another 18. But my camera is just falling to pieces. The strap of the case broke and it fell off my horse once, then I carried it in my pocket but it fell out of there once or twice. I think I shall have to get a new one. However, it's done pretty good service since I came out. I wish I could see those photos as they look to you. They must look so different when you've never seen Canada. Can you see the difference between Jarvie country and the Peace and Battle River country? How much more clear and sparkling the air is up here? I have become so accustomed to the vividness of this country, the marvellous colourings and clear sharp outlines, that I can't quite get back my original feeling of astonished delight.

When I get back to Battle River, I'm going to buy some traps to do a little trapping, I think. Ermine preferably!! Did you know ermine was only weasels in their winter coats??? I didn't. They've all changed colour now. The sparrows have turned white too.

Sorry! this is all the paper I've got.

Do write again.

My Dear Lena,

Oh, you'd be tickled if you could see me trying to keep house in my spare time. Canada is a funny country to keep house in and up here in the wilds you can't get half the things you need when you need them. You have to buy vast quantities of everything. I buy 50 lbs. of flour, a side of bacon, 30 lbs. of sugar, and a box (40 lbs.) of apples at a time!! And I've booked my winter's supply of beef – the hind leg of an animal that's running round the prairie at present but will be killed as soon as it's cold enough to freeze the meat. Can't you see me tackling 100 lbs of beef??? When I get it, I shall just hang it on a nail outside the house. It will get frozen hard and keep all the winter. As a matter of fact, I shall have to get it sliced down to the bone soon after I get it because meat freezes so hard in the winter that you can't cut it. You have to chop it with an axe!!! And now I've got a cellar I'm getting 3 sacks of potatoes, a sack of carrots, a sack of turnips, and a sack of onions. And I hope that will do me for the winter!

I still buy things in smaller quantities than most people. I haven't got used to big quantities yet. Up here lots of people buy their whole year's groceries at once. They call it "grub-stake." It took me weeks to discover what they meant by grub-stake, but the reason they do it is this: Trappers earn quite a lot of money during the winter. When they sell their furs in spring they get $1,000 or more. But after, they don't get any more money all the year. So, while they've got the money they buy their grub-stake. Then, whatever happens, they won't starve even if they've spent all their money before they've earned any more. Lots of farmers do the same. After threshing, when they've sold their grain, they get some money but they know they won't get any more for a year, so they get in huge stocks. But wouldn't the grocer be surprised if you went in and bought a 5 lb. tin of baking powder?

I've not had much time for cooking lately. I've been out all day and only home for supper, bed and breakfast. But I'm gaining weight all the time! Oh, you might tell Daddy I eat a vast plate of porridge for breakfast every morning, will you. I know he'll feel more satisfied if he knows! I also eat bacon, 2 eggs, fried potatoes, stewed fruit, bread and butter and honey for breakfast most mornings too!! I always cook twice as many potatoes as I need so that I can have them fried next day!

I'm going to send this letter by air mail and post one to Mother and Daddy by ordinary mail at the same time. Let me know how much time it saves.

It's rather late (10:30 p.m.) so this will only be a short letter. I'd meant to write a really long one tonight. Finished supper at 7:30 p.m. and was just starting to clear up when two men arrived and they've only just gone. They were more "People of Importance," inspecting the district and including me in the sights. I do get a lot of them and they all ask the same questions: How do I like Canada? Is this going to be my first winter? Don't I get lonesome? Am I not afraid of living by myself so far from anyone?, etc. I'm glad these arrived after dark and couldn't take photos of me. Mr. Wilson, Mayor of Peace River, called on me one morning just when I was busy cleaning up and took me outside "to have my photo taken with the Mayor, to send home." I've got the print; you shall see it in due course. I look even more dirty and untidy than I felt!

I should have left this letter till tomorrow but there's a committee meeting here in the afternoon which will take up some time. Did I ever tell you about the committee of four bachelors who look after me? They're priceless. I've put the fear of the Lord upon them, told them that if ever my water barrel is empty, or my wood unsplit I shall quit work and go for a holiday! They do amuse me. They're all different nationalities. There's old Bill Tyson, the village blacksmith. He's a Yankee, aged 60. Then there's Bill Asmussen. He's a Canadian but his parents were Danish, I think. He's young and good-looking and a magnificent horseman. And Charles Plavin, he's an old Russian who has lived in Germany and the States, and who is one of the most interesting men in the district. And the fourth one is Tellef Lien, a Norwegian, aged 36. He's going to teach me to ski this winter if we can find a suitable slope. They all talk English – but quite differently – and old Plavin gets awfully excited and jumps about. The others hate him. I thought there'd be bloodshed last time they met!!

Well, it's not winter yet. The chinook has been blowing steadily ever since that big rain till today. But today the wind has gone round to NW and the thermometer is dropping fast, so we may be going to get snow. The northern lights tonight are more wonderful than ever I've seen them. They spread across the *whole* sky like a great bunch of streamers starting in the NE and waving about in all directions. I can see them from every window.

Well – I'll write again soon.

~: *11 November 1929*

Your letters of October 13th and 21st arrived last Friday. Dudley seems to be a very good place for mailing letters, better than anywhere except Manchester and London. The letter from Weston should have arrived a week before but didn't. I'm always awfully glad to get your letters and know you are so well.

I'm just waiting for the kettle to boil, so that I can wash up my supper things and get to bed. (It's 9:30 p.m.) It's getting cold again tonight and there's a gale coming up from the west. We've had another week of perfect weather, cold at night (down to 10 or 15) but sunny and warm in the day.

You can't think how weird it feels at night, living all by myself in this little house. I've got the whole valley to myself. There's not a light to be seen. All around are old burnt-off tree trunks, very white in the moonlight, and the Spruce trees are intensely black against the sky and make a noise like the sea in this wind. The sound of the river has almost gone, now it's freezing over. It feels as though Brutus and I are utterly isolated in the middle of this immense country.

There's something overpowering about the size of Canada. I get the sensation sometimes that these people are tiny beings struggling with their backs to the wall against something enormous that is bound to beat them. And when I see acres of land cleared and broken I feel a queer sort of triumph and then, seeing the Battle River country from one of the surrounding hills, I realise what a little scratch on the surface it is. All round, shutting it in on every side, is bush and forest and muskeg, unmapped and untouched.

That's something queer about Canada. I keep noticing it – not only that it is big but that you can't help feeling all the time how big it is. Even though you can't see more than a mile or so around, you still feel that it goes on for thousands of miles. I can't make out the cause of it. It seems to be something apart altogether from one's knowledge of geography. Do you get what I'm driving at or does it sound merely mad?

Kettle's boiling. I'd better wash up.

~: *Tuesday Nov. 12th*

This is a funny beginning to a letter. But I was in a funny mood last night, the effect perhaps of reading "Wuthering Heights."

What a very long time my letter of Sept. 19th took to arrive. Did you notice by any chance what day it was posted? A half-breed took it out for me. The roads were practically impassable after the rain. I don't know how many days it would take.

~: *Thursday Nov. 14th.*

I don't seem to be getting on very fast with this letter. I keep getting interruptions.

Yesterday I took advantage of a very warm fine day to wash the three pairs of curtains in this room. (Why, oh why, did I choose biscuit colour?) Between carrying in the wood and the water, doing the washing, carrying in more wood to heat the irons, ironing curtains and sewing on their 42 rings and putting them up, they took half the day.

Oh, you pampered beings who get hot water by turning the tap, you should just try this life! Getting water from a half frozen river is really exciting. You see, the ice gets thinner and thinner as you get nearer the water. It's hopeless unless there's a handy rock. Well, there are lots of rocks, as you'll see from the photos I sent you, but they're awfully awkwardly arranged! Also, standing on a very rounded rock covered with a thin layer of ice while you reach over to get a bucketful of water is no mean balancing feat, I assure you. Even when you've got your water, turning round on aforesaid slippery rock and then stepping from one slippery rock to another to get to the bank has its excitements. I went through yesterday, I mean one foot only, but goodness, it was cold.

Bother! Have just missed a truck that might have taken this letter out if only I'd finished it sooner.

The mail is in tonight or tomorrow. I don't know whether I shall go over tonight to see. It's been snowing all afternoon. They're going to move the Post Office 4 miles north to Rousseau's in a week or so, now the Post Office 6 miles south (North Star) has been opened. It's obviously unfair to have two offices 6 miles apart and then nothing for the next 18 miles. Think of doing 36 miles in mid-winter just to see if there are any letters for you! Of course I shall have to do 8 miles but then I'm reasonably certain of having some letters when I get there.

It started snowing very heavily this afternoon. I thought we were in for 3 or 4 feet of snow but it stopped again. When I went down to feed Dan the river was half frozen and the ice snow-covered. The water was a sort of blue black colour and it was snowing hard. It looked just like one of these American films. It only required a woman staggering through the snow clutching a baby!

These half-breeds are funny. Last week one of them called me out late at night to see a baby who was teething. (I didn't go. I've met the lady and the baby before. She thinks that as she doesn't intend to pay anything she may just as well call me out as come down to see me.) Today, a half breed brought a boy of 6 with *pneumonia* 12 miles in an open Ford car in a blinding snowstorm to see me! I suppose he didn't know it was pneumonia, but with a feverish child, getting pain in his chest on breathing, and with a respiration rate of 50 to the minute you'd have thought he'd have suspected it, wouldn't you? He told me that the Kiddie's breathing began to get faster at dawn this morning. As a matter of fact, the kid's jolly bad. He was an elegant pale blue when I saw him. I don't like his chances. I'm glad the snow has stopped. I'll be able to get a lift in a car tomorrow. I promised I'd get out on horseback (it's only 6 miles away) or if the snow was too deep to get a car through.

I've had a stroke of bad luck. I've lost my camera. I carry it round with me a good deal and had had a moose hide case made for it. I imagine the strap must have broken. I didn't miss it for 2 or 3 days after I last remembered using it, so it may be anywhere over 30 or 40 miles of trail. I've put up a notice in the store. That's all I can do. I haven't time to retrace my steps. Those three days and the snow will have covered it by now. I'm hoping someone has picked it up. I don't want to have to buy another, though I'd been thinking about it before.

But I've spent a lot of money this month. I bought a gas-lamp when I was down in Peace River. It burns gasoline (petrol) and gives a brilliant white light.

Did I tell you I did a quick dash to Peace River and got two teeth filled? Luckily, there's a very good dentist there. I spent a most enjoyable evening playing bridge till 2 a.m. with Dr. and Mrs. Robinson and Mr. Wilson, the school inspector.

I'm busy teaching the pup to talk. He's getting on quite well. He now says "please" before I give him anything. Unfortunately, I've been teaching him at meal times, having no other time to spare, and it's rather encouraging him to be a nuisance. But he is fun to train. He sits down and lies down and shakes hands when I tell him to. He's awfully heavy, though, and overbalances when I try to teach him to sit up. He brings me his dish when he thinks it's meal time and he asks for the quilt when he wants to go to bed. (I cover up my camp bed with an old quilt for him.) He's very good company. I don't know what I'd do without him.

Did I tell you Mr. Plavin's remark when he saw that photo of Mother? "She is a very handsome robust lady – what?"!!! I thought mother would like to know.

I do meet some priceless people on this job, visitors as well as patients, and now I've got yet another class of visitors – men enquiring how to get to various places. This is the penalty for having a pretty good all-round knowledge of the district and a home-made map, compiled very laboriously from land office lists with the names of the majority of the people on it. So newcomers, generally unable to speak English, go to Bissette for direction and Bissette saves himself much time and trouble by assuring them that I have the only map in existence and sending them over to me! You see me dragged from my bed in the early hours of the morning (i.e. at 8 a.m.), expecting nothing less than a broken neck, greeted on the doorstep by a Ukrainian who enquires if I am the doctor – in other words says "Meeses Doktor"? and when I say I am, bursts into Ukrainian. I assure him in my best Ukrainian that I don't understand and get another burst of Ukrainian. (All this on the doorstep at temperature of 10° F, me in my dressing gown.)

Eventually, he either gives me a bit of paper with his section number on it or makes me understand the name of the man he wants.

Then I get out my map and, having found the place, tell him how to get there. It's often 10 minutes work to explain, pointing in the different directions and showing him how many miles on my fingers! It's difficult to be sure they understand because they all say "yes, yes, yes." It's often the only English word they know! I know a few words of Russian, Hungarian, Polish, Ukrainian and Cree but I get them mixed! But all the Eastern Europeans call me Mrs. Doctor. I don't know why. Still, this game of directing people is all very well. Three times in one week have I been fetched out of bed. Oh goodness! I do laugh when I remember how I used to pine for fresh air and exercise this time last year.

This is just the life for me, you know. I haven't been quite so busy lately and so Dan has been very frisky. He tried to run away with me last week!! (I was riding without a bridle or bit. Somebody borrowed mine for a couple of days.) I may say I let him run and, when he showed signs of slowing down, I kicked him on again. I did the 10 miles to Second Battle River in 20 minutes less than usual! He won't try that game again in a hurry. But it's a great sensation galloping across open prairie. And now the pup can keep up. We have some great times.

I can't see myself settling down in a town after this. Of course, there are times when it isn't quite so enjoyable. For instance, coming back from the Second Battle on this same journey, I had to go and see an old man with heart failure who had moved from the house I'd previously seen him in and was not on my map. He can't speak a word of English. The Hungarian who directed me could speak a little. I found the place eventually, after taking an unnecessarily long way round. I asked at the house if there was a quicker trail to Rousseau's and was put onto a trail going S.W., told that there was only the one trail and I couldn't miss it and I was to keep on that till I came to the telegraph poles and then follow them south. Sounded simple and saved me a good four miles. It was quite dark and exceedingly cold and I'd had nothing to eat since breakfast. I wanted to get home quickly and so I started off.

Well, ½ mile away the trail branched S and W. Obeying the first rule for getting about the prairie (i.e. whenever there are two trails and you're doubtful, take the most used one), I turned south. Another ½ mile, no telegraph posts. Then I saw a light ahead but

50 yards from the house came to a creek. It was not more than 5 feet wide and would have been quite easy but for the fact that it had frozen over 2 or 3 inches thick and Dan wouldn't cross. Thinking the people might have a bridge or dam across it somewhere, I followed it along a little way but could not find one. So, I called out at the top of my voice and tried to rouse the people in the house, without success. I turned round to retrace my last half mile and couldn't find the trail I'd come on!!!

After hunting around for about 5 minutes, I got back on to it and went back to the fork in the trail and started off west. Went about a mile along it, not a sign of any telegraph poles. Gave it up as a bad job and decided to go back to Keleman's and then take the trail I knew. Well, I risked a short cut from the trail I was on. (You'd have thought I'd have learnt sense by that time, wouldn't you, but I hadn't.) The trail petered out in a bog! Mercifully the bog was frozen pretty hard so I cut across it and aimed for the trail I knew! Remember it was quite dark – cloudy, no stars, no moon, no northern lights, open prairie and bush, no fences or houses – and I hit the trail exactly where I expected to!!!

I thought my troubles were over but I'd forgotten this creek. It runs right across Big Prairie from the hills to the Peace River and is bridged in one place only – where I had crossed on my way up and 2 miles further east than the trail I was now on. So, of course I came to the creek that I'd had to turn back for and couldn't get across. I kicked and kicked but Dan wouldn't try it. I got off and tried to lead him across. The ice cracked ominously before I got half way so I gave it up and tried yet another trail I knew. Went back a little way, then decided to cut across prairie to get to it – and once more got lost!! However, I found a narrow place in the creek, got Dan across it and then I was all right, only six miles home on a good trail. But I got home at 11 p.m.!

All this seems very involved. I've drawn you a sketch map. It may make it clearer. I discovered when I got to Rousseau's and on to the telegraph line again that it was just so dark that you could go between two poles without being able to see either of them or the wire, so I possibly missed the line in that way.

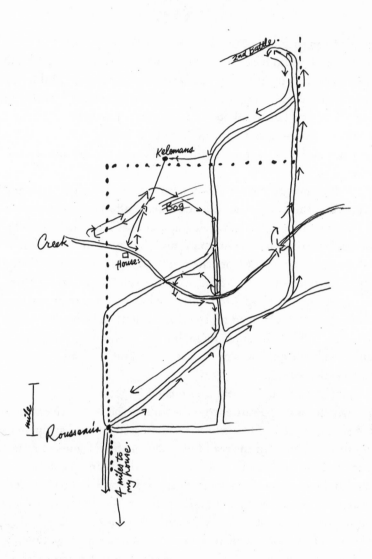

~ Saturday Nov. 16th

Well, I have had a day of it! Started with two patients before breakfast and have been at it ever since. Set a fractured femur for an Alsatian puppy this morning!

The little boy with pneumonia is doing awfully well. I went out to see him this afternoon and had a glorious ride. It was a perfectly lovely day.

I hope to get this down to town tomorrow.

Your letter of November 3rd has just arrived. Really, the mail service is extremely good for this time of the year, isn't it? I thought it would take a day or two longer crossing the Atlantic during the winter when boats had to take the southern route but 18 days is excellent time.

I'm sorry you've been imagining me in the depths of winter all this time when I've been enjoying such marvellously fine warm weather. It's beginning to get colder now and we've had a little snow this week but I've not felt cold yet. It's beautifully dry and sparkles in the sunlight. I must remember to get some dark glasses next time I'm at the store. My eyes were quite tired by the glare yesterday and snow-blindness out here is not uncommon.

Last night there was a beautiful sunset and a perfect "alpine glow" on the hill across the river. Do you remember that perfect one on the Jungfrau?

The river is frozen over now, and there is a little snow on the ice. It looks very beautiful from the hill to the east, a shining white ribbon. The ice is only about 5 inches thick yet but it freezes right through before winter is over, except in the very deep patches. The roads are exceedingly slippery and cars and wagons have made them like glass in places, particularly on the hills. The roads are very narrow down these hills by the river and I've already told you how exceedingly steep the hills are. These trails are scratched along the side of the slope and there is not more than 6 inches allowed for skidding! They put the fear of the Lord upon me in wet weather and they're much worse now. Somebody will certainly go over one day.

Yesterday morning I lay in bed gazing at a snow-covered world, thanking heaven that I hadn't anybody really ill on my list and even the little boy with pneumonia could be left for a day or so. He's getting better so rapidly. I got up and made my breakfast and, before I'd eaten 2 spoonfuls of porridge, a car arrived. Patient a boy of 13, Hungarian, whose "throat was swollen inside." Tonsillitis. Temperature 103. I looked at his chest and sure enough, scarlet fever!!! 8 miles in a rattly Ford car with temperature of 103 – and the outside temperature just below zero!!

I shot him off home to bed, told them to come back and fetch me in an hour's time (there wasn't room for three in the car) and hurried to finish my breakfast. Got as far as bacon and eggs and another car arrived: the little Frenchman from the garage with frozen feet. (Silly idiot was wearing leather shoes.) Thawed those out, fed him on cake and coffee, washed up, dispensed the necessary medicine, throat paint, serum, disinfectant for the scarlet fever kid and just got done before they arrived for me. Went and inspected the isolation and sanitary arrangements, warned them they were liable to $100 fine if they left their ¼ section or allowed anyone else to enter it, put up a large quarantine notice and gave the other kids serum all round. Then went and saw the kid with pneumonia who only lived 1½ miles from there.

Went home to find a message awaiting me that George Robertson's baby was very ill and that Joe Hansen who lives next door to George Robertson had pneumonia!! George's car had broken down and he hadn't a team and wagon, so the only thing seemed to be to ride. It's 3 miles away by the short cut, and 3¾ to 4 miles by the road. I decided I must have a meal before I started to ride over. The temperature was just below zero and dropping rapidly. I was just hauling in some wood to keep the heat going while I was away, when another car arrived: the little Frenchman again. He'd left a pair of gloves in the morning. Hearing where I was off to, he offered to take me in his car but warned me he'd broken his battery during the day and so had no lights! However, I assured him that I knew that trail so well that I could find my way blindfolded. (I've had a baby with a big abscess in his neck, a boy with tuberculous meningitis, two cases of whooping cough, a baby with bronchopneumonia and a confinement along that trail!!! Oh, and a man who died of TB too. I'd forgotten him. And there are only 6 houses.!)

But, it's one thing to find your way along a well marked cart-track on horseback and altogether another to pick out the way when it's entirely covered by snow and no-one has been along it and in a car going fairly quickly. However, we got there quite safely. It was only just 6 o'clock and not very dark. Sure enough, Mr. Hansen had pneumonia. Temperature 104.5. Looking after him took about an hour. He's a bachelor and had only been looked after by two other old bachelors who happened along. It took me about ¼ hour to make his bed. It was just a jumble of blankets (6) and coats when I started. It's a great life having to do the nursing as well as the doctoring! You should have heard the other two old blighters enquiring if I'd come and tuck them up if they were ill?!! I threatened them with a dose of castor oil and they shut up.

Then I went and saw George Robertson's baby. It was pretty bad and took me another ½ hour. So, by the time we started back, it was 7:30 p.m., absolutely dark, no stars, moon not up. However, we got on pretty well. We slid backwards down two steepish hills and had to back and take another run at them. In fact, we had to do that three times at the second and did an elegant sideways skid whose real beauty I didn't appreciate till I saw the tracks today! But we got here all right, radiator boiling merrily but that's a detail.

I do see life, don't I?

~: *Friday Nov. 22.*

I went across to the store to get some gasoline and came back with a ham on one side of my saddle (14½ lbs.) and a vast hunk of beef on the other side (12 lbs. cost 9/-) and carrying a gallon can of gasoline in my hand.

So I've just had a huge supper of steak and onions and am almost comatose as a result. I certainly was not cut out for a vegetarian. My cooking has taken a turn for the better. I've had an awful month or so. I never knew whether what I put in the oven would come out cake, pastry or dog biscuit!! The pup has been getting fatter and fatter! I couldn't even toast a piece of bread without burning it and I invariably broke the yolk of my fried eggs.

By the way, this is a bit of the letter I had from the Department last night.

> "You will be interested to know that we have a report of the excellent work you are doing, sent in through the Police Department."

I can't help wondering whether this had any connection with a really decent supper which I achieved for P.C. Babyface!!! It was one of the evenings when things went right, more or less. It certainly was the only piece of work of mine he saw.

Oh goodness! There are such lots of things to tell you, I don't know where to start. I could write about six pages a day if I'd time. It's such a fascinating community to be living in; now I'm getting to know people all the gossip is so much more interesting. For instance, the latest excitement is that Jim Schamehorn has shot four of Bill Grey's pigs who were on his (J.S's) land. Well, that sounds more or less straightforward till you know that Jim's daughter, Lucy, ran away from home Xmas Eve last year to marry Ned Grey, Bill Grey's son. She ran away because they absolutely refused to allow her to marry him. He is a half-breed and a Catholic. They are Canadians of German extraction and virulent Protestant and have a violent aversion to "breeds." Since she married, her father and mother won't have anything to do with her and she won't have anything to do with them, though they live on adjacent sections.

My own situation was rather delicate a week or two ago. I'm on good terms with both families but when Lucy increased the population with a boy she still wouldn't have her mother in the house (even if her mother would have gone). Mrs S. used to waylay me on the road to enquire about the infant and Lucy and Lucy didn't want me to give her mother any information. When I told Mrs. S what a lovely baby it was, she snorted and informed me that it was a "breed." Feeling won't be improved by this pig shooting business, whatever the police decide is the law on the subject. This open herd law business is an awful difficulty you know.

The kettle is boiling so I'm going to wash my hair.

~ Saturday Nov. 23rd

I washed my hair and washed a woollen jumper and then it was bedtime.

And now I've just been interviewed by four "people of importance" and never had the sense to ask them to take this letter down with them so that it would catch Tuesday's mail. Now if I post it tomorrow, it will leave by Friday's mail. Isn't it maddening? However, I think I shall have to take to posting my letters here. They'll take a long time but you will get them every week and I know you must get worried when there are gaps, though as I've told you before, if anything happened you'd hear long before my letters stopped arriving.

I hope to goodness those photos have arrived. They should have done long ago. They're exceedingly precious because, of course, I've no duplicates of the ones I didn't take myself. Miss Brighty promises me some she took the day I arrived here but they haven't come yet. I've some 20 more to mount. I'll do them tomorrow and send them out with this mail if I've time.

My camera has been found. Mr. Keleman has it. That's about 8 or 9 miles away and I haven't time to go after it. He forgot to bring it when he came to the store. Glad I haven't got to buy another.

How much did the Carnival realize ultimately?

Thanks ever so much for the Argosy. I wonder if you realised when you read that tale "Among the Corn Rows" how marvellously true to life it was? But for the scenery, that might have been Battle River Prairie. Oh heavens! Don't I know it all? Crackers and sardines and "biscuits" and mice. Did I tell you about the old Yankee bachelor who taught me to make biscuit? I can make it almost as well as an American now. It isn't a bit what we call biscuit. It's really baking powder bread, little crusty loaves that you split and butter and eat hot. Very good – and exceedingly indigestible! I was taught to make them of flour, water, baking powder and salt, the absolute minimum, you see. (Some of these men live on less than $100 = £20 per annum for food and light.) They're more attractive with lard and milk added, of course.

It's a cold grey day. I should think we're in for a heavy snow fall. Grey days are very rare up here. It's funny how they alter the scenery. It looks much more like England now! Much smaller.

I wonder how Mac is getting on. I suppose she's in S. Africa now, nice and warm.

I've ordered some skates but they have not arrived yet. Peace River didn't stock any big enough for me! I wish I'd learnt to skate. I am told that the best way to teach yourself is to push a chair along the ice! I've warned the people living along the river that if they see me solemnly pushing a chair down the river they're not to think excessive hard work has gone to my head. I shall merely be learning to skate!

Oh, this is a funny life! It's funnier now than ever. You should see me hopping out of bed at 3 a.m. or 4 a.m. every morning to stoke up! I'm wondering whether to take to sleeping in my living room when the really cold weather comes and I have to stoke two hourly. You see, it isn't only me. I'd take the risk of waking to find the house below freezing point but all my drugs would freeze and perish if the house got too cold. And my heater, even when filled with wood, won't stay alight more than 4½ to 5 hours.

Dudley seems almost unbelievably tame and safe compared with this and yet I suppose one runs a much greater chance of sudden death crossing High Street than riding out here.

I'll try to get this out today. Failing that, it will have to go by mail tomorrow. The telegraph office is built so I'll be able to wish you a Merry Xmas by cable with luck.

⌁ 27 November 1929

Here are the remainder of the photos. I don't suppose I shall have any more to send you for a month or so. I only got my camera back from Keleman's this week and haven't taken any more than are here. However, with the other lots I've sent you, you should be able to get some idea of the country.

I'm very busy again. No more scarlet fever, thank heaven, but lots of oddments and a very bad axe wound in a man's foot that I have to go and dress. (It's four miles away.)

Life continues to be exciting. If anything, it gets more so!

I got lost last night. Sheer stupidity, of course. I had two visits to do, knew the trails to both of them. But, as one was 4 miles due north of the other I decided to aim north instead of going round by the trail. The positions were like this:

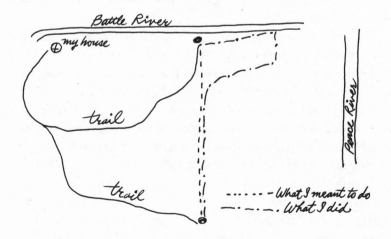

You see how much it saved? Well, I knew nothing of the intervening country, had only crossed it once (on my way in from landing on Peace River) and it turned out to be anything but flat prairie. I got into a slough, went due north along it for a distance of perhaps ½ mile, and then the wretched thing turned east, and I couldn't get out of it because the banks were steep and thickly wooded. It was getting dark very rapidly, too (5 p.m.). The slough got narrow and then very bushy and then we came to a number of fallen trees and Dan fell over one and plunged into the bushes and I simply had to duck my head, to avoid getting my glasses smashed, and hope for the best!

Then, we managed to get out of the slough and up the bank. Out of the frying pan and into the fire, it proved. The windfalls were piled feet high. They came up to the horse's chest. It took about ½ hour to do 100 yards and then we got to the top of the bank. (It was only about 50 feet high.) I looked north and there was the river!!! By this time, I wasn't quite sure whether it was the Peace River or Battle River I was looking at but I soon realised that I must have come on to Battle River much further east than ever I'd been. So I turned west, thinking that if the worst happened I'd get down to the river and go along the ice till I found the part I knew. After a ¼ mile, I found a trail, followed it and came down on the house I was aiming for in a few yards!!

But this business of steering by the Pole Star is harder than you'd think. And now it gets dark at 4:30 p.m. I have to do some of my journeys late in the dark but I must cure myself of this habit of trying new trails late in the afternoon, particularly when I mean to go through uninhabited country. I can never resist exploring. Of course, it wasn't my sense of direction that was wrong that night. I knew which way to go, all right. It was the physical necessity for taking the line of least resistance that was the trouble.

But by Jove! I do sympathise with those poor surveyors. They told me that they came through a wide belt of windfalls from the north and did about a mile a day – and that a long, hard day's work.

I haven't time to write any more. This will catch Friday's train from Grimshaw, I hope.

It's 10:30 p.m. and I'm just waiting for the kettle to boil for my hot water bottle and then I'm off to bed. But I thought perhaps I'd better start a letter now because in future your letters are going to be scraps written at odd times, I'm afraid. In fact, you may get cut down to a weekly post card if this weather holds. You see, I'm learning to skate. With the aid of my next door neighbours, two stalwart young bachelors named Jim and Cyril (surname unknown, I don't think I've ever heard them mentioned), I spend all my spare time staggering up and down the river! It's a fascinating amusement, isn't it? There's a stretch of river nearly ½ mile long and from 100 to 200 feet wide of smooth "black" ice, perfectly clear. You can see every stone and shell through it and so smooth that it reflects the starlight just like water. It really is a perfectly lovely spot.

The weather is unbelievably beautiful. The chinook is blowing again. There is no snow. The temperature went below zero one night but mainly it's between 10° and 35° F which feels very much warmer than an English December. Of course, you have to wrap up well. I'm still doing all my work on horseback. Dan was sharp shod last week so doesn't slip on the ice now.

I've been quite busy again but it seemed to be slacking off a bit yesterday and I was congratulating myself on having no visits to do today, therefore plenty of time for skating. However, "the best laid plans," etc. I've seen six patients today and had a call from another one 10 miles away in the bush so I shall be busy again tomorrow.

One of today's patients had ridden 90 miles. He did it in 24 hours!!! Only stopped three times to make tea! And till you've ridden through heavy bush like that with branches hitting you in the face in the dark, over a trail which has to be known before you can see it, you can't appreciate what a journey it was. It would take me three days, hard going. Incidentally, I'm the nearest doctor and he tells me there's a settlement of nearly 300 people there, nearly all Indians and breeds; it's a trip I may have to make.

I'm sleepy. I got up early this morning, had swept up and got breakfast before sunrise!! Doesn't that sound well? It rather spoils the effect to add that sunrise is 9:30 a.m. and I've been getting up between 9:30 and 10 a.m. lately! Daylight is very short now, about 9 a.m. till 4:30 p.m. The evenings seem very long but my new neighbours play cards every night so I expect I shall survive this winter. I'm almost beginning to wonder if this winter is a myth. I've been expecting it daily now since the middle of September. But we're still having weather that's almost too beautiful to be true, it's so marvellously sunny.

We're going to have a Church here soon, United Church of Canada = Presbyterians + Methodists, I believe. They're going to start building in a few weeks. It will be a great joy. Rev. Selkirk was here yesterday talking about it. I met him in Peace River last time I was there. He's quite nice but I hope we get someone younger and more energetic up here; the man they get is going to determine almost entirely whether it's successful or not.

Most of the people here are just neutral. There's almost every variety of Nonconformist and Anglicans and Seventh day Adventists etc., etc., but they'll all be prepared to sample any non-Catholic religion. (The Catholics have just built a church on Little Prairie and are going to build one on Big Prairie soon. They are numerically much the biggest crowd here. All the breeds are Catholic.) And there's an enormous crowd of Americans. One of the student-preachers up here this summer spoke of them as the "Godless Americans" and I think he was about right. They haven't even a tradition of Sunday church-going, and in other ways too they seem fairly godless.

The telegraph office is to be opened next week, we hope. I shall cable you for Xmas, if it isn't too expensive.

We have also acquired a barber. He's living in Joe Bissette's bunk house at present but as soon as he's built a shack he's going to start a Pool Hall!! Aren't we getting civilised?

There are great stretches of the district that were unbroken bush when I came in and now I find houses, fences and patches of land cleared. I hardly even ride over the same trail twice. Everywhere people are busy fencing their land, forcing the trails to follow the road allowances.

Well, the kettle has been boiling for some time. If I get time tomorrow I'll add to this.

❧ 5 December 1929

Snow, snow and more snow! There's a drift about 2 feet deep in front of my house and between the door and the wood pile. It has been snowing steadily for nearly 24 hours now.

I came back 12 miles after dark last night (and it *was* dark), riding right into the teeth of a NE wind, snowing hard, tiny stinging snowflakes as sharp as needles. My great fear was that I should get lost on the open prairie because the trail was covered over, but I didn't. I made record time, as a matter of fact.

I've spent most of the morning pulling teeth. A man walked 20 miles in the snowstorm yesterday, found me out and so waited till this morning. He wanted 10 teeth removed!! My hat! Nearly all the crowns had gone, leaving just black stumps and there were great abscesses all over the place. The roots of the canines were nearly an inch long and the others very little shorter! And when I'd done it, he'd got to walk 20 miles back!!!! However, I got 'em out all right. Thank God I'm not a dentist.

Dr. Sutherland is up from Peace River today, coroner's inquest. I'm hoping to get this letter taken to post by him. Here comes another patient!

❧ 13 December 1929

I'm having a really hectic life this week, careering round in sleighs, temperature varying between -10° & -40° F!! (42 to 72 degrees of frost.) So far I've got my nose, my cheek and my left thumb frostbitten, but not badly, and I'm enjoying life "just fine," as the Canadians say! I've hardly had an hour in my own house for days. The worst of it is, there are lots of exciting things happening and I could write a 50 page letter straight off without having to stop to think. However, it is now 2:30 a.m. so I'll stop.

❧ December 18th

I'm sorry it has been so long since I wrote you a proper letter. Things were pretty busy for a few days. Result: I haven't written a single Xmas letter. My report for November has only just gone in and I'm running short of lots of drugs because I'd no time to order more.

The worst of it is, the most interesting things always happen to me just when I'm too busy to write home about them. I'm really having an infinitely more exciting time than it must sound in my letters.

For instance, I only realised when I was mounting that last lot of photos to send home that I'd never told you about the week just after the rain and being rowed across the flooded river in a rapidly sinking boat to a maternity case. (I arrived just ten minutes before the baby.) The boat, you see, had been high and dry all summer and the wood had shrunk in the sun till there were gaps between all the planks. I thanked heaven I could swim!

Last week I met three extremely interesting women. I was busy washing up, looked out of the window suddenly and beheld three women on skis, attired in the most approved skiing suits, etc.!! The effect was about as startling as that of three women in Lido pyjamas would be in Ednam Road! They came in and I learnt that they were from *Malvern* and had just come out from England! They were busy *walking* from Peace River to Fort Vermilion, 300 miles, with the mail!!!! They are known round here as the three mad Englishwomen. It certainly is the most surprising way of spending a holiday that I've ever heard of.

Louis Bourassa, the half breed I told you of when I met him on the boat in July, takes the mail up every year, usually down the Peace River on the ice. But this year we've had such a marvellously warm fall that the river had not frozen over completely, so he was going overland. Sounds simple enough till you realise that the pack trail via Keg River to Vermilion is not wide enough for sleighs. He had about 2 tons of mail and was taking 4 flat sleighs, so he was going up the line the telegraph men had cut till he came to the end of that and then going to *cut* 30 miles of trail to Keg River and then take the wagon trail to Vermilion!! Even then, camping out for a few nights in unexplored forest full of moose, deer, bears, foxes, timber wolves, etc.wouldn't be so bad but there was the prospect of it turning cold at any moment.

They left here on Saturday Dec. 7th. Sunday the temperature began to drop, Monday it was -35° F, Tuesday it dropped to -45° F (77 degrees of frost) and a north wind blowing. You can have no conception how cold that is. They hadn't, I know! I hadn't much idea, though I knew a bit from what the trappers and others have told me. However, I heard that Louis had to give up the overland route as the telegraph crew had just come down to a belt of heavy timber. So they came back to here and went down the trail to the river. I hope they get to Vermilion all right. The temperature has never been above zero since they left. Most days it's been from 20° to 30° below zero.

You can't imagine how cold that is. It makes your eyes and nose water and they promptly freeze. My eyelashes often freeze to my glasses. Your nose freezes inside till you can't breathe properly and if you open your mouth to breathe, you get an awful tight feeling in your chest. You *cannot* keep warm by walking and even when you run and are hot, your face freezes. Everything you breathe on gets coated with ice. If you try to cover most of your face with a scarf, it gets frozen to your face within half an hour.

If you warm up in the house before going out and your hands get damp, then your woollen mittens are stiff with ice inside the leather ones before you've been out for long. Metal gets so cold that if you touch it your hands stick to it and blister, just exactly like a burn. All the windows get frosted, not just pretty patterns like they do at home, but ice half an inch thick.

I've been frozen half a dozen times – my nose and thumb last Monday, my nose several times since. It's skinning very elegantly now. Today I got three fingers frozen just carrying in firewood!

The woollen jumpers arrived on Dec. 6th – absolutely providential. I can't imagine what I'd have done without them. They fit beautifully. I hope to goodness they won't shrink much when I wash them. They will take rather a lot of washing, being white, but I don't mind that a bit.

Poor Daddy! It's nothing short of tragic when a pun as brilliant as your "queer" one misfires! I feel for you! All my subtler jokes go astray up here, the Canadians have a sense of humour as poorly developed as the Americans!

Sorry to hear about the burglars in the neighbourhood. Didn't Mick bark when the policeman wandered round the garden? You should have my pup, he's *some* watch dog, puts the fear of the Lord into most of my patients. He's got a beautiful deep growl that almost frightens me sometimes! He's getting pretty big, too – 28 inches at the shoulder. I've re-christened him "Smoky." It's the most appropriate name you could imagine. A half breed called him that when he saw him and I adopted it.

Now I must get supper.

Starting a 40-mile ride with Dan.

My Dear Winifred,

It was nice to get a letter from you. Thanks most awfully for the plays. I shan't feel so desperately "off the map" when I've read them. I'm beginning now to miss civilisation quite a lot. There's hardly a soul up here who is even semi-educated like me.

The school teacher and the priest are a little better than the rest but the teacher is a weird young man who has tried his hand at almost everything from mining to lumbering. The priest, Father Brudginski, is really very interesting. He is a German, an Imperial German, whose people had enormous estates before the war. He has travelled a good deal, speaks many languages, was in German S.W.

Africa till last year and is very interesting on the subject of the British as colonisers. He says we're very bad, worse than Germans, that we shall soon be tipped out of S. Africa by the Boers, whom we've made the mistake of half-educating. He says that the Boers will turn out all English officials, that we should not try to colonise by sending out officials who can be removed from office, we should send out farmers and the more the better.

I expect he's right. Certainly the English are infinitely the poorest colonisers in Canada. The Germans and Norwegians are the best, then the Central Europeans. But the trouble with the latter is their different standard of living. As a Canadian said to me, "You can put a Ukrainian on a stone pile and he'll get rich"! He's about right, too. They live in pigsties, on the minimum amount of poor food and are prepared to work all the hours there are. Consequently, they're reducing the standard of living and wages all over Western Canada as they're coming in vast hordes and providing almost unlimited cheap labour.

It's really quite a serious situation. I had this conversation with the Father last Monday; we were travelling in a sleigh to a sick Hungarian baby. The baby's father came down to my place, told me about the child and said he'd call for me in about two hours. I couldn't make out why. (He didn't talk much English.) Two hours later he appeared with the priest and we went off. Then, when we got there I had to wait another hour while they christened the infant before I could get at it to treat. It was 3 weeks old and had pneumonia. Strange to say, it's recovered, whether due to my efforts or Father Brudginski's, I don't know.

This is a great life, but oh the cold! You don't *feel* cold, you just freeze. And the agony of thawing out frozen fingers beats anything I've ever felt. You feel so utterly helpless, very tired and very weak and tearful. It's a ridiculous sensation. I've had a really hard week, 4 nights up, a slow maternity case, any amount of travelling in sleighs, the temperature round 30° of Frost in the day, colder at night. I got awfully sleepy from missing so many nights and keeping awake in the sleigh was an awful effort. And yet, to have gone to sleep any time would have been almost certain to lead to a pretty severe frostbite. My house keeps warm enough but I have to stoke the fire two or three times during the night. Even with the fire on day and night I still had to thaw out the ink to fill my pen before writing this. It was frozen quite solid.

Melting snow for water is funny, too. It takes so long, and if you don't put water at the bottom before you start to thaw a bowl of snow *it burns*!! Now explain the physics (chemistry) of that! It *does*. I didn't believe it till I tried, but you get water that tastes burnt if you don't put a little water at the bottom first.

I'm sorry I haven't been able to write to you for Xmas, but I simply hadn't time.

~: 24 December 1929

This will probably be a very short note. I am expecting the Police to call in for my mail on their way back to town and they'll be here any minute. I meant to write a long letter but have been busy writing reports, business letters, etc. so haven't much time left.

The pudding, sweets, etc. came up by Thursday's mail – pudding basin broken but pudding intact, praise be! I also received a magnificent cake from Auntie Edie. I wish she could have seen the expressions on sundry old bachelors' faces when they tasted it; cake like that had never been seen before in Battle River Prairie!! I regret to say it's nearly all gone. I've had an awful lot of visitors lately!

Don't you worry about my having Xmas "all on my lonesome." No jolly fear! I'm going out nearly every day for the next week and I've mortally offended lots of people by accepting other people's invitations first. I don't think Bill Schamehorn will ever forgive me for going to Slim Jackson's for Xmas day!

I've also received a most magnificent box of chocolates. It would look magnificent in Dudley. Up here it positively takes your breath away. And I've had lots of things from people in Canada that I hardly know!

It continues to be chilly. Zero is the highest we've seen for over two weeks. It snows a few inches every night.

I did 35 miles by sleigh yesterday and 48 miles by sleigh on Friday but I'm not really very busy. The little baby with pneumonia (did I tell you about him? they sent for a priest and kept me waiting while they christened him before I could get a chance to treat him!) has recovered completely. Children as well as adults seem to have an amazing staying power up here.

I'm managing to keep pretty warm. I hardly ever feel cold when I'm out but that's the catch about this climate. Your nose or a finger can freeze while you feel quite warm. I nearly got badly frozen the other day. I went out at 11 a.m. expecting to be back at 5 or 6 p.m. but didn't get in till 3 a.m. and everything in the house was frozen solid. I had to take my mitt off to unlock the door and by the time I'd done that and turned the door handle my hand was beginning to freeze. I was so cold I could hardly get the fire going. I'd left my lunch and gone out in a hurry in the morning and everything on the table was frozen. Canned milk, ham, *bread*, oranges, apples, butter, the tea in the teapot and every spot of water in the house, of course.

If I sleep all through the night all the water freezes before morning. Usually I go to bed about 11 p.m. or midnight, stoke up again about 4 a.m. and get up at 9 a.m.

But still I wouldn't come back for anything!!

The Police are a long time. If I'd thought they'd be as late as this I'd have started to write tidily!

I'm getting to know the tracks of lots of animals in the snow, mice, weasels, mink, deer, moose and jack-rabbits.

Oh – police!

~: *27 December 1929*

My Dear Uncle Albert,

Your parcel came up by last night's mail. Thank you ever so much. The dog collar was a marvellous thought. You might have had television.* I'd asked the village blacksmith only last week if he could join another bit of leather on to the old one for me, as it was getting too tight even though I'd made a hole at the extreme end. But yours is a really aristocratic affair. It adds quite a tone to the establishment!

I wish you could see Brutus. He really is one of the most attractive dogs I've ever met. I can't imagine life without him. He sits beside me at meals and says "Please" most politely when I offer him anything and won't touch it till he's been told he can have it. He'll even hold a biscuit in his mouth without chewing it till he's told he can. But I can't get him to do that with meat yet. I've never met anything with

* Mary saw an early demonstration of this new technology before leaving England.

such an enormous appetite. He never refuses anything. Today he's had 8 lbs. of mush (cornmeal porridge), a loaf of bread, about 2 lbs. of beef and a big bone, all the odd scraps, but he still looks hopeful when I go to the cupboard! And the man I bought him from told me to give him as much as he'd eat! It can't be done.

He's just the right size for a dog team now. Everyone seems to think I ought to break him in but he'll be too big and heavy next year and so it's hardly worthwhile. I should like a dog team They are much the fastest way of travelling in the winter. A team of dogs (3–6) and a sleigh can average between 60 and 90 miles a day, as compared with 40–60 miles for a team of horses and a cutter, and 30–50 miles with a saddle horse. Brutus did 40 miles in fairly thick snow the other day and was quite fresh and chirpy at the end of it. (More than I was. I got frostbitten.)

I do realise I'm having a marvellous time up here. It's hard work occasionally but I'm getting a thrill that would be worth paying for and I'm seeing the North West as it really is. And of course I'm not like these poor devils of emigrants. I can always leave it when I want. If I were tied down I should be complaining by now!

You know, I'd never recommend anyone to homestead in Canada. Farming out here is just as uncertain as anywhere else and this homestead entry, with a unit of 160 acres, practically forces men into growing grain which is notoriously the biggest gamble of all. There are a good many families up here now who are a good deal nearer to starvation than any I've ever seen in England. And as for housing conditions – well, two families (6–10 people) living in a one-roomed house 10 ft. × 12 ft. × 7 ft. is not even considered over-crowding!

There is no paid work whatever to be obtained in this district at present. Almost the whole of the community is living without money – carrying a load of feed for a sack of potatoes; saving and splitting 10 cords of wood for $30 worth of groceries; clearing 20 acres of brush for your neighbour and he'll break 5 acres for you next spring, if he doesn't forget or trade his plough or lose or sell his horses or decide to leave the district or quarrel with you in the meantime! And so on.

There are no roads. There is only one school which accommodates 30 children. There are between 150 and 200 children of school age scattered over 800 square miles. Sixty per cent of them can't even speak English. The school inspector told me that the average retardation of the 30 children who are at school is 4 years!! So, the adults of the district in the next generation will have the education of children of 10.

Living is exceedingly expensive. Clothing is expensive and of infinitely more importance here than in England. You've got to have woollens and lots of them. You don't just catch cold if you haven't, you freeze to death. Woollen goods are much more expensive and of much poorer quality here than in England.

So, I don't blame any comfortably unemployed man in England for staying there!! It's certainly no use telling him fairy tales like the emigration pamphlets do. Hang it all, every man they get out here under false pretences – and that's what it amounts to – is going to write to all his pals at home to warn them not to come. It's obvious that the emigration figures are going to drop rapidly when they let unsuspecting men and their families come out to this and then write home about it. Supposing you were unemployed, would you come up here after what I've told you? Even though the emigration authorities did tell you of all the fortunes that had been made out of the land?

I've only sampled one isolated bit of Canada, I know, but this Battle River Prairie is being advertised all over Canada as the coming district, a second Peace River country, a land flowing with milk and honey, etc, etc. Sometimes I feel like writing to the Daily Mail or some other excitable rag and getting them to insist on the real facts being published in these emigration pamphlets. Then if men came out they wouldn't be reduced to stealing, breaking windows or in other ways getting themselves jailed, so that they could be deported back again!

And yet, it's marvellous country. It's the way they are trying to develop it that is wrong. All this advertisement is mad and bad. Since the Premier came in this summer and boosted the Battle River country in the papers, there's been a long stream of settlers pouring in, a sort of modified gold rush. Lots of them have no money now, and remember, there's no money to be made between now and next September, so I shall be having some more "starvations" on my hands.

Goodness me! This is a very long letter. I'm getting into the habit of writing long letters. I've always so much to tell them when I write home.

My Dear Auntie & Uncle,

It was very nice to get your letter of Nov. 30th the day after Xmas.

I'm feeling pretty stiff tonight. I spent part of the afternoon skating and an almost equal part of the afternoon sitting on the ice! You see, we've had a "chinook" (pronounced she-nook), a warm SW wind, which sent the temperature up from -10° to +40° F overnight and melted most of the snow. The chinook is still blowing but the temperature is down below freezing point, so all the melted snow on the river has frozen and there's good skating again. I did about two miles this afternoon. I'm getting better at it gradually! Poor old Brutus hates the ice. Nothing will persuade him even to put his feet on it. He ran up and down the bank howling like a lost soul and he's got *some* voice. I bet that howl carried four miles each way!

He's very restless tonight. He knows I've got a big hunk of moose meat outside. My friend, Mrs. Blue, brought it for me this afternoon. He's a funny dog. He's quite well-behaved, he never steals, but the way he dallies with temptation is a great joke.

He'll walk up to the table, put his nose within an inch of the meat, take a deep sniff and then sigh and walk away. He lies down for a minute and does it again. Then comes and puts his head on my knee and sighs most soulfully. Then back again for another sniff!

But even when he could easily reach it, he won't touch it. I wouldn't be without him for anything. But goodness knows what I shall do with him if I come back to live in England. What on earth would he do in a little garden when he's used to running around a district of 600 square miles?

What should I do, either, if it comes to that? Honestly, the thought of a street and tramcars gives me a headache after having a whole river valley to myself. The nights here are marvellous. Utterly silent. The snow is a mysterious sort of deep blue colour under the northern lights. The stars nearer and brighter and sparkling fiercely in the cold. I used to lie and listen to the "quietness" at New Milton at night. The silence here is as different from your quiet as that is from Birmingham's eternal racket. You can stand here and listen for 10 minutes without hearing the slightest sound.

I love the long sleigh drives, too, and the jingle of the bells and the squeak of the runners on the packed snow. Of course, this chinook has absolutely ruined the trails. First of all, it blew so hard that snow drifted 3 feet deep across the trail in places, then the snow half thawed and then froze again so that now these drifts have a crust of ice over them which is just too thin to bear a sleigh. Which makes very slow going. I had a 10 mile drive last night and not more than 4 miles of trail were passable. We kept having to make detours over the prairie.

Your garden should be a great joy next year, I wish I could see it but I'm afraid I shan't manage a visit home till 1931.

~: *30 December 1929*

My Dear Lena,

Thanks ever so much for your letter and the shortbread and Edinburgh rock. It's a good job you can't see how fat I'm getting! I really am. And I've had 9 lbs of chocolates given me this Christmas, too! All the things Mother and Daddy sent me arrived safely.

My cooking is improving gradually. I learnt how to roast chicken last week. A nice young man came to supper. (At least he was a patient and I asked him to stay to supper.) Of course the men out here cook as well as or better than the women, so he was going to show me how to roast chicken properly, Canadian fashion. Well, we got on all right but first of all forgot to light the fire in the cook-stove (the heater was on but that doesn't heat the oven) and then we forgot to turn the damper so as to heat the oven. So for over an hour the chicken sat in a cold oven and did nothing!! However, we had supper at 10:30 and it was very good and we were so hungry by that time that we could have eaten it even if it hadn't been!

I learnt how to pop corn on Xmas day. Hot pop corn with salt and melted butter is awfully good.

But, you know, when I come back to England I shall have forgotten how to lay a table or eat a meal properly. You see, out here they economise in washing up. You have one plate (usually tin), one knife, one fork, one teaspoon and a cup (no saucer) and with those you eat soup, meat and potatoes, stewed fruit, pie, bread and butter, and drink coffee. After all, as one man said to me, if the plate's clean enough for soup, it's clean enough for potatoes! When I'm home, I don't eat fruit off the plate I've had meat and potatoes on but my visitors do. It doesn't matter how many plates there are on the table;

they eat everything off the one! Some old bachelors out here eat out of the saucepans, frying-pans, etc. that they've cooked in. That saves washing up any dishes at all!

I've had about 10 lbs. of moose meat given me today, steak from a young bull moose. I *am* looking forward to supper. It's the most delicious meat.

Brutus was called Brutus before I bought him. I never changed it because I couldn't think of any better name for him. Sometimes I call him Smoky, which is the name that the half breeds gave him. It suits him very well. He's getting bigger and bigger. If I ask him if he is hungry he stands on his hind legs and puts his paws on my shoulders and wags his tail and says "Please." And he knows the difference between his right paw and his left too. Uncle Albert has sent me a frightfully swell collar for him, with his name engraved on it – and my address – but he's not likely to get lost. He's known from Peace River to Fort Vermilion.

~ *31 December 1929*

I'm very energetically answering letters, making a desperate effort to start 1930 with less than 100 letters owing! Really, my mail this Christmas has been of simply staggering proportions! Literally so, when I had to carry a big sackful back on Thursday last, with a gale blowing drifts three or four feet deep across the trail! I've had more letters, cards and presents from people in Canada than from people in England!! Cards from people I'd only met in the train! Now I'm busy trying to write and thank everyone.

People are nice to me really.

I'm awfully sorry to hear that young David has Scarlet Fever. Very hard luck. I hope he's recovered by this time. It's a long job, though. My case up here remained a one and only, thank heaven! This new scarlet fever serum is marvellous stuff, much better than the brand I was using in England. Steve's rash disappeared within 12 hours of giving him the dose and since the 3rd day he's been perfectly well, no temperature or anything else. I've had an awful job to keep the family quarantined.

You don't sound at all enthusiastic about my photos. Don't you like the look of Battle River? It's a lovely place, really. It grows on me more and more. I should hate to have to leave. I hope the Government won't move me next summer. I am to have a government inspector in here shortly, am going to try and get a car out of them. If I can't, I shall have to get another horse in the spring.

I'm hoping to get down to Slave Lake to see Dr. Rodger in the spring. I couldn't manage it this fall because I had too many maternity cases in the offing. I'm fairly well-booked up from now till the end of May but am hoping to get off for a weekend in June.

I don't know when I shall get my Summer holiday or quite what I shall do with it, unless you and Daddy would like to make a trip out?? If you don't, I think I shall go north. The Rockies would be desperately expensive, the Alpine club costs a young fortune to join and I'm more and more attracted to the unexplored North West. I meet so many trappers and people who tell the most marvelous yarns about the North. However, it's a long way away yet. Though I've been out here over 6 months now and it hasn't seemed very long.

It's most amusing. They're going to make me a Coroner, I think!! Female Coroners must be awfully rare birds. I've never heard of one. It'll be awfully funny. When one of my patients dies and I don't know the cause, I refuse a death certificate, report the doctor to the Coroner, order and perform a post mortem, summon a jury, instruct them to return a verdict in accordance with the medical evidence and pick up my fee. Simplest way of making money I've met yet. All my patients who die will die unexplained deaths in future!!

Now I must write my report for December to the Powers that Be, about 3–4 hours work. I'm feeling frightfully virtuous about staying in tonight. There's a dance on. I'm going out to Dunc. MacLean's tomorrow and possibly to a dance the next night. Oh dear, and I never told you what a topping Xmas party I went to. Ah well, perhaps I'll have time next letter.

My very very best wishes for 1930.

⌁ *4 January 1930*

Dear Daddy & Mother,
I had another big mail today. That makes between 80 and 90 letters and parcels during the last 3 weeks! Do apologise to all the friends and relations I ought to have to written to and haven't.

I can't remember my letter of Nov. 11th etc. I seem to have alarmed you unduly. I've never been so badly lost that I couldn't have retraced my steps if the worst had happened. And now the snow is about and it's so cold that getting lost would really be dangerous, I'm never out on my own very far from home. I have to be fetched by sleigh to all my patients, so that I am always with someone who knows the trail well. And usually the sky is clear and I can steer quite well by the stars now. (A proceeding that's harder than you'd expect, by the way.)

It's bitterly cold now. About 30° below zero and a strong NE wind that goes through my 5 layers of wool and moose and hide and fur as though they were thin silk. When I went over to Bissette's for my mail this morning there were about a dozen men in the store and, as I went in, there was a positive chorus of "Well, is it cold enough *now* for you, Doc?" You see, I've been ragging them about this winter they've talked so much about and told them it's not nearly as cold as an English November. Of course, I assured them that today wasn't anything to make a fuss about but didn't mention that I'd got my nose frozen before I got to the bridge from my house!

Daddy's cable came by mail today, too. Our line is through, all right, but we haven't got an operator yet!! I may say that there's a man in the district who can operate, so if I have to get an urgent message through I shan't have the slightest hesitation in using the line. But of course I couldn't for Xmas.

There's going to be trouble about our mail service before long, I'm afraid. Bill Schamehorn will almost certainly have to give it up. He's had two horses go sick already and it's costing him more than he gets out of it. If he throws it up, we shall have to go back to the once monthly with a two months' gap in spring – awful thought.

My days are fuller than ever. I've now got the job of doling out clothes to the destitute. Very necessary, too. But frightfully difficult to decide whether the twelve children of a lazy father are more needy than the four children of a hard working man, when all are equally inadequately clothed for this weather and the supply of clothing is limited. I've seven big sackfuls to go at but they're not nearly enough.

I'm writing this now so that it can go down tomorrow with the mail. It looks to me as though we're in for a heavy snowfall and when we get it the road will be blocked for motor traffic probably till March.

My Dear Winifred,

Your letter, calendar and the book of plays arrived yesterday. Thanks most awfully. I enjoyed the other plays immensely. I'd love to have seen one of them or, failing that, to have someone to discuss them with.

It's a glorious day today—25 below zero but perfectly still, not a cloud in the sky, the snow sparkling in the sunlight and a clear sky-blue in the shadows. This blue colour on the snow is simply marvelous. I can't get used to it.

I've just had my dinner (I stayed in bed till 11 a.m.), window and door wide open and the sun streaming in. I think I must go for a walk. It's really too good to miss. Going for walks out here is anything but the simple thing it is in England, though. I shall have to re-dress myself. Before I can go out, I must put on about 6 layers of wool! Actually, a wool vest, woolen combs. (ankle and elbow length), thick wool knickers, breeches, a thick wool sweater, three pairs of woolen stockings, cloth puttees, moose-hide moccasins, a thick woolen coat, a moose-hide coat, a thick camel hair and wool scarf, a wool cap with ear flaps, camel hair and wool mitts, with big fur and moose hide mitts coming almost to my elbows on top. And if I were going out in a sleigh I should *add* my big blanket-lined leather coat, my traveling rug, an enormously heavy travelling robe and a charcoal heater for my feet!!! And even then get frost-bitten, probably! Alas! My nose will never be the same again. I've had it bitten three or four times already!

Later

And at that point I got called out to a case and have only just got back (7:30). And sure enough I did get frozen – nose, cheek and one thumb! It's a great country. I've a maternity case due next week 18 miles away, may a merciful heaven prevent it being any colder. I've got maternity cases booked every 2 or 3 weeks from now till June, all in different directions. You just imagine riding from Birmingham to Burton-on-Trent in a sleigh or on horseback to a case!

I wanted to write you a really long letter this time, but I've got to go and get some bread from Mrs. Waines, and I shall take this across to mail at the same time.

~ *12 January 1930*

My Dearest Mother,
Read the enclosed from the Powers that Be. Half an hour after I got that, Miss Phillips arrived! I don't know whether they thought I was dying of overwork or going loopy from loneliness, but anyway here we are! All my house has been turned around and swept and dusted for me, all my papers tidied up and put away (I wish I knew where) and we're going in for texts and Bible reading!!! And, oh mother dear, there is *not* room in one house 18 ft. × 20 ft. for yours truly and *any* other woman. Two months of it. Just think! I'm off for a holiday as soon as the other confinement I'm waiting for has come off. One came off yesterday.

Think of me.

P.S. She can cook though.

COPY OF LETTER FROM SUPERINTENDENT PUBLIC
HEALTH DEPT., EDMONTON. JAN 2, 1930

"This is just a line to let you know that the Minister is anxious for you to have assistance in your district. Of course, you know Dr. Bow and I have realized that the pressure of work up here is great and during this cold weather practically impossible for one person to attend to and look after their own health.

Miss Phillips, a nurse who has been relieving for Miss Conlin for a short time is leaving to be with you on Monday's train the 6th, inst. I shall tell her to make her own arrangements to reach Notikewin from Grimshaw.

Miss Phillips has been relieving in several districts. I think you will find her a very agreeable and companionable person, and that she will also be of real assistance to you."

My Dear Daddy and Mother,

The weather changed suddenly last night. The temperature shot up from 20 below to 18 above zero and today has been delightful.

Bill Tyson brought Dan over this morning and I went off and saw four patients, did a 7 mile circle over Little Prairie. Oh, the joy of riding horseback again! Dan has been getting all the hay he could eat and oats twice a day for 6 weeks, and very little work. He was so fresh it was sheer bliss to be on him. I could hardly have made him walk if I'd wanted. We went plunging through the snow drifts on the open prairie. I had to break trail a good part of the way. And, oh, it was great fun. I love to feel a horse enjoying a run like that. If it's as warm as this tomorrow, I shall borrow him again.

My mail last night was the smallest I've ever had and nearly all demands for money, $25 gone west in subscriptions. It does grieve me. There was no letter from you. The last was Daddy's from Dec. 22nd. I imagine that Xmas mails and the awful storms you've been having in England may account for the delay. I really do seem to be getting the best of the weather up here. We have had less snow and warmer weather than anywhere in northern Alberta. But this place looks so near the top of the map (and the North Pole) that the Powers that Be imagine it must be intensely cold and have sent me the most *magnificent* fur cost you ever saw! It simply buries me. I'm going to get Miss Phillips to take my photo in it. It really is very kind of them, though quite unnecessary up to the present. However, I travel round in it looking like Jewish Financier or a Theatre Manager and enjoying myself immensely.

I hope to go down to Edmonton a week on Monday, arriving there Jan 29th. I shall stay there 4 or 5 days, I expect, then come back, stopping off at Jarvie, Kinuso (to see Dr. Rodger) and Peace River, making about two weeks holiday altogether. It's a bad time of the year to travel. It may be warm or it may easily be 60 below. However, with everything up here very slack and Miss Phillips here to carry on, it would be a pity not to take the chance.

I shall feel so funny in a city, and wearing skirts. You know I'm still wearing breeches even though not riding horseback. It's so much more comfortable, particularly when walking in deep snow.

Our telegraph operator begins to function tomorrow. If all goes well, I shall send you a wire first time I go up there (it's 4 miles away) just to let you know we are at last in touch with civilisation.

P.C. Solway (Baby-face) has come up here more or less permanently, to the great annoyance of many of the residents. His "office" is only ½ mile from the centre of the moonshine industry, so we may have a little excitement in store. I shall have to be jolly careful. All sorts of information comes my way which is certainly best kept from the police! He always calls in when he passes, to the amusement of everyone. (He is engaged to be married and will be as soon as he's settled up here. But they haven't all found out yet and, of course, as I'm the only unmarried female over 21, they're very anxious to find me a husband!)

Life continues to be rather trying. I couldn't bear it, having an assistant I mean, but for the thought that it will give me a chance to get down to town. The district is very slack at present. Not enough work for one, much less two.

I've got three men dying of TB and a couple of sick children and an old woman of 80 with heart failure and that's about all. The old lady is booked for the next world, I'm afraid, and there's little I can do. She is Ukrainian, doesn't speak or understand any English and is an *obstinate* old woman. All these Central and Eastern Europeans go to bed in their clothes. They sleep on the mattress and cover themselves with an enormous feather "comforter," a sort of feather bed 3 feet thick. No sheets, no blankets. Now this old woman was wearing sundry cotton and woolen vests, a marvelously hand-embroidered linen blouse and a thick cloth skirt. Well, she's pretty bad and couldn't move much and I didn't want her to get bed sores to add to her troubles, so I told her grand-daughter she was to give her just a cotton or woolen nightgown. However, the old woman wouldn't hear of it. Told them to tell me to go away and stop bothering her!

It's a difficult life. The breeds go to bed *completely* clothed, even wearing their moccasins. Consequently, it's difficult to tell, when you descend on them unexpectedly, whether they're staying in bed as you told them or merely hopped in when they heard you coming! I've got two breeds with TB who'd get better, I'm convinced, if they'd only do what they're told. I'm getting a good deal of work amongst the breeds just now, you see. Little Rachel L'Hirondelle is getting better. Everyone knows she had TB and was expected to die and, now she's out of bed and gaining weight, they think I can cure even consumptives who've been coughing up blood for weeks. If I could only get them earlier, they'd have a chance, though physically they're rather like rotten apples – all right to the outside appearances but just as soon as they're ill they go to pieces, absolutely without resistance.

However, I've got hopes of one lad. He's gaining weight, stopped coughing (he'd been coughing up blood) and his temperature has been normal for three weeks. If he recovers, he'll be about the first breed in the district to do so. They regard TB as we do the plague – inevitably fatal. There's no need to enquire about TB in the family. There is *always* TB in the family. This boy is Boniface House. (By the way, he's the lad who brought me in from Battle River Landing. There are lots of photos of him and the wagon.) He is 23. His mother died of TB 3 years ago. His brother Pat, aged 21, was the first death I had up here, in August. Absolutely hopeless when I first saw him.

Bon has suspected he'd got it all the summer but didn't come to me till December when he'd started coughing up blood. His younger brother Frank, aged 18, had been trapping up on Hay River (200 miles away) but was brought in about 3 weeks ago. He's dying of TB. There is one other boy, aged 14, deaf and dumb. Pat's wife has a cough. Nothing more, as yet, but I fear the worst. Bon's little son is doubtful. They all live in one house and their wives and families, with half a dozen other breeds.

That's typical. There are half a dozen families being wiped out at the same rate that I know of. And that's what I'm up against. One wonders sometimes if it's worth treating them at all. Yet you can't let them die just because their father and mother or grandfather and grandmother, happened to be different colours. They're decent people enough.

I've done a good deal of reading during the last few days. Miss Phillips does all the chores and all the cooking and I just lounge around and see two or three patients a day and enjoy myself. I'm even beginning to catch up with my letter writing!

I think this ought to keep you going for a while. I didn't intend such a long letter, but just kept wandering on.

Much love to everyone.

P.S. Am enclosing a cutting from Monday's Edmonton Journal. They are talking of sending the unemployed *up here*! And we've got people starving already.

~ *23 January 1930*

The mail came in this afternoon and once more I had to borrow a sack to get it home! The magazines, music and C & C with mother's letter of Dec. 29th all arrived. Thank you very much for them.

Sorry about this cable that I am always promising and never sending. We have just (2 days ago) got an operator and next time I go north I hope to send you a message. Things have been delayed owing to the last 30 miles of the trail from here to Peace River being blocked up by snow-drifts for the last three weeks. (Thank heaven I have not had to send anyone to hospital. Have been fearing it ever since I knew the road was blocked.)

We have less snow up here than almost anywhere in Alberta and really I could stand any amount of this weather. Day after day of brilliant sunshine – cold but not that horrible damp miserable cold that you've been getting –and the snow lit up at night by the moon or northern lights makes night sleigh journeys very attractive. My feet and hands are hardly ever cold and I've not had my nose badly frozen since before Xmas.

I am sending Lena a combined Xmas and birthday present. They are moccasins made by the Beaver Indians. They are not like the ones I wear, of course. Mine are laced up, to wear in the snow, but that's the sort they wear indoors. I've just got my own Indian ones. They're lovely – beautiful beaded flaps all round and as soft as deerskin. The breeds can't make them like that.

Things are pretty slack up here. They would be, now I've got an assistant. I don't know when I shall get to town, was hoping to go on Tuesday but am still waiting for a case. I've washed and darned 5 pairs of silk stockings today in preparation. I haven't worn them since I came up here! I'm really getting quite excited about going out and having a bath! Do you realise I haven't had a bath for 6 months!! I shall wire for bathroom with bedroom, I think, instead of the other way about! I only hope I shan't get run over or anything. Really a city is awfully dangerous compared with the backwoods!

I have just learnt to snowshoe. You know, on those long tennis racket things. They are easier to manage than you'd expect and you can make amazingly good time over deep snow.

Unfortunately, I was out snow-shoeing along the river yesterday afternoon and came back to find that those three English women I mentioned, who went to Fort Vermilion in December, had called on their way back to Peace River but hadn't been able to wait for me. I was very disappointed. I hear they had a marvelous and exceedingly adventurous trip. (Their names, by the way, are Pugh, Powell, and Lister and they come from Malvern, in case you ever hear of them in England.)

It's awfully good of you to send out all these magazines, etc. It must be costing you a young fortune in stamps but you should see the way they're appreciated when I've finished with them and hand them on! A man took a bundle of them up to the telegraph camp last week. He had to walk 40 miles (and had just done 10) but still wanted all I could possibly spare. And four or five other families are always waiting on my doorstep after mail days. There are some Hungarians who simply love *London Opinion*! I can't believe they understood more than a quarter of the jokes, but they always ask for them.

Great excitement two days ago. Our little policeman (Baby-face) chopped his ankle with an axe. (While splitting wood with which to heat water for a bath. I told him he should give up trying to bath, as I have.) I stitched it up for him with great enjoyment!

I don't know how my letters will have been arriving lately. I've been writing more than once weekly (Jan 1st, Jan 7th, Jan 12th, Jan 17th, and today 23rd) but they may come all in a bunch. With the roads so bad, the mail is a bit erratic and the trucks more so.

I really am getting no end of publicity these days. I've just heard that there's another article about me in the Edmonton Journal. You should read some of them. They're priceless. A year or two out here and I may become quite famous! I haven't heard any more about being made a coroner but live in hopes!

The breeds with TB, or suspecting TB, continue to come in numbers – 3 new cases this week, all of them fairly early. It's most remarkable how they've all started coming this last two months. It would be simply great to be able to get it controlled and prevent it spreading to the children.

It is now 11:20 p.m. so I think I'll go to bed.

I am on my way down to Edmonton for a few days. We have been
passing along Lesser Slave Lake for the last two or three hours. You
remember the last time I passed it was on my way north in July, it was
a misty dawn and I saw very little?

It is a marvellous lake, about 70 miles long and I should think
about 15 miles wide just here. There are mountains on the other
side and the whole view is amazingly like Barmouth Estuary or the
Cumberland coast. I must say I envy Dr. Rodger at the moment. A
lake, mountains, forests (real forests, heavy timber). Kinuso looked
a fascinating little town, set down in a big clearing, a railway, mail
twice a week and she's had lots more exciting cases than I have.
However, I don't know that I'd change. There is a certain thrill in
being right up north absolutely cut off from civilisation and railways.

I've been having a really exciting time since I last wrote to you.
I very nearly ended my bright young life on Saturday. Mrs. Stobough
(the lady I was waiting for) lives 17 miles south of my house. Two men
came for me in a car early Saturday morning, while it was still dark.
It was snowing and had been snowing steadily all night and there was
a strong north west wind drifting the snow across the trail. We set
out, 4 of us, and before we'd done 2 miles had to dig our way out of a
drift. It only took 10 minutes. Still, we were in a hurry and it seemed
a good deal longer, so the man who was driving tried to make up and
was going along the new road faster than he would ordinarily have
done. The loose snow made the trail very difficult and we skidded
wildly from side to side every few minutes, then suddenly with an
awful crash found ourselves in the ditch, the car almost buried in the
snow and tilted nearly onto its side.

The ditches on this new road of ours are 5 feet deep and 7 to 10
feet wide in some places, to drain the water off where the road goes
through muskeg. The ditches are full of snow and level with the road
so that it is quite impossible to tell where one ends and the other
begins. We were none of us hurt luckily (Triplex glass saved a good
deal of trouble, I imagine) but, owing to the tilt of the car, the gas
wouldn't go into the carburettor and we couldn't move the car. We
were then six miles from my patient and that was the nearest house!
So there was nothing to do but walk, 6 miles in a snow storm over a

trail covered with loose snow, attired in heavy fur coats and carrying all my kit. However, we got there. The baby had been born ½ hour but we finished things and cleared up, had a huge meal and came back. A lovely baby and everything O.K., so nothing else mattered. And what could be more enjoyable than a six mile walk before breakfast?!!

It was quite obvious that the trail would soon be unfit for any motor traffic so, when I heard that two trucks were going to try to make the trip to Grimshaw on Sunday, I sent a message that I'd like to go, too. So, they picked me up. We had a lovely trip. That NW wind was still blowing. We had to detour miles through bush where the road was impassable, breaking down fences where necessary! At Dixonville (the new settlement at Whitemud, only they won't call it Whitemud), one of the tires blew out and we had to stop for an hour. The last twelve miles to Grimshaw have been practically impassable for three weeks but we were prepared to walk that far if the worst happened!

Ten miles out of Grimshaw we had to abandon one truck. So, with 6 passengers and about two tons of grain (on a ton truck), we tried to make that last 10 miles. I don't know how many hours it took or how many drifts we were dug out of – I lost count of both – but finally we got within 500 yards of Grimshaw when the gasoline gave out! (12 gallons for 60 miles!!) So we only had that little way to walk. The snow was knee deep. We had to climb a fence to cross the railway track and I tore my skirt. Then suddenly, without warning, we were all up to our waists in snow. We'd forgotten the ditch! We struggled out eventually and walked across to the hotel, feeling just a little tired (it was then midnight) and the hotel was full to the doorstep! So we had to go to a little rooming-house, managed to get three rooms, very lucky.

On Monday, I went to Peace River by freight train and last night caught this train to Edmonton. One way of starting a holiday, isn't it? How I shall get back, I don't know. But if I can't get in, Miss Phillips can't get out so I shall just play round in Peace River till spring!! However, I expect I shall be able to get back with sleighs or a dog team. And I simply had to get out. Another week with that woman would have sent me out of my mind! She's a good nurse, I believe, and quite a pleasant soul, but apart from medicine we hadn't a taste in common. Incidentally, she couldn't cook any better than I could. When she came she said she was going to do *all* the cooking, she *adored* cooking etc., etc. Needless to say, I let her do it. But, if I couldn't cook steak any better than she does, I'd get a housekeeper. She hates the idea of living alone, has had a bolt put on the door!! She'll make *some* district nurse when she gets a district. I hated leaving poor old Brutus to her tender mercies but I couldn't bring him with me.

These steam-heated trains are awful. I keep having to go out to the end for a breath of air. And I slept awfully badly, too hot even with just a thin blanket. I'm used to spending a good deal of my days outside and my night in a bedroom that is rarely much above freezing point.

I am considering buying a second-hand boat I saw in Peace River!! 27 ft. long, 60 h.p. engine. It would be nice for a holiday to go down to Fort Vermilion, then to Chipewyan and down to Fort Resolution on Great Slave Lake. I could get there and back in a month. The north country attracts me more and more. There's something very fascinating about the country north of Peace River.

They tell me that wherever I go after this, however beautiful and warm the winter is, I shall get homesick for this snow and the cold winters for the rest of my life. I think they may be right. I certainly have no desire to exchange this weather for the sort you're getting. And there are men up here who have left good jobs in the south, California, Japan, S. Africa, because of this desire for the clean sharp cold and the snow.

This train is just too slow or too fast. It goes slowly enough to let you glimpse tracks in the forest but just too fast to see what they are. We have left the edge of the lake and are going through open forest, a little bit like the New Forest, with big open stretches of muskeg and red willow bushes.

I'm going to have a busy time in Edmonton. It will take several hours each day to remove 6 months' grime! Then I want to see what I can get out of the Government. I want all sorts of things, from a car to a hospital! Miss Conlin (nurse at Jarvie I stayed with in July) has had a bad accident and is in hospital, will be there for weeks, so I shall spend most afternoons there.

Then I want to see some ice hockey. And I shall have to go to the talkies and the theatre and any concerts there are. And shop, of course. So I don't expect you'll hear from me for a while.

~ *The Corona Hotel*
Edmonton
1 February 1930

My Dear Uncle and Auntie,
I am down in town for a few days holiday. It's lovely being in civilisation again. I arrived here Wednesday evening.

I was in the "House," listening to some of the speeches on Friday. I'm beginning to get really interested in Alberta's politics, now I understand more about them. The probability of free homestead entry being stopped is not a rumour. It's almost a certainty. I'm more than ever glad that I came out when I did. Battle River Prairie is probably the very last bit of Canada in which pioneer settlement, far from a railroad or telegraph, will be allowed to occur. And a very good thing, too, in some ways. And yet pioneering does bring out the very best (as well as the very worst) in the people who do it. Of course, the withdrawing of homesteads will give Battle River yet another fillip. Every available quarter will be snapped up. It will be people's very last chance of getting free land.

I tried Brutus with "that's mine"/"that's Brutus's" but he didn't understand. But I can put meat on the floor under his nose and tell him not to touch it and he won't. He has just discovered how to open the door. He turns round and sits against it and it flies open! When I was coming down a steep hill on Dan the other day, he slithered and half-sat down in the snow. The pup brightly seized him by the tail! Whether he was very intelligently trying to act as a brake or merely taking advantage of Dan when he was down, I don't know! But the effect on old Dan was surprising. He tried to kick and gallop both at once and we got to the bottom in a rush!

I was out to the Whittaker's (the people I bought him from) tonight. Big Brutus, who won 7 prizes in the Edmonton show July last, is not nearly as attractive as the pup and not in anything like such good condition. Of course, a small garden and exercise for an hour a day can't be as good for a dog as long runs behind horse or sleigh every day. I shall try to bring young Brutus down to the dog show this summer and see how he stands. His waist line, like his owner's, is not as slim as it should be. I shall have to diet him.

I went to an ice-hockey match on Friday, Edmonton v. Calgary. It was thrilling. If ever you get a chance to see one, don't miss it. The speed is amazing and the whole thing terrifically exciting.

It's really very funny how things have changed since I came out. I was just Dr. Percy then, now I'm "Dr. Percy of Battle River" and everyone seems to know about me! This country is a bit like America for publicity. Would you believe it? The daily paper announced on Wednesday that I was arriving that evening from the north to attend the opening of Parliament next day! I'm getting an awful swelled head.

~: *Friday, Feb. 7th*
  In the train

I had a lovely time in Edmonton, met lots of interesting people and spent nearly a month's wages in a single morning's shopping!! Civilisation really has its advantages and, once I got used to wearing shoes and skirts again, I felt quite at home. I had a 3 hour chat with the Deputy Minister and I think I may manage to get a hospital and a car for Battle River within the next year!

When I was in the office, they got a letter from Mrs. Cole, District Nurse at Wanham, saying that a couple of cases up there required a Doctor's attention, so they sent me. I left Edmonton Monday, got to Wanham Tuesday a.m. (it's an 18 hour journey) and have had a lovely 3 days – a 30 mile trip by sleigh into the Bad Heart Valley and back yesterday to do the aforesaid minor operations. And now I'm on my way to Grande Prairie. This is a 4 hour journey out of my way but it's a pity not to see all I can. A Member of Parliament is going to meet me and take me round and to see the hospital (a new municipal one). Then I come back tonight on this same train and go back as far as Kinuso, where I shall stay with Dr. Rodger for three days.

The more I see of Canada the more I love it. There are miles and miles of forest here. And you know how fascinating spruce trees look in the snow in Switzerland? These are like that, but wilder. The dead trees lie and rot where they fall and make the whole thing more primitive and impenetrable than ever. One could get absolutely lost within 100 yards of the road or railway track. Mrs. Cole's house is in

Finding a way home from Peace River.

the middle of an uncleared ¼ section. The sound of the wind in the trees all round was lovely. There are lots of moose in the forests there. We saw half a dozen fresh tracks crossing the trail within 3 miles.

Coming back last night by moonlight (we got home at 7:30 p.m., but the last 1½ hours was dark) was wonderful. The trail is narrow and winds in and out between thick spruce for miles. It was so quiet and mysterious, the wind making just a little sighing in the tree-tops and dark mysterious shadows, moving slightly, alongside the trail. Quite suddenly, without any warning, one of the horses shied wildly and they set off at a wild gallop. Mrs. Cole stopped them eventually, when they'd pulled us off the trail into a patch of deep snow, but they were horribly nervous afterwards. I suppose they saw or smelt moose. I told you how horses hate moose, didn't I? I'd hate to try and get old Dan through that forest. He's always jumpy at night and all those stumps and shadows and the smell of moose would be too much for him.

This is the part of the country that Dr. Johnstone is so keen on, she worked in the Wanham district a year last summer. I can understand her loving it. It is much more beautiful than Battle River Prairie. And yet, I've grown to love the wide spaces up there.

I was invited to leave B.R.P. and spend the summer with the clinic. It was tempting in some ways. I told you what an exceedingly jolly crowd they are and camping out is a great joy, but I refused. I'd sooner have my dog and my horse and my own little shack, and I've really grown quite fond of my half-breeds and Ukrainians.

We have been travelling through unbroken spruce and poplar forests for three hours now, and yet on the map it's only a tiny stretch. It's impossible to grasp the size of this country. I've been talking to an Englishman, ex-school-teacher. He's cleared up several difficulties.

Cottonwood trees = Aspen poplars

Balm of Gilead = Black poplar, etc.

I've been very puzzled about these. He has also sorted out for me spruce, tamarack and Jack Pine (all varieties of what we call spruce). There are lots of tracks here – ermine, jack rabbit, coyote. They're very fascinating. I wish I could get the breeds to teach me all about them.

Jove! There is the most amazing collection of moose tracks along the railway here. For ½ mile or more we've been passing them. They've been feeding on the long grass in the ditch. You can see the way they've scraped away the snow with their feet.

When they walk, they leave a long sliding sort of track, cleft in front and with a cleft point at the back. Cattle tracks are cleft in front but they haven't that long double point at the back. Jack rabbits leave a funny track, big marks made by the hind feet which come down in front of two little marks left by the forefeet. Weasels (ermine) leave a very tidy track, just as if you'd pressed two thumbs into the snow side by side. The gaps are fairly long. Mice leave the same sort, but very tiny. They disappear into wee holes in the snow. Deer leave awfully tidy little tracks. They put their feet down straight and lift them out clearly and they're very evenly spaced.

That's enough about tracks. Hope you weren't too bored. One can't help being interested in them out here.

I've bought a harness for the pup. I'm going to teach him to pull a sleigh. His brother in Edmonton can pull Mr. Whittaker, who is about 6 ft. 4 ins. and broad in proportion. Young Brutus ought to be able to haul my groceries home from the store, I should think! Whittakers have about 14 Great Dane pups this year!! Out at the farm, of course. They've only got their Brutus in town. Young Brutus is a better dog than his brother I believe. He's certainly in better condition.

We seem to be getting somewhere. I'll stop. Oh no. This is Sexsmith. These little Canadian towns are exactly alike. There's the hotel; a rooming house; a garage; two or three stores; a bakery; a bank; the railway station with a 6 foot platform, a little wooden hut, ticket office, etc.; grain elevators; oil tank and water tank. They're unbelievably dull. When Battle River gets to that stage I shall quit.

~: Postcard From Peace River
11 February 1930

Well, I've got back so far and now the excitement begins. I've got to do the last 100 miles by sleigh! The temperature has dropped 30° in the last 24 hours, it's snowing and there's a gentle north east breeze! I'm going to wear all the clothes I've got and hope for the best.

~: 14 February 1930

I got home last night after an exciting and very amusing trip in from Peace River. I was very glad to find everything O.K. I'd been terrified Miss Phillips would set the house on fire, as she couldn't manage my gasoline lamp. Delighted to find your letters of Jan. 5, 12 and 19th awaiting me.

The fireless cooker on which you sent the booklet is certainly a great idea but what fireless cooker would stand an eternal temperature below zero and continue to cook? And incidentally the hottest of dinners wouldn't help if the house was cold. I've had my fingers frozen once while trying to light a fire in the stove after I'd been out longer than I expected. No, I get on just spendidly. I have given a duplicate key of my house to the Waines and they stoke the heater 4 hourly when I'm out. It's really essential. This house goes cold within an hour of the heater going out and in 6 hours the temperature inside can drop from +60° to -10°! As for porridge, I use quick Quaker Oats. They cook while I lay the table and make tea.

I love your idea of the four committee men sweeping the snow from my doorstep. They live 2, 7, 6, and 11 miles away!! I don't often see them. They meet about every two months.

Gee whiz! I like mother's idea of the police being unnecessary up here at any time of year. We have now got "Baby Face" semi-permanently, worse luck. He is a little nuisance!! But we need a policeman, all right. There's any amount of theft, moonshine, out-of-season beaver and muskrat trapping, and destitution for him to look after.

The sweater and long-legged wool combs. you sent probably saved me from very severe frost bite on Wednesday.

When I went down to Edmonton, though I only took my weekend case and had little room to spare, I took a pair of those combs., 2 pairs thick stockings, thick wool knickers, a white sweater and moccasins, much to Miss Phillips' amusement. But I assured her that if the temperature in Edmonton touched -50° F, I'd paddle round the main streets and even into the Government buildings in moccasins rather than get my feet frozen. As it happened, Edmonton was having a warm spell (+10° to +40°), so was Wanham, so was Kinuso. So I could wear silk stockings, silk undies and thin frocks in comfort! Much more comfortable than the same clothes at same temperature in England.

I left Kinuso Monday night, temperature +38°, but began to feel cold in bed in the train and had to cover my bed with my coat. At Peace River it was zero, a north east wind and snowing. Ugh! I almost got my legs frozen before I got to the hotel. Then I began phoning round to see how I was to get to Battle River. Roads absolutely blocked to cars. It had snowed steadily for days after I left. However, someone told me George Robertson and Slim Jackson were about town, so I hunted round till I met them and they were going to start back in the afternoon, taking an old winter trail which angled NW from Peace River, across 3 lakes, and cut into the highway about 10 miles south of the Whitemud, missing Grimshaw and the 30 miles of badly blocked road entirely. I don't think the lakes will be marked in any map you have. The biggest is not more than 4 miles by 3 miles and surveyors would hardly notice those!

So at 5 p.m., we started, temperature still dropping like a brick. We made the 9 miles to Webbers' (George's wife is a Webber) in 3 hours and it was -45° F when we got there! Jove, it was cold. If I hadn't piled on every stitch of wool I'd got before I left Peace River, I'd have been frozen solid. Next morning we set off again, Mrs. George (surname), a sister-in-law of George Robertson, aged about 19, coming along too to stay with her sister. It was -39° when we set out. I think I told you how slowly the horses go when it's really cold. Four miles an hour was about all we could average. We lay in the waggon box, two at each end, all our eight feet on the heater, and with piles of blankets and feather beds on top.

About 2 p.m., after crossing the first lake, we came to a little trapper's cabin in a marvellous place, great trees all round and a wonderful view of the second lake between them. There was no one at home but of course the door was not locked (that's unwritten law in the winter in the north), so we camped there for lunch. I wish you could have seen the stove. It's the first real trapper's stove I've seen – all made of *mud*, about 6 to 12 inches thick, with a tin stove pipe at one end and a sheet of tin with two holes in it for the top. No door, of course. We got a terrific fire going, then set to work to thaw out sandwiches, butter, jam, sardines, biscuits – all frozen stiff, of course.

We got on the move again at 4 o'clock (horses had to have 2 hours). It was not till then that I discovered that neither George nor Slim were exactly sure of the trail. One had been over it 8 years before and the other 10 years before!! However, as someone once said, you couldn't lose George Robertson anywhere between Peace River and the North Pole, so we hoped for the best! The second lake was 2 miles wide, the snow had drifted 3 or 4 feet deep and it was very heavy going for the horses. We crossed the third lake at sunset. The trail from there was gone, absolutely blotted out. Windfalls and new young trees had just covered it over!! (It hadn't been travelled for about 6 years).

Sunset, 40° below zero, so there was nothing for it but to *make* a trail. Slim and Dick Norquist went ahead and George drove. I would never have thought it possible for a sleigh to go through a thick wood like that and have to cut down so few trees. We had 3 miles of that before coming to the old trail again! It took hours, We thought we were in for a night in the bush, at 40° below, with insufficient bedding. Of course, I've always wanted a night in the bush but not at that temperature, with snow up to your knees or more. We were 20 miles short of where we'd intended to get to but at the first house we came to we stopped. Again, the owner wasn't at home but we made a fire, drank lots of his coffee, had a vast supper and were just sitting around smoking when the owner came home! He was a delightful old chap, had known Slim Jackson years before, so that was all right. It was a one-roomed house, one bed. So Mrs. George and I had that and the men all slept on the floor. Mr. Swink (the owner) was very funny when he offered us his bed, said he didn't think we should find the blankets too dirty. He'd only had them 3 years!!!!

Next morning (Thursday) we started off again, only -32°, and we made the last 40 miles home, changing teams at the sawmill.

In all the 2½ days, I never got so much as a finger or the tip of my nose frozen! It was perfectly lovely lying there in blankets, only my face out, watching the sky and the trees. It was brilliantly sunny each day and the snow was sparkling and squeaky.

Now I must go to bed. I've got heaps of things to tell you but I may be able to get this out tomorrow.

~: *21 February 1930*

Mother's letter of Jan. 26th came last night. I don't know why it took so long.

I was going to write you a long letter today but I spent the afternoon mounting and labelling photographs and now there's not much time left before I must start to get ready to go to a dance. Little Prairie School is being opened officially tonight, with a dance and "concert"!! All the local talent! I hope nothing turns up to prevent my going. It ought to be a shriek. I was going to accompany some songs but the MacLeans firmly refuse to lend their piano (and I don't blame them) and Joe Becker's organ is completely beyond me. I tried it in the summer sometimes but we never got through a single piece without collapsing. You see, at critical moments I invariably forgot to pedal!

I got rid of Miss Phillips on Monday. I've never been so glad to see the last of anyone in my life. Really, it was worse when I got back than before I went. She'd rearranged all the furniture, was drying her washing in the dispensary and the whole place was dirty. And she talked – and talked – and talked. "The Ride of the Valkyries" is a marvellous record for drowning chatter. I was reduced to putting it on several times!!

At any rate, it was a case of one of us going. I've never felt so tempted in my life to quit and come back to England. However, it's all over now and I've got back to a state of real good temper. And I've cleaned the house energetically and washed cushion-covers and things and it's beginning to look decent. This letter will explain the disgruntled tone of some of the letters I've written lately!

The weather continues coldish, below zero all the time. We are apparently having rather an unusual winter. The cold is unusually continuous and there is very much more snow than anyone remembers. It is three or four feet deep and drifted badly in places. Two waggons have gone over the edge on the hills this week. No one hurt, luckily. But the days are lengthening marvellously. I don't need the light on till 6:45 p.m.! There is a little warmth in the sunlight now, too. It's funny to think that there's only another month of real winter to go.

I went tobogganing with the Robertsons on Wednesday. It was good fun. We all got tipped out on a bank, though, while the horse dashed off with the toboggan!

I got a white pencil in town and have written under all the photos, so you'll know what they all are. Aren't the enlargements of Bill Tyson good? Brutus always has his nose white with snow these days. He digs with it! He loves the snow.

Do keep these photos carefully, won't you? I'm paying an extra 1 per cent each to get "guaranteed fadeless" prints and lots of them can never be replaced. And when I'm an elderly spinster with a pug and a parrot it'll be interesting to look back on them and remember all the excitements I survived!

Now I've got just an hour to fetch in wood and snow and iron my frock and bath (in a basin) and change.

> ❦ *McNamara Hotel*
> *Peace River*
> *25 February 1930*

Here I am in the "big city" again, after another exciting sleigh journey. I brought a man with a fractured skull down to hospital in a caboose. He was working on the telegraph outfit, 80 miles north of my house, when a tree he was felling dropped on his head. It took them from Friday night to yesterday (Monday) at 6:30 a.m. to get him out to me and he was so bad that I didn't dare keep him up there. I was afraid he was bleeding inside his skull and would probably die on the way out. But, if I'd kept him up there and he'd died without anyone attempting to operate (I haven't a trephine, only an amputation saw), I should have felt that I'd taken his last chance away. All very worrying to decide what to do at 6:30 a.m. However, we got him down here alive and he seems to have stopped bleeding. And though his pulse is only 38, he may recover. The X-ray plates are exceedingly good. There's a long branching fracture and the bone is depressed at one end.

The old chap was in a terror on the way down. We travelled all night, did 90 miles fairly heavy sleighing (there was another 12 inches snowfall last week) in 19 hours, 13 hours driving and 6 hours rests, all with one team of horses. That's exceedingly good time. We were going to change teams twice but were not able to get horses.

But he was difficult to look after, exceedingly irritable in spells, tried to get up and go for a walk! Would suddenly sit bolt upright on the camp bed. All this in a small tent on the top of a rocking sleigh and we had to have a stove inside the tent, of course. I was terrified that I should drowse off and he'd sit up and a jolt of the sleigh would send him headfirst onto the heater! Gee! I was glad to get him into the hospital. You ought to have seen the outfit. It looked so quaint at night, the little tent, lit up inside, looking a sort of glowing orange colour, crawling over mile after mile of snow, with the northern lights shimmering and swaying above us, pale apple-green and gold edged with mauve. It was a perfect night. I should have enjoyed travelling outside all the time. And luckily it wasn't cold, only about zero!

We start back tomorrow at 6 a.m.! I've another maternity case due the day after tomorrow. I hope to goodness I shall make it in time!

Did I tell you I was getting books, both fiction and general literature, from the University Extension Dept? They've a wonderful library and I get anything I want and only have to pay postage. It makes a great difference. I don't feel so utterly cut off from education now. It was awful getting cut off from books. I've been buying them steadily but one or two books per month were very short rations for me.

Peace River is a funny little hole, but on a night like this the little lights in the houses on the hills look like fairy things and the snow is a deep blue colour in the twilight. I am very tired after my trip, particularly as I didn't get home from Friday night's trip till 6 a.m. on Saturday, and I had a very heavy day, starting at 10 a.m. to this man. And last night I didn't get more than ½ hour's sleep.

So I'm going to bed.

Your letters of Feb 2nd, 3rd and 9th arrived yesterday. I am sorry you were so worried about my letters not coming. I was afraid there might be some gap owing to the state of the roads. Roads are still blocked to car traffic but not too bad for sleighing. They tried to clear the roads round Grimshaw with a snow plough but the drifts were too deep.

I have just finished my supper, or dinner rather. I actually achieved a 4 course meal!! And I'm now topping it with coffee and a cigarette and am feeling much too full to think of washing dishes. I was very hungry. I've been seeing patients all day and had no time for lunch. It's usually the way when I've been out for a day or so. I've pulled 5 teeth!!

One of the breeds with TB died while I was out. My old Hungarian who had heart failure in November and recovered went and failed again while I was away, so they took him down to Peace River. I must have passed him on the road. I'm disappointed at losing him. He was a very satisfactory case to treat. He responded so dramatically.

I'm off to the Third Battle tomorrow, starting at 7 a.m. Thank heaven, it's light fairly late now. Last time I went up there with the policeman, we got lost in the bush. Beyond the Second Battle is a difficult district to find your way about in. There are practically no landmarks.

The temperature remains about zero but there is more warmth in the sun. I think I'm beginning to get sunburnt! The glare of the sun on the snow is considerable. I've got two cases of snow-blindness.

Dear dear! I've got so many things I'd like to tell you about. They've been accumulating for weeks! I never told you about the Indian Reserve at Kinuso or the Indian Boarding School at Indiana on Slave Lake, did I? Dr. Rodger and I went with the policeman (Heale) in a car along the lake. He only meant to go 9 miles but the chappie he was after was always "in the next village," so eventually we got to Enilda!

The Indian School is an amazing place – Catholic, of course, and state-supported. (It's a Federal Government affair and Ottawa is largely French-Catholic.) It looks like a huge hotel beside the lake with wide balconies and lots of windows, painted white and green. The old father is French, unshaven, amazingly fat and incredibly dirty. But a delightful old chap for all that. He breeds silver foxes in his spare time!! He's quite the most worldly priest I've ever met. The nuns who run the place and do all the teaching are equally surprising – young and bright, very thrilled with the new radio someone had just presented, chatted brightly to the men. In fact, were normal teachers but most abnormal nuns. They took us all over the place.

There are 120 little Indian kids there, all ages from 4 to 16. Poor little beggars! It's a lovely school but you can't wonder that they hate it. Who wouldn't sooner sleep rolled in a blanket beside a fire in a great forest than in a little white bed in a dormitory? And such a dormitory! Doubtless the cubic space per child is correct but the floor space isn't. There is just room to walk between beds and there are 50 or 60 beds in the room. The ceiling is very high but the room looks so overcrowded. The children are only allowed to speak English. Poor little kids! You know it seems rather terrible to see the "noble red-man" being cooped up and dressed like in an orphanage. Not that the Crees are a particularly attractive brand of Indian. They are not very different from the Cree half-breeds up here. Still they are Indians and did once fish and hunt and trap over all this North country.

You know, I can't help feeling that we gloss over the bad behaviour of the British in history and only draw attention to the good we did in some parts of the world. Hang it all! What right had we to wipe out the inhabitants of North America? They never did us harm. They were happy enough living their own lives and were a fine and healthy race. Then we come along and seize parts of their country and live in it and because they fight, send out armies and slaughter them, driving them back to the west. Then trade with them and give them alcohol and religion and subsequently proceed to shut them up on little reserves while we divide up country amongst the surplus population of Europe.

The traders and early trappers have left behind them a degenerate race of half-breeds with the weaknesses of both races, with absolutely no resistance to TB. And now, although we've thousands of square miles of unoccupied land, we gaze with covetous eyes on the Indian reserves because they are good land. In southern Alberta there is a big Indian reserve. The Indians have been told that they must either farm it like homesteaders or be moved off. They would like to move them farther north where we can't settle so easily. Kinuso is very anxious to get rid of its reserve. It's a patch of good land stretching from the railroad to the lake. Two reserves north of the Peace River were sold this summer. It all seems very unfair and I suppose the same thing exactly happened in Australia and New Zealand and to a smaller extent in S. Africa. Yet when I read it as history I rejoiced over the victories against the horrible scalping, tomahawking Red Indian.

The longer I stay away from England the more amazed I am at its different appearance from this distance. The way we go round patting ourselves on the back for our noble treatment of the native races in our colonies and "our great Dominions." You know the sort of thing. You should hear the way Canadians talk of the British. There is almost an anti-British feeling and they seem to think England is populated by a race who lives on the dole and is incapable of work.

I never told you about the opening of the school house last week and Charlie Plavin singing "Rocked in the *Craaaaaaaaadle* of the Deep," completely out of time and tune, the audience writhing in agonies all through it. They did a play exceedingly well. I've seen it several times in England – "The Grand Cham's Diamond"* – but they'd translated it into Canadian and it gained a good deal of pep. The dance was a squash and went on till after 5 a.m. They were still dancing when I left at 5:15 a.m.! I must be getting old. I was utterly weary of it by 3:30 a.m.

You know, you don't realise what a tiny house I'm living in or you wouldn't talk so brightly re: Miss Phillips and getting my toes trodden on. Imagine yourself living, cooking, eating, sleeping, working in a house only a little bigger than the dining room at home, with someone with whom you are utterly incompatible. Nowhere to go outside to get away. I'd have gone off my chump had it lasted for long. And, as for keeping the house warm while I was out, she came with me to all my cases. She was furious if anyone came with a cutter or sleigh that would only hold two, and it's always difficult to take another person to see anyone who's ill. They don't like it and it involves a lot of explanations. And the breeds are so shy at the best of times that a third person reduces them to silence as often as not.

And she was so abominably self-assertive and was so darned careless, too. Pushed one of my white sweaters I was airing over

* A one-act play by Allan Monkhouse.

the back of a chair before I was going out, right against the stove and ruined it. Broke the end of the camp bed. Broke some other oddments. Anyway, she's gone and I've recovered from the effects pretty nearly.

Do you realise it's just over a year since the advert in the B.M.J. appeared? Just over a year since I started riding lessons. I mean to ride in the horse races in June here if I can get a horse. Dan is too old. I shall have to start training soon.

~: 8 March 1930

I have done quite a lot of travelling by dog team this last week. It's an amazingly smooth comfortable way of travelling and the speed is remarkable. It's very quiet. One lies at full length in the little sleigh and the sensation is almost like drifting downstream in a canoe, with the shoosh of the sleigh on soft snow sounding like water. I came back from a case at 5 a.m. yesterday – only 3½ miles but you couldn't see the trail at all by starlight and the snow seemed almost bottomless. The trail had only been broken that day, over soft snow 3 or 4 feet deep. With a team and sleigh it would have been an awful trip but with dogs one just lay down and drowsed and gazed at the stars and they found their own way. Dogs are marvellous. They'll follow a trail when it's under two feet of fresh snow.

Teaching Brutus to work was most amusing. The first day, he pulled backwards and howled with rage steadily for two miles. Next day, he ran with the others but obviously under protest. Yesterday, he began to pull. He'll make a good dog next year. I shall get a couple of well-trained huskies to go with him.

I've got lots more photos and shall be sending you another batch in a week or so. My camera is working well again, thank goodness!

I am very stiff and sore tonight, having been riding this afternoon – only 10 miles but the trail had drifted over badly and it was very slow, very hard going. I imagine Dan gave me a good imitation of a camel ploughing across the desert. It certainly was the slowest and the most tiring ride I've ever done. I could have got there faster on snow-shoes. It was to the same case I was out to with dogs – a maternity case. I was there Thursday for 12 hours. The people are Ukrainians, speak no English. There was only a wooden bench to sit on and nothing to read or do for hours. When the baby was born, we had to wrap it in a dirty old cloth skirt. They hadn't so much as a binder, napkin, blanket or clean rag! I've just taken over a complete outfit, from vests to socks and bonnet. Poor little beggar – his skin was chafed already. He's a lovely baby but I hope I don't have many more as difficult as that. It's no joke when there's no assistance whatever and no one to translate.

My old pal Kolyna with the heart failure is back from Peace River. (I told you about missing him on the way back from Peace River.) When they got there, they found the hospital closed for scarlet fever, Dr. Agnew in hospital with severe burns from a gasoline explosion and Dr. Sutherland off with blood poisoning from a septic arm. Consequently, Peace River has now neither Drs. nor hospital. So they brought him all the way back!! That's 200 miles in an open sleigh for a man who is blue-green and swollen all over with heart failure! He ought to have died, but of course he hasn't. They're awfully tough.

I've lots more letters to get off before the mail tomorrow and I shall be out all day going to see old Kolyna (18 miles on horseback but the trails are bad). I really mustn't stop to write you any more.

~: *14 March 1930*

I am really exceedingly fit and am beginning to lose a little of my winter fat. I am now 4 lbs. heavier than the day I landed in Quebec and 14 lbs. heavier than I was when riding hard every day last fall. But I shall soon get a few lbs. worn off if it goes on as it has done this last week. I've been really busy. Did a 40 mile trip on horseback yesterday at 15 below zero! At least it was that when I started. It warmed up a good deal during the afternoon and was 12 below when I got home. I'm very stiff today, of course, but I've two 30 mile trips for tomorrow and the next day which will doubtless wear off most of it.

It's amusing to remember that a year ago I couldn't even canter safely and ached after an hour's riding in a riding school! My new leather chaps are still rather stiff and I have some difficulty in getting on to the horse in them but they are exceedingly comfortable and warm to ride in. They keep the wind out so well. I'd have been frozen yesterday without them. There was a keen east wind all morning. I now go out on horseback covered from head to foot in fur and leather.

I've got a proper fur-lined Yukon cap. No-one recognised me at first, thought I was a man!

As regards frost-bite, there's no permanent damage. I've never been badly bitten, only to the skinning stage (like bad sun-burn) on my face, and my fingers and toe were merely swollen and painful for a day or so. I've come through the winter very well indeed, thanks to my terror of frost-bite making me super-careful.

Brutus is having a lovely time. I got the bones of half a moose for him the other day. They'll keep him going for a little while! He is a ripping dog. I never have to bother about him following. He will stop for a second when he crosses a fresh rabbit or fox trail but always comes after me without being called. He invariably comes when he is called, too. He's always healthy, his nose is cold, his coat is sleek, and he eats as though he's had nothing for a week. Yet, I can put meat on the floor and tell him not to touch it and he won't. Oh, altogether he's a model of all that a dog should be.

I am writing to Edmonton for a book for you, written by a woman who is homesteading up by Sheridan Lawrence's place near Fort Vermilion.* Then you'll see what interesting letters I *might* have written if only I'd exaggerated a bit! It's true enough in lots of places and the main story is correct. I've met people who know her. (Sheridan himself, of course, on the boat down the Peace. He is the Mr. S. of her story and was simply furious at her exposure of his daughter's marriage to a breed.) But lots of it is just imagination. The place she's living in is as closely settled as this, so I'm told. And if it weren't, a woman who can't find her way ¼ mile through the bush has no right to be in this country. And no one but a fool would try to homestead with a man of 70 and a child of 12. However, I think you'll find it interesting. She describes the country and the breeds infinitely better than I can. (Though needless to say she didn't hear the Cree war-whoop. They haven't got one! And McCarthy, the policeman referred to at the dance, forgot to take his weapons that night so he says!)

It is now 3:30 p.m. I'm going to have lunch!! I didn't breakfast till 11 a.m. as I had a patient earlier.

---

* Hilda Rose, *The Stump Farm: A Chronicle of Pioneering* (Boston: Little, Brown and Co., 1928).

Having had lunch, I decided to go across to the store and then
I called in for bread and stayed listening to Waines till half an
hour ago. He has an infinite number of yarns to tell and needs no
encouragement. He went all through the S. African war and then
was 10 years in India in the army and afterwards went all through
the Great War. He's been a keeper, a stud groom, etc. to Lord Irwin,
the Duke of ?, and several others. His father and brothers are all of
the same type, so he knows all the "nobility" and their little habits
and can talk about them indefinitely. She was a lady's maid part of
her time and comes from the same type of servant family. Quite
interesting to listen to. And they love an English listener who is
properly impressed by these titles and the great estates they mention,
instead of Canadians and Americans who don't know the difference
between them and the post-war profiteers and can't see that it
matters as long as the cash is there.

There's a dance tonight to which I'd meant to go, but I'm too stiff.
People going past and seeing my light keep calling to take me, so this
may sound rather disjointed.

Do you remember my telling you I'd set the leg of an Alsatian
puppy just before Xmas? He saved a man's life last week. Carl
Holden and a pal and this pup were out on Little Prairie and saw a
hole in the snow. They thought there might be a fox or marten down
there and poked with a stick. They felt something but it wouldn't
come out. So Holden said, "Here give me the stick. I'll soon make
him come out." He *did*. Out came a large black bear, exceedingly
peeved at being disturbed! Their only gun jammed in the excitement
and the bear was practically on to Holden when the puppy interfered
and kept the bear interested just long enough for the men to shinny
up a couple of trees!! And there they sat, gun on the ground between
them and the bear running backwards and forwards foaming at the
mouth! (Bears can climb trees, too. I saw the marks of bear claws
on a poplar only a month ago. He'd gone 20 feet up.) Eventually
one of them managed to get the gun and shot him. It was only a .22
but he got him through the ear and killed him. Some shot! My trip
yesterday took me within a mile of the place all this happened.

I've had no chance to learn to ski. There are very few pairs in the
district and no suitable slopes for a beginner except up at the Third

Battle. The lad who was going to teach me lives 13 miles away. I haven't seen him since the fall.

I think I told you more about Kinuso when I stayed there. Battle River certainly has its compensations. I'd hate to live in the village like Dr. Rodger has to; and though her house is a very superior 4-roomed bungalow with a verandah, there were other occupants (bed bugs) which took a good deal of getting rid of, so I've been spared something! She has neighbours with whom she can play bridge and there is a good radio across the road, which makes up for some things.

I didn't buy the boat I spoke of in Peace River, fearing that possibly 59 of the 60 h.p. might be dead! And besides, I'd got some new ideas for my holiday by the time I got back from Edmonton. I don't know a bit what I shall do. I may yet go to Aklavik (on the Arctic), down the Mackenzie and back by plane. The pup is a problem, though, because I should hate to leave him. And he's no lap dog. He requires about twice as much food as I do.

He's lying on the rug now sleeping, an expression of intense bliss on his face, his feet twitching. When anyone comes he barks furiously. I have to put a finger through his collar before I can open the door. He frightens strangers.

The book you sent me, Scott, is made much more interesting by having seen dog teams at work up here. I know just how he'd feel. I hate seeing them whipped and they howl so horribly, the wolf strain I suppose, but yet they seem genuinely fond of the man who works them.

It's supper time – 9 p.m. – so I'll stop this.

~: 15 *March 1930*

My Dear Win,

I got your letter of Feb. 23rd the day before yesterday and the one of Feb. 16th last week. You're a dear to write me so often. Lots of people who wrote to me at first are stopping because I'm so long in answering and my mail, apart from papers and magazines, is beginning to be mainly chits from the Department and the Workmen's Compensation Board and advertisements. And it's most depressing when you have to wait a week for your mail, and get quite excited about it, to find that out of 20 envelopes you've only got 4 or 5 real *letters*! And honest Injun, I haven't got much time for writing to people.

Oh, I shall have to take to getting up early I suppose.

I've been pretty hard-worked lately. The population has been increasing rapidly! Midwifery out here is *some job*. The people are so far away. It takes so long with a team and the roads have been impassable to cars since the end of January and probably will continue so until the middle of May. And between now and then I've got 5 cases booked – 1 mile, 7 miles, 11 miles, 20 and 22 miles away! It isn't the actual confinements that are such a problem. It's visiting these women afterwards. You can't just leave them and hope they're all right. Often there's no one but me to wash mother or baby!! That's why I'm having to ride sometimes now. It's my only way of getting to see them. It's much too cold for riding half the time. I got caught in a blizzard this afternoon. The snow suddenly swept down like a thick mist. I could hardly see the trail but luckily I was only a mile from the house I was aiming for.

Oh, it's a great life, but it's no job for a woman. However, no man would tackle it because of keeping house in his spare time and it's not sufficiently well paid for a man and his wife. And in any case there are any number of openings in towns in Canada where there aren't any worse hardships than the lack of hot baths! So I suppose they'll continue to employ women.

They're going to cut down the spruce trees round the slough south of my house to build my barn. Isn't it tragic? It will spoil my beautiful view. But it's no use arguing. They regard the slough as a blot on the landscape because it can't be broken up and cultivated! Even at night, when the trees cast queer black shadows on the snow by moonlight, they can't see it as anything but "that – slough." You never saw people so blind to beauty in your life. Their idea of a beautiful road is a long straight dirty road, well graded, deep ditches on either side, with a telegraph and telephone line and fenced, with no trees likely to fall across the track, and with little wooden towns, eating house, beer parlour, store and pool hall, about every ten miles.

Oh Lord – they're *hopeless*.

I don't know what sort of weather you're having in England but whatever it is, thank heaven for it! You should just try this! *Real* winter. In spite of the fact that I've been in all day with the heater on, I've had to light a fire in the cook stove and open the oven door to try and get the house warm! I've never had to do that before, not even at 45° below zero and it's only 10 below now. But there's a northwest gale that seems to come through the walls! It's been like this for two days.

Monday was fine and warm (i.e. about 10 above zero), began to chinook in the afternoon. I got called out to another maternity case (my 3rd in 10 days) and went as I was, with just my fur coat over and didn't bother with rugs as the man who fetched me had one and the house was only four miles away. I was out there all night. At about midnight it began to get cold and at 5 a.m. the most terrific blizzard swept over us from the north. Well, I waited till 10 a.m. and the wind went down a little and then I *had* to come home for I knew my house would be freezing up. I hadn't left the key with the Waines as I'd expected to be home in the evening. So we came. 4 miles in ½ hour (the wind was behind us most of the way) and when I got home the tips of all my fingers, both heels, and part of my right ear were frozen!! Not badly, I'm glad to say, but bad enough. The house was frozen up; everything solid. The Waines had been more or less wringing their hands on my doorstep knowing what would happen!

The blizzard continued all day, the temperature somewhere between 10 and 25 below zero. Today has been clear and sunny, but still with that infernal wind almost cutting your head off. Tonight the lights are blazing overhead – brighter than ever I've seen them, I think – a clear *cold* sea-green colour. So it will probably be colder in the morning.

The trails are hideously dangerous. That two or three hours chinook on Monday melted the surface of the snow and then it froze so all the slopes are clear smooth ice, bad when you're walking but deathtraps to sleigh teams and saddle horses unless they're sharp shod.

Don't think I'm grumbling. It's all in the day's work. But I wish this wind would let up for a while.

Oh, a great piece of news! Our little policeman, Babyface, has got the sack!! Came to say farewell this morning on his way south. His greatest trouble seemed to be that he didn't know which of his sins had been found out!! He got a telegram recalling him to Peace River and that's all.

A man named Hayward, a lanky excitable Irishman, is being sent up in his place. I met him when I was down in Peace River. I hope he's got more sense than the last one. Of course, the district is buzzing with excitement about it.

I hope the mail gets in tomorrow. A little doubtful with trails so bad, I should say. It's ridiculous how excited one gets for 24 hours before the mail comes in. I shall finish this after the mail arrives but wanted to get some of my letters started before Friday. It makes it such a rush when the week's correspondence has to be done between Friday and Sunday. And yet, I hate writing a letter on a Monday and not being able to post it till the following Sunday.

~: *March 21st Friday*

The mail arrived at noon today, bringing Daddy's letter of March 2nd. Oh, don't you worry. *That* wasn't my summer holiday I was taking in January, no jolly fear! That was an "extra," a present for a good girl! Three weeks holiday, travelling expenses and a locum provided! Very kind of them. Very kind of them. And quite good policy too. The nurse who left here just a year ago, after being in from the June before, went out with a broken arm and was then in the hospital (at their expense) for nearly three months with a nervous breakdown. She'd had her mother living with her and keeping house for her too.

But they needn't have worried about me. I don't let the isolation get on my nerves. And I am much younger than the nurse and get all the kick out of the sidelines – riding, trying to skate, snowshoeing, skiing, etc. I had my first lesson on skis yesterday, from Tellef Lien, a Norwegian. It isn't nearly as easy as it looks. It seems to me to combine the difficulties of skating and snow-shoeing. Even on this little slope, from my house to Waines, I managed to sit down twice! I can't see myself ever getting to the stage of jumping.

I've just had another set of excellent photos returned, so I've now about 35 to mount and send to you. They really look frightfully "Frozen North"ish. Particularly the dog team ones.

It's depressing to think of the Priory fields being built over. There will still be the Castle and the Wren's nest, of course, but they will lose a good deal when there is no view over the fields to the town. That's one thing about this house. Although the district is filling up so rapidly and all the adjacent "quarters" are occupied, I can only see the roofs of 4 houses and shall only be able to see one when the leaves are on the trees.

There is talk of a big area west of me (starting 3½ miles due west) being made into a Game Reserve. That will mean that those lovely forest-clad hills will remain untouched, for which I shall be very glad. I am hoping to do a little exploring up there later on. There is a lake only 6 miles west that I want to see and there are some old pack trails I've heard of from trappers that will be fun to explore. I shan't be nearly so tied down to the district this year as I was last and I shall be able to get much further on horseback in a day.

I have had a present of a beaded moosehide camera case from a breed woman. Really quite a lovely thing, done with my initials D.P. in beads!! It took me a few seconds to get the D.P., of course: D.P. = Doctor Percy!!

I'm thinking of having a fairly extensive addition to my house soon. Give me the benefit of your advice on these suggested plans will you?

You see, I want it fixed so that patients do not have to pass through the living room to get to the dispensary (their muddy boots causing me a great deal of hard work) and also not to have to cook in my living room in the presence of any visitors I may have because it always puts me off! And I want a verandah, screened, to enable me to live outside and sleep out in summer. I thought if the dispensary door opened from that then people could wait on the verandah when I'm busy. Then a door in the kitchen would enable me to get in wood and carry out ashes and dirty water without going through the living room.

I shall have to have an extra heater, of course, next winter. I don't know how much the additions will cost. I'm getting Slim in to figure out how much timber it will need when he comes in at the weekend.

I've had my third small mail running today, only 7 letters and 4 papers and some drugs. I'm fed up. I don't know whether to make an effort to write more or whether to stop writing altogether, till everyone writes in alarm to know if I'm dead, or eaten by a bear!

It really is very sad, though. I'm getting lots fewer letters than I used to in England and I certainly write more, though not so many as

I should I suppose. It's very pathetic when all your friends forget your existence, when you've only been away 9 months.

It's snowing again.

~ *26 March 1930*

I'm afraid I'm rather a hard person to please. Last time I wrote I was complaining of the weather being too cold. Today, I'm grumbling because it has begun to thaw at last and is also pouring with rain and I need Wellingtons even to wade out to the wood pile! My house is surrounded by a miniature moat! The earth looks awfully dark and dirty after seeing nothing but beautifully clean snow for so long. My floor is filthy. I've had 10 people in so far today (it's 4:30 p.m.) and they and the pup have brought in an enormous amount of mud.

I have been very busy for the last few days and have done several long rides to the north. I'm getting hardened again to riding, thank heaven. But Dan is a mean old devil!! He's very fit and fresh and thinks he can do what he likes. Did I tell you he bucked Bill Tyson off twice? He nearly got rid of me on Monday. I went so far forward over his head anyway that when I came back the horn of the saddle tore my breeches almost from knee to waist! That's going to take *some* darning I can tell you. I'm going to have to ride him with curb anyway for a while. I can hardly pull him up with the present bit and I've got to teach him who is boss.

There doesn't seem much news to tell you. The new policeman has come in and shows signs of being a bit more sensible than the last. The new church (United, i.e. Methodist and Presbyterian) is being built very rapidly. They hope to have it finished for Easter and are starting in brightly with a BAZAAR!! The fact that no one has any money to buy with, even if anyone had money to buy materials for makings things to sell, doesn't seem to worry them any and they propose to charge $1.00 each for admission and supper! The cash, of course, goes to furnish the Manse. We don't know yet who is coming in as minister.

The lumber has just been delivered for my barn. (I'm not having it built of logs after all.) I hope they get it built tomorrow. Then I've got to have my house and place where the garden is going to be all fenced in. That can't be done till the ground thaws out, which will not be till towards the end of April, I'm told. I shall get a piece of land broken for a flower garden. My vegetable garden is going to be combined with the Waines, so that I shan't have to get anyone to work it for me. Potatoes, carrots, parsnips, turnips, radishes, lettuce, peas, beans, cabbage, cauliflower, rhubarb, onions and celery would take more work than I am anxious to do!

Hurrah! It has stopped raining. Now I'm going to wade over to the barber's and get a hair cut!

~ *Friday March 28th*

Well, of all the mad climates! All last week was bitterly cold. This week it began to thaw on Wednesday, then began to rain and yesterday and today have been wonderfully fine and the temperature *70° in the shade*!!

And you should see the trails. Bottomless slush. You know what a mess an English 3 or 4 inches of snow is when it melts. Imagine 3 or 4 feet of snow melting suddenly with the earth still frozen so solid that water cannot sink into it! I've been out riding each day, and today could only average 3 miles an hour on horseback!!

My barn is built. Eight men came and did it for me yesterday. It has had a fire in it today to dry up the melting snow on the floor and after Monday it will be fit for Dan.

The mail came up yesterday. Your letter leaving Dudley, March 10th (2 a.m.), arrived here March 27th (5 a.m.). That's very good, isn't it?

I am enclosing a letter I received this mail from Miss Powell, one of the three Englishwomen who went to Fort Vermilion in December. I can't remember whether I told you that after missing them when they called here on their way back, I caught them up at Peace River, on my way out for my holiday, and we spent a very interesting day together.

In reference to the Alexandria Falls, in case I didn't tell you of it, that was my idea for my summer holiday at the time I met these people. No white woman has ever been there yet, and to my disgust they were proposing to go! They started out, after I left Peace River, to go to Fort St. John, Fort Nelson, Fort Liard and then across to the Alexandria Falls on the Hay River, and back via Great Slave Lake and Fort Vermilion. An exceedingly interesting and distinctly adventurous trip, the trails being anything but well-travelled. However, as the letter explains, it didn't come off. I am very relieved to know that they are now skiing over glaciers in comparative safety!!

Fort Nelson sounds attractive! No doctor for 300 or 400 miles. I wonder if they'd pay me any more than the Government of Alberta? (This place is getting very civilised; they're going to start a railroad in here next year, we're told.) And even their nearest doctor, at Pouce Coupe, is as far as I am from railroad or hospital. It's an amazing country, isn't it?

Did I tell you when I came here in the summer about a young Anglican missionary with his wife and child on the same boat, on their way to Fort Vermilion? They came out with Louis Bourassa with this last mail, passed through here yesterday and called, but I was out. I'm awfully sorry about his leaving Vermilion. I hate to see a missionary labelled "Quitter."

McArthy, an Anglican parson I met in Peace River in the fall, has also given it up this spring, after little more than a year. Both of them married, too. I can imagine how they felt. I've felt that way myself! But heavens, if I can stick it, batching by myself, surely they might when they've someone to live with.

Oh, the winter is trying. For two pins, I'd have dropped this job myself once or twice lately but now spring is coming I feel better.

You can't imagine the effect of the *silence* here at night in the winter. I've lain awake at New Milton listening to the quiet and always there were lots of tiny sounds, but here it can be absolutely silent. Sometimes I stood outside when I went to get in wood at night and listened and listened and heard *nothing* except my own breathing. It was almost like some exceedingly refined Chinese torture! Then I've gone in and put on the gramophone, Beethoven's Fifth Symphony usually, as a sort of protection against silence! Don't think I'm going daft. I'm only trying to give you the sort of impression it makes. I began almost to hate the northern lights. They made the snow look such a queer greenish colour, and they swirled and waved so silently. I haven't felt like this very often but it's a rather overwhelming sensation when it comes. One feels so insignificant and helpless, as if the whole of nature is antagonistic.

The mails for the next 6 or 8 weeks, till the trails are dried out, will probably be exceedingly erratic. I expect this will get out safely as the ground is still solid under the slush, but when that thaws – !! So don't be alarmed even at a month's gap.

⌒ *29 March 1930*

Dear Win,

I've two letters of yours to answer – March 3rd, just after your weekend at Dudley, and March 7th. I was glad to hear some news of the family from an external observer.

Thanks also for the information that Daddy and Mother are still enjoying getting long letters from me. I don't want to bore them.

I wish you could afford to come to Canada this year. There are lots of marvellous trips that I might do with a companion that I can't very well do alone. And you'd *love* my dog. I'm getting keener and keener on him. He really is amazingly intelligent and the greatest pal. I wish sometimes that his feet were not so large. He carries in an outrageous amount of mud nowadays but large feet are a sign of good breeding in a Great Dane.

Oh, the greatest joke! There is a school up at Rousseau's corner (4 miles N) which had a man teacher last year. The new school year starts in April and the trustees engaged a woman teacher. They were so keen on having a woman that they didn't even bother about her qualifications! There are several old bachelors among the trustees and of course they got a good deal of ragging. (The real reason they wanted a woman was so that they could have things all their own way. The man was not very easy to manage.)

Ten days ago, the telegraph operator said he'd had a wire from his pal the operator in Peace River and the woman was 45, grey-haired, wore spectacles and had a wooden leg, and she was coming up with the mail!!!! Of course, we waited in great excitement and when the mail came there was no teacher! It was just a rag, of course. But when an authentic wire came that she was coming with this mail the excitement was really terrific. And when it arrived, the teacher was a M A N!! All the old bachelors in the district shaved and spruced up and waiting at the store to greet the lady. Can't you just see them? And their faces when the man arrived!

Why a man? We don't quite know. But probably the Powers That Be got some inkling of the reason for the trustees wanting a woman.

The man they'd had was a good teacher but knew his own mind and went on strike, shut the school in the fall till they paid him his wages and they didn't love him.

I had a really big mail again this week, a good sackful. As a result, I am 100% more cheerful. Also, the weather has broken at last and the snow is disappearing like magic and there's a foot of water over the ice in the river. The river will break up about the middle of April, they say. I had been getting desperately tired of winter.

I have spent half this afternoon peering down a microscope hunting for TB, and finding it. The amount of TB up here is horrifying. I think I told you about the House family. The Mother died of TB 3 years ago. Pat died of TB last summer, aged 21. Frank died of TB a month ago, aged 18. Boniface has it and had been in bed since before Xmas, and was getting better but is now running round the country killing moose, etc., and will undoubtedly flare up again before long. Bon's baby, aged 12 months, was taken ill about 4 or 5 days ago and when I saw him this morning showed fairly unmistakeable TB meningitis. And Auguste, the youngest brother, aged 16, is deaf and dumb and I had to aspirate a TB abscess in his neck last week! It's simply heart-breaking. And during the last week I've also collected two new cases amongst the white population – a man of 31, dying fast, and a doubtful case a girl of 6 who was living in the same house as the young Norwegian boy I sent out to a sanatorium just before Xmas. I'm also looking after two more certain cases and three more doubtful cases and the population of the district is only 1200.

I've had an awfully interesting series of cases lately. And I saw the worst rickets I've ever seen in my life. The interesting thing is this, that baby was born up here, a country where the average sunshine per year is over 2,000 hours, was breast-fed for 7 months and then given lots of fresh cow's milk (and of course the cows run loose in the sunlight) and yet she has rickets.

I've got some exciting books from the library this week. I've also got lots of letters to answer and so much dispensing to do, so this is all this mail.

~: *4 April 1930*

Spring has come with a rush. The snow has almost gone, the prairies
are knee deep in water, all the creeks are pouring water and the
beaver dams are full. Down here by the river are dozen of waterfalls.
There is about a foot of water running over the ice at present and in
a few days the ice, which is still frozen to the bottom, will rise and
break up. There is a good deal of excitement about the bridge and
some doubt as to whether it will stand. One end (the far side) is
already very seriously weakened, as the water rushing down from the
sloughs has washed away a great deal of earth and undermined the
support. The weather is very fine and very warm – there has been a
strong S.W. wind for several days – and the music of all the streams
and waterfalls and the cries of the returning birds is delightful. Geese
have been flying north for several days, in much smaller parties and
flying lower than when they left. I saw a red-headed woodpecker and
a hawk yesterday and two bluebirds today.

I am pretty busy at present but thoroughly enjoying splashing
round the country on Dan with Brutus swimming valiantly behind.
Swimming is no exaggeration. He has had to swim across several
creeks!

The mail was very late getting in owing to the bad trails and I have
been out all day, so didn't get my letters till 8:30 p.m. And now the
store has to close on Sunday and I shall have to take my letters across
on a Saturday, so that this week I've only 24 hours in which to answer
all my mail. As I've a three month's report which will take hours to
write, I'm hoping I can avoid doing any visits tomorrow.

I received Daddy's letter of March 16th today. The incoming mail
seems much more satisfactory than the outgoing. I'm sorry my letters
are so irregular. They have been posted regularly.

I've had quite an exciting week. The old man with heart failure
died on Monday. Very sad, as he was just getting better. I can just
imagine Daddy's expression and remarks when he reads that! He *was*
getting better. The swelling of his legs, etc., was decreasing and he
had lost his elegant blue-green colour. And then he went and got an
embolus and departed. Monday night I had to take a woman out to
hospital, Berwyn Cottage Hospital (6 beds, Catholic), as Peace River
was closed. We started off in a sleigh but the chinook was blowing
hard and by the time we had done 24 miles the roads were almost

Caboose serving as ambulance.

bare of snow and quite impossible for sleighing. We were going to change to a wagon but Mr. Gives thought he could get through with a car, so we tried it and did very well as far as Grimshaw. Twice we buried ourselves firmly in the deep snow in the ditch and had to be pulled out with teams and twice the car turned completely round on ice-covered roads, but otherwise we were all right. From Grimshaw to Berwyn, the trail was from 3 to 5 feet deep in snow still, so we had to take to a sleigh again.

In Grimshaw I met Mr. Pritchett. You remember the letter he found and forwarded in the fall? He is an old Englishman, out here 20 years. He had met Dr. Rodger in the fall and had driven her from Slave Lake to Kinuso when the roads were bad. They had to drive along the railway track and one of the wheels came off just as they were trying to get off the track because of a train coming!!! Dr. Rodger told me about it. He is an interesting old chap.

I came back from Grimshaw with lots of "civilised" food – oranges, grape-nuts, honey, lemon-cheese (lemons being unobtainable, I couldn't make my own), dates, canned strawberries, raspberries, etc. – and so am living in great luxury, when I've time. Meals are very erratic. I didn't have my supper till 10:30 p.m. (I started this letter while it was cooking.) As this was the first meal since breakfast and I have ridden over 20 miles during the day, I was exceedingly hungry

Trying to get a patient to Berwyn hospital by car, April 1930.

and ate so much that it would be inviting nightmares to go to bed till midnight, so I'm continuing this.

I had a letter from Dr. Rodger today. She does have a thrilling life. Another aeroplane trip to Edmonton. I must be slow. All my patients seem to be capable of removal to hospital by less exciting means.

I am hoping to get some duck-shooting towards the end of the month. This of course is strictly against the law (i.e. out of season) and therefore can't be indulged in anywhere the policeman is likely to come. But up along the Third Battle River, away from the trail, it is quite uninhabited and I should get a chance. The only difficulty is passing the policeman's house with a gun! I think I must start carrying it round regularly and tell him I'm afraid to travel without it!!

It isn't midnight yet but I'm so sleepy I can hardly keep my eyes open. So, I'll give up the struggle and risk nightmare. If I have any time I'll mount some more photos to send to you tomorrow.

Saturday

Managed to make time to mount rest of snaps. I'm quite proud of some of these, but I do wish I'd remembered to take off my dark glasses before that one of me on horseback was taken. How do you like the chaps?

~ 11 April 1930

I am scribbling this while watching a maternity case! I'm up to the eyes in work. This will be the third night running and I've done 78 miles on horseback in the last 48 hours, too! The roads are frightful. I've a 40 mile trip again tomorrow so don't see any other chance of writing. The mail is in but I've not had time to get mine yet. I've certainly justified my existence this week! The population of this district is increasing at no end of a speed. The birth rate must be nearer 30 than 16.

Wednesday I was out all day, got home at 12:30 a.m. – very cold, it was freezing hard – to find a man waiting to take me to a case 20 miles away. So, had to repack my bag, snatch a biscuit or two and start off again. They'd had to send for me to go on a saddle horse as the trail was impassable to anything else (they have two cars), miles of it under water, and a couple of creeks to swim! When we were two miles from our destination, a man met us and told us they wanted us to hurry, so I did the last two miles of a 45-mile-day at a dead gallop. Found the lady pulseless, cold and clammy, so it was a darned good job we hurried. Stayed there till 6 p.m. (from 4 a.m.) and got in at 10 p.m., looked to the horse, made supper and went to bed.

At 1 a.m., a voice outside my window, George Robertson – Could I go and see his wife? He thought she had appendicitis, and the trail to his place was only fit for a horse. So I dressed, packed my bag and off again. Sure enough, Alice was starting an acute appendix. Was arranging to take her down to Peace River to hospital when Mr. Black arrived at George's – Could I come at once to his wife? He'd had to follow me over to Robertsons,' taking an extra hour, so we hurried on. Back home to fetch my bags, and then a 9 mile hurry up there! And here I've been all day and look like being most of the night! And tomorrow I must go and revisit the lady with the Haemorrhage (i.e. a 40 mile ride).

Who wouldn't be a Doctor?

I hope to goodness George has got Alice down to Town safely.

Oh, I do wish I'd got my mail. It's frustrating to be sitting here with lots of time for letter writing and yet not able to answer any.

> ~ *McNamara Hotel*
> *Peace River*
> *16 April 1930*

The rush continues. I've had 1½ nights in bed in the last eight days, and have done 180 miles on horseback in the time, and also 100 miles down here with an acute appendix.

I am just waiting for a bath. (This hotel has running hot and cold water. A bath costs 75 cents, i.e. 3/-.) Then am off to the hospital to give the anaesthetic while Sutherland operates on the lady and then am off back to the Battle.

The roads have to be seen to be believed. We've had another heavy snowstorm. I did 35 miles on horseback over the prairie in a blizzard on Monday, so thick the snow was like fog. Got lost but mercifully the horse found his way back to the trail.

We had to bring Mrs. Guttau (the appendix) out with a sleigh pulled by a caterpillar tractor!! It was that or a plane. And as she was 17 miles from a telegraph office and also there being no place where the plane could land within 5 miles of her house, it was quicker the way we came. I kept her nearly unconscious with morphine, but, oh Lord!, you don't know how trying the rat-a-tat-a-tat of a caterpillar is till you've done 70 miles behind one.

I am posting this down here, as shall have so much work to do when I get back that I can't promise to write this weekend.

Seventy miles behind a caterpillar, April 1930.

~: Thursday
Grimshaw

Have just had breakfast and am sitting in the Chinaman's getting
warm and waiting to find out if I can get back in today. We pulled
out of Peace River at 5:30 a.m. this morning. Couldn't start last night
as the snow had melted so much that no car could have got over the
mud. We got on splendidly this morning. Only had to dig ourselves
out of one mud hole, had to change a burst tire and had to stop
another time because the petrol pipe clogged up. So we did 17 miles
in 2 hours, excellent time for this part of the world! I hope I can get in
tonight. I've left cases up there I'd have said it was impossible to leave,
if this case hadn't been so bad that I had no choice.

I had 6 hours in bed last night and feel a different being. Now I've
got to go and see a patient here. My practise is extending rapidly!

I really have had an exceedingly exciting week. I nearly got
drowned on Sunday, crossing a deep creek.

You see, to get to Ashworths' (20 miles S.E. of my house), I have
to cross Jack Knife Creek. Well, it's deep and swift at present. You'd
almost call it a river in England but it will be almost dry by fall. There
are two bridges over it and both had gone out with the flood. Of the
three trails possible that cut out two, the creek being uncrossable at
these points without a bridge. The third trail is the shortest and just

crosses the creek at a narrow, fairly safe place. Thursday, in going
to Ashworths' the first time, we swam the horses across easily and
coming back by myself I had no difficulty, though was more than a
little scared. Sunday, I was on my way to see her again and the creek
was 1 or 2 feet lower and I didn't anticipate any difficulty, having quite
forgotten that by that time the bottom had thawed and washed out
badly. So the horse got in but couldn't get a footing in the almost
vertical wall of mud the other side and nearly drowned me trying to,
so we had to swim up stream and get out same side. Water was only
up to my waist, of course, but rather chilly as you can imagine, as the
snow is still melting in the bush.

So there I was, soaked to the waist, *still* on the wrong side of the
creek!! Well, there was a man loading hay the other side, who had
nearly drowned his team the day before, so he hauled my horse over
with a rope, while I walked over on a couple of thin poplar poles,
which incidentally rolled over with me and tipped me in again!!! But
I didn't get much wetter! And then I had a 4 mile ride to Ashworths'
in my wet clothes and the wind was from the east. Don't marvel that I
haven't had pneumonia. I certainly should have done if I'd had time!

Coming back at night I took a long trail through 2 miles of shallow
water, to get to a place where they'd mended the other bridge, after a
fashion.

I'm still enjoying it, in spite of minor mishaps like this! Tuesday
morning, 5 a.m., while riding through the bush I saw a big bull moose
fairly close, about 500 yards. The horse drew my attention to it. She
nearly jumped out of her skin. I was riding one of the Guttau's horses.
They brought a spare when they came for me as they knew how Dan
had been worked lately.

That's three spare horses that have been brought for me in the last
week. The only difficulty is that I've no spare legs to ride with.

~ *26 April 1930*

At last – touch wood – things are beginning to slack off a bit. I've
been desperately busy since I got back from town last Sunday. I had
an awful time getting back – 43 miles by truck, at 2 miles an hour, 2
miles to the gallon!!! The mud was beginning to dry and was simply
glutinous. The truck even had to plough its way down hill in low

gear!! I don't think we went a mile in intermediate. Then, 1½ miles the other side of the saw mill, we stuck for good. So, I walked to the mill, hired a team and wagon as far as Lays' (18 miles from home), borrowed a saddle horse from there to Guttau's and another saddle horse from Guttau's to get home. Landed in at 1 a.m. after doing the last 13 miles over unspeakable roads, in the dark, with a rain-sleet-snow storm beating in my face. When I got home, my boots were frozen to the stirrups and my stockings to my boots! I couldn't feel my feet at all! And I arrived to find notes under the door, pinned on the door and lying on the table – 7 more or less urgent calls!! Including one to a baby unconscious and in convulsions, dated Friday!! This on Easter Sunday at 1 a.m. I decided that if the child was still alive it would wait an hour or two and if it wasn't there was no point in getting there at 3 a.m. So, I started off early next morning. The kid is recovering I'm glad to say, though she's still pretty bad.

But every day till yesterday I was at it as hard as I could go. Last night, I took a holiday, played bridge with the new parson, the telegraph operator and Mrs. Rousseau. Had quite good luck and thoroughly enjoyed it.

The new parson, Mr. Parker, is going to be a success, I think. He is young, not more than 30 I should say, an M.A. as well as a B.D. He rides, swims, skates, canoes and shoots. His wife, who is coming up in June, is Southern American (Missouri), also a university graduate, keen on riding and swimming. They dance and play bridge and don't object to baseball on a Sunday. In fact, he is helping to promote the team. So the Powers that Be have sent us the right type, thank goodness.

By the way, let me correct the mistake I made about the Fort Vermilion parson. He has been recalled to Peace River. He didn't just quit. I knew he disliked Fort Vermilion and therefore accepted the information that he'd quit without bothering to verify it.

Later

The mail has just arrived with your letters of March 30th from Dudley and April 7th from Barton. Glad to know you're having a holiday. I hope the weather was good, likewise the golf. Your descriptions of the flowers down there make me quite homesick, for – although spring is coming with a rush here – we haven't got past the occasional blade of grass yet, except where the sloughs and pools are receding and the black mud is being covered by a haze of green just like a new lawn. The birds are arriving by the million – geese, cranes, thousands and thousands of wild duck, blackbirds, bluebirds and lots of tiny birds about the size of wrens that I can't identify. Hawks are common and I've seen one eagle.

The river is rising rapidly, about 3 feet yesterday. The ice has gone out down there but Ted Waines says there are great chunks as big as a house higher up. Doubtless, it is the break-up there that is causing the rapid rise here. I expect the ice will come down shortly.

I have seen a few mosquitoes already. I fear this will be a terrible year for them. No-one has ever seen so much water about as there is at present. Still, I shall get broken in gradually this year.

For the last two nights it has not frozen, first time since October!! Until then it froze hard every night, as I knew to my cost. I had a number of night rides and very tough going they were, too. For miles we had to plough across half-frozen pools and sloughs, ice up to two inches thick, the horses' feet going through into a foot of water and bottomless mud, very slow and very tiring going.

The man with the fractured skull is recovering. He is still cross-eyed and seeing double but has regained his hearing, can walk about and remember everything except for the week after the accident. He has no recollection of the journey to the hospital.

~ *26 April 1930*

Dear Uncle and Aunt,
Well, I have weathered the winter safely, a little fatter but otherwise none the worse! Spring is just starting here. For the last two nights there has been no frost. Previously, the temperature at night varied between 0° and 20° F, while it was 60° or 70° F during the day. Ploughing started in one or two places yesterday but in most places won't start for another 3 days as all the frost is not out of the ground yet. You see how short a time this leaves to grow grain. Frost can be expected in September, often comes earlier. That's what makes the whole business such a gamble. So, from the beginning of May, men out here have to work about 16 hours a day, ploughing and seeding and cutting even at 11 p.m. It is light almost all night. Even now there is enough light from the

sunset to see the time by your watch at 10:15 p.m. The long days make growing much faster, so the further north you go the earlier the grain is ripe. But that is just about balanced by the earlier frosts.

The wild ducks are here in thousands, on every pool and slough. It is a wonderful sight when you come on a couple of hundred suddenly and they all fly up together. I haven't had time to have a try at one yet but I think I shall have to borrow a shot-gun. A .22 is no good unless you're an exceedingly good shot.

Brutus is beginning to be a nuisance. He's growing up rather fierce, which is strange when he's hardly ever tied up. He not only barks when anyone comes but he goes up to them growling savagely and looking horribly dangerous. I should be scared stiff of him myself if he were someone else's dog. He even prevented a man from knocking on my door one day. (Sunday morning, 2 weeks ago. I'd let him out and then gone back to bed to sleep.) Every time the man put up his hand to touch the door, young Brutus seized it firmly!! Finally, the man had to shout through my bedroom window!

When he takes dislikes to people I have to hold him while they get into the house and even then he lies and growls at them till they go. He takes no notice when I tell him to stop. He's held his own quite well in several minor fights, which I don't mind. I should hate to own a dog that size who couldn't. And he's a marvellous watch dog. He won't let anyone touch anything of mine, or my horse, unless I tell him it's all right. When I was down in Peace River, I left him at home. And he followed Mrs. Waines round the house growling when she went in and did some cleaning up and lit a fire for me. And when I'm at home, he spends his time trotting backwards and forwards to see her and keep an eye on me. But I wish I knew how to stop him being quite such a fierce watchdog. Have you any suggestions? You see, there are many strange characters up here and a good watchdog is essential, but I don't want him to do more than bark.

(By the way, two Ukrainian lads I gave a meal to once, and to whom he took a frantic dislike, were taken to jail by the policeman last week for stealing!!)

Dan is in splendid shape, though I am working him very hard. Grooming him is not quite such a task now. He's shed most of his long winter coat. He's frightfully skittish and great fun to ride. I've had some marvellous gallops.

You will perhaps have seen my letters home and know that I had a chilly swim in a creek two weeks ago. I learnt yesterday that I had a narrower escape than I had realised. Duncan MacLean (the husband of the owner of the piano) and Cecil Taylor were nearly drowned there two days later. A horse was drowned and three other horses had narrow escapes. Neither of the men could swim, but my being able to swim would have been little use when I was wearing heavy leather chaps and coat.

I've had a lovely big mail this week – about 30 letters, papers, etc. and another good set of snaps. My camera has been working well for the past two months.

~: 3 *May 1930*

This week has been almost as busy as the previous three and I have half a dozen visits to do today. So this will be a short letter, I expect.

Poor old Brutus got trodden on by a horse on Monday night and two small bones in his foot are broken so I've been having to travel without him. It will teach him to keep out of the way! We were riding very fast (I got called to see an old man aged 72 they thought was going to die before I got there but he's up a ladder building the church chimney today!!) and Dan kicked the pup right under the feet of the other horse. He had to follow the rest of the way, 3 miles, with his injured foot as I couldn't stop to look at it. It is getting better rapidly. He is using the foot a little today but he does hate staying at home when I go out; I could hear his howling when I was exactly three miles away the other morning!

I've just come back from another maternity case. I got called out at 6 a.m., dressed, collected my tools, saddled Dan and arrived at the place at 6:50 a.m. (2½ miles away) to find the baby born, washed and the lady energetically scrubbing the floor!!!

The baby was born at 5:45 a.m. After scrubbing she was going to get breakfast and then do the washing! I told her in signs, as she speaks no English and her husband only a few words, to go to bed, but she didn't want to. And when I told her husband she should go to bed for seven days he translated to her and they both roared with laughter! They are Ukrainians of the poorer type, living in a 10 × 8 feet mud hut. The furniture consists of a stove, a plank bed covered with straw, with big feather pillows as coverings, and a shelf with a cup and a saucepan and a pie dish. (There is no table and no chairs.) I expect they have some food somewhere but I didn't see any signs. I must take a photo of the place some time lest you think I'm exaggerating!

Do you wonder the British working man doesn't get on in Canada? He would no more tolerate those conditions than fly, much less make good under them. The B.W.M.'s education and upbringing are dead against him in this country. He starts at the same sort of disadvantage – competing with the Central Europeans with their lower standards of living and longer hours of work – in Canada, as he does in world trade. And as far as I can see, the Ukrainians, Ruthenians, Hungarians and assorted Slav races that I can't sort out are the ones who are going to make good out here. Even living as they do, they regard Canada as a sort of Heaven on Earth. They live on practically nothing and they work 16 hours a day on it.

The women and children work in the field with the men, entire families. Even children too young for school are busy clearing and piling brush just now and they get along at an amazing speed. It seems to me that even though the numbers of emigrants from Central Europe are limited so as to keep a higher proportion of English and Scandinavian peoples coming in, yet before long the Slavs will be the dominant race in this part of Canada. They're tough and they're prolific and they can make a success of farming on land no Englishman would touch. Also they never believe in paying when they haven't got to. (Lots of them have some cash, more than the English-speaking very often.) I do something for them, tell them how much and they consider they've done all that is necessary when they've said, "No have got, Mrs. Doctor, thank you, Goodbye." And then they come again next time, quite happily, expecting that the benevolent government which gives them land will continue to give them free medical service indefinitely. You should see their expressions when I get them on to split wood! Or demand payment in eggs or butter!

This payment in eggs is getting rather a nuisance. When eggs were 50 cents a dozen it was all right. But now that they're down to 20–25 cents and the price for pulling one tooth is 4 dozen eggs, it's getting serious! I pulled 3 teeth for a Ukrainian woman the other day and she's going to give me eggs!!! But really one has to make them pay whenever possible. You can imagine nothing more annoying than charging a man $2 for a job which would have cast him $15–$20, apart from hospital fees, if he'd been in town, being told that he has no money and will pay in the fall after his crop is threshed, and then happening to go into the store an hour later to find him taking out a roll of $50 or $100 to pay for groceries. One almost feels like getting cash in advance! Of course, the money doesn't go to me. It makes no difference what proportion I collect. Still, I do feel mad about it sometimes. As an ordinary Doctor one can always refuse to go next time but out here that's impossible.

I got my well dug at the beginning of the week and I've got about three feet of clear, soft, good-tasting water only 10 feet down. Very lucky. Water is one of the great problems up here. Those wells which have been dug on Little Prairie are so alkaline that the water is undrinkable. Even cattle and horses refuse it. And it's so hard that it can't be used for washing. Other wells have soft water but it's black and undrinkable. Other places, there is no water even at 100 feet, so people continue to drink creek water. I've eight cases of severe diarrhoea along one creek in Big Prairie. Two children nearly went west, but they take no notice when I tell them to boil their drinking water! They're all breeds, old-timers, and because the water was always safe before, they cannot understand that the hundreds of new settlers coming in make any difference. And I defy anyone to get the idea of germs into these half-breeds' heads. I get awfully mad with them at times but it's no use. They're like children. They remember for an hour or so and then forget till you come again.

Oh, I learnt the Cree for aspirin the other day. It's pronounced taystigwanan moskeke = headache medicine. I'm a moskeke wenou = medicine man. The preacher is an ime wenou – Sunday man! I'm getting on!

~: *7 May 1930*

Dorothy Round is doing marvellously. I'm awfully thrilled. Do go on sending me cuttings. The Times and the Observer are rather brief on the subject of Tennis. I should love to see some of those matches. They must be awfully exciting.

It is wretchedly cold and grey today. It hailed yesterday and snowed on Sunday and is still very cold at night. (Relatively warm compared with winter but still often down to freezing point or just above.) This climate is all very well for a time but when you start getting snow in September, and are still getting it in May, you begin to get rather tired of it. Too much like the Arctic, where the year consists of Winter and July. I'm beginning to wonder whether I can possibly stand another winter.

Part of my trouble is that I've had another busy week, 4 nights up out of 7, and I started Monday badly by having to fill in two death certificates before breakfast, a depressing business anyway and particularly so when you're feeling Monday-morningish!

However, things are getting slacker at last. I've only done 10 miles on horseback in the last two days, as compared with an average of 20–25 daily for weeks. I slept for a couple of hours in the afternoon yesterday and had 10 hours in bed last night but, although it's only 9:30 p.m., I'm getting sleepy again already. I really feel I could sleep for a week.

I'm already awfully tough, you know. A month like the last one would have killed me last year. The amazing thing is that I've only lost 2 lbs all the time. I'm still 12 lbs too heavy. Yet, it isn't lack of exercise, nor even excess of food. Still, it's cheering to see that Schoolbred's have invented a new O.S.,* the "stylishly stout." I imagine that it will just do for me!!

There isn't really any news for you this week. The pup's foot is getting better rapidly. There is a big lump but I'm afraid there always will be some deformity because he won't keep off it. He hardly limps at all now and bounces round as energetically as ever. He is a year old this week and is 28 inches high at the shoulder.

Our beautiful highway is now more or less useless. The road has been washed away on either side the Whitemud Bridge so that the only way to get in and out is to take the old trail round by the Clear Hills. I suppose this will delay the grading of the road from Little Prairie store (6 miles south of here) to the 2nd Battle, as they will have to stop to put in a new grade at Whitemud. The trails up here are still much too wet for cars, and even wagons are getting into difficulties if carrying much of a load.

* For "outsize." Schoolbred's is a London department store.

The river is dropping fast. Some of the rocks are showing now. I have a patient across the 2nd that I should see but am waiting till I can cross on horseback. They are using a raft and making the horses swim at present.

~ 9 May 1930

My dear Lena,
I have just been across and fetched my mail and read the letters, and now I'm writing while my supper cooks. Not that there's much cooking about it. I'm having canned beefsteak and onions, canned corn, potatoes, canned fruit and coffee (also canned). Doesn't sound very attractive, does it? But I assure you I'm lucky to be able to buy the canned stuff. There is nothing fresh to be had and there won't be for two months or more. No vegetables. No potatoes (but I've still got half a sackful down the cellar). No fruit, not even apples. No lettuce or celery or tomatoes or cress or anything like that. No bacon or ham, both stores have sold out and we can't get any more because the Whitemud River has washed the road away on either side of the bridge. No fresh meat. I had a goose and two ducks last week but haven't been shooting this week.

So you can understand what a bad time the people have who have used up all their vegetables and potatoes and who can't afford to buy any canned stuff. Food up here is very expensive. My supper is going to cost about 4/6 and there will be enough for lunch tomorrow out of that. But people with families can't even afford butter or canned milk. Lots of places I go to they have bread and tea (no milk or sugar) or bread and Golden Syrup and coffee for a meal.

Last Saturday I got called out to a man who had been found unconscious outside his house. He was living alone and there wasn't another house nearer than 1½ miles away and not any woman whom I could get to look after him for 5 miles round. So I had to stay there myself. In the house I found flour, sugar, salt, baking powder, cloves, lard, rolled oats and coffee and of course a stove to cook with. How would you have liked to start in cooking meals for yourself for two days with only those ingredients? I had to feed the pigs too! The old man didn't need cooking for. He'd had a stroke and was unconscious. He died on Sunday night.

There's a man just come to live in this district, two or three miles west of my house, who has 21 children!!!! And on his way up here he adopted a half-breed boy because he said he could just as well look after 22 as 21!!!! There are some funny characters in this country.

I've been trying to trim Dan's mane with a pair of scissors this afternoon. It should really be done with shears. I've only managed a kind of ragged semi-shingle because he wouldn't keep his head still!

~ 16 May 1930

You'll have to forgive the dirty paper. It's impossible to keep anything clean. The dust today is simply awful. No one would believe that I'd swept and dusted this room only 4 hours ago. There is grit ½" thick all over the floor! Even with doors and windows shut (which would be intolerable today, it's 70 in the shade), the grit still gets in.

I'm waiting for the mail, late again. Goodness knows why this time. Except for a few bad mud holes, the roads are in excellent condition. Cars are running at last. We had a lot of people in from Peace River and Grimshaw yesterday. Motor salesmen (3), Government officials, police, land seekers and surveyors. I suppose the rush has now begun. This district is becoming famous all over Canada.

I'm fed up with it. I've had another busy spell. I've got an outbreak of dysentery from drinking creek water. The creek is fouled by barns, stables, pig sties, privies and manure heaps, but is the only source of drinking water in that region. One man tried to dig a well but at 80 feet it began to cave in and he hadn't got water, so he gave it up. The others haven't even tried. I've had 10 cases and one death, a breed kiddie aged 3 and I've had two other children, aged 3 and 4, who had convulsions with it and who had very narrow squeaks. The last case was Florence L'Hirondelle, aged 4, who went to bed apparently quite well and by the time I got there at 7 a.m. was delirious, having convulsions every few minutes and looked like departing this life at any moment. I was in and out of the place for nearly 48 hours but I think she's going to pull through now.

I did a sanitary inspection very solemnly with a policeman yesterday and am making all these people shift their pig sties, barns etc. Gosh! Shan't I be popular? Some of them are old timers whose barns have stood there for 5 or 10 years. But it didn't matter when no-one lived below them. They can't realize how the situation has changed. There were less than 300 people in here 3 years ago. Now there are 1,500 and more coming in every day.

This water question is the big problem in this district. Wells are expensive things to drill or dig and when the chances are that they won't find water, or will find undrinkable alkaline stuff, you understand them using water from a stream.

I'm going to have to keep my well locked, I can see. There's a nasty dirty Ukrainian just come and helped himself to a drink out of mine – drinking out of the bucket, of course. I went out and told him what I thought of him and that I'd have given him a cup if he'd come and asked but all I got from him was "No ferstan" (or something which sounds like that and means "I don't understand"). Heaven knows what nasty disease the man may have. And these central Europeans are all dirty.

~: 21 *May 21st 1930*

I'm writing this while I heat the water for my hot water bottle and bath. I've just come home (10:30 p.m.) from doing my day's visits. I felt pretty chilly on the way and thought it must be freezing again (there was 2″ of ice on the water this morning) and I've just looked at the thermometer. It's 24° F!! For the third week in May, that's really the limit. I suppose it will be down to 15° before morning. What's the betting I get called out about 3 a.m.? I'm glad to say all my patients are recovering. I've still plenty of work to do but it's not so worrying.

I've just got 3 dozen oranges from Rousseau's. They're only little ones, and cost 3/6 a dozen at that. Still, they're worth it. I'm going to retire to bed with two oranges, a towel to wipe up the splashes, and a novel, just to celebrate getting home before midnight for once! There's a dance at North Star tonight. I nearly decided to go but perhaps I'd better sleep when I can.

Poor old Dan is beginning to show signs of wear. I've got to have a second horse or a car pretty quickly – I can't bear to work a horse to death. The district is petitioning for a car for me. I don't know if I'll get it. Half my work is on trails I couldn't get a car over, but if I can rest the horse (and myself) two or three days a week it will be something. The road engineer was in today too, so we'll soon be getting the main road graded.

Mrs. Waines is buying a cow in a few weeks so I'll soon be able to have fresh milk every day. It will be simply great.

The water is boiling.

This isn't your weekly letter. This is an extra. I'm sending several things out by the preacher tomorrow and thought I'd write you a note.

He's going to fetch his wife.

⌁ 26 May 1930

If you want a really good reducing exercise, let me recommend digging a garden, preferably out of virgin soil full of the roots of a great forest which has been burnt down! I dug a patch about 3 feet square this afternoon. I only went about 2 feet deep, perhaps less, and I removed 4 bucketfuls of trees roots from that bit. The garden is anything but smooth and elegant now but I've planted some sweet williams I had given to me and some columbines and I planted a little spruce tree in one corner. I now need a week in bed to recover.

It has been raining on and off for two days, lovely warm rain, quite heavy at times and soaking right down in the ground. It was beginning to be very necessary, too. It's almost the only rain we've had and although there are still bad pools and mudholes in the roads from the snow, yet gardens and fields were pretty dry. Seeding is nearly finished everywhere now, and south, on Little Prairie, the grain is already three or four inches high.

Mother's letter of May 4th came by this last mail.

Things have been very slack since Thursday, and about time too. I've got the house fairly straight at last but have still any amount of mending, washing and sorting out clothes. I think I can safely put my winter things away, now, though the telegraph operator's wife, who came in on Saturday, said they'd had a heavy snowfall in Edmonton on Thursday, 3 or 4 feet drifts over the roads in places!

We're getting some very nice people into the district these days – two new teachers (one male and one female), a telegraph operator (whose health broke down in a busy city office) and his wife, both very nice. The policeman and his new wife are awfully nice but won't be in permanently till fall; and there's the parson and his wife. Very different from last year when the elite of the district were the storekeepers and a couple of old bachelors, all addicted to moonshine and poker!

A good many homesteaders coming in this year are quite nice people, too – young and comparatively well educated, with the better-class Canadian standards of housekeeping and diet. And these Canadian and American women who take diet deadly seriously are amazing. They know more about calories and vitamins than I do.

There will be a tremendous lot of land broken this year, probably 20,000 acres! It's all being cleared and burnt off now. Lots of new tractors are coming in and are working 18 hours a day! I can hear a tractor at work across the river. It will be going at 11 p.m. and will be on again before I wake. Very different from breaking with horses, though of course lots of them still do it that way. I love seeing them at work, one man driving 4–6 horses and guiding the plough, too. It is a great picture, but the breaking is never so even as when they use a tractor.

I don't know what's going to a happen about my house just yet. Thanks very much for your plans and suggested alterations. You've given me several new ideas. I want to talk it over with Mr. Petersen before deciding exactly how it shall be done.

My well is even a greater joy now it has cleared completely. There was a faint milkiness from fine suspended clay at first, and a faint taste from the green spruce wood of the cribbing. (I may say it was such an improvement on water I'd tasted in Canada that I didn't even notice these things till they disappeared.) Now it's absolutely sparklingly clear and ice cold, infinitely the best water I've tasted in Canada. Edmonton water is river water, contaminated by sewage and heavily chlorinated to make it safe. Clyde water was very alkaline and quite undrinkable, however thirsty you were. Jarvie drinking water was carried from a well and stood in a small tank till required. And I've been living on dirty river water, yellowish or brown, often muddy, full of crawlies and, even when boiled and filtered, not very attractive.

Water is one of the things I never appreciated at home. I liked it, but I never thought when I turned on a tap and got good clear *safe* water what it would be to have to manage without it.

The dysentery outbreak appears to have died down completely; the last two cases have recovered and there hasn't been a fresh case for 10 days, praise be!

Taking a patient to Peace River hospital, May 1930: 80 miles in 20 hours.

~ *McNamara Hotel*
  Peace River
  30 May 1930

Here I am in Peace River again, after the most abominable trip out. I do have the worst luck with roads. This time it was a half-breed boy with a gangrenous appendix and peritonitis and it took us *20 hours* to do 84 miles in a car!!!!! Last Sunday, that trip could have been made easily in 3 hours. But it rained almost all day Monday and Tuesday, and Wednesday it rained heavily for about 3 hours. We had 2½" rain in that time and the highway was just bottomless mud. If I had had any idea how frightful the road would be, I'd have demanded a plane. It would have been justifiable but I thought we'd probably make it in 6 or 7 hours. However, we got the lad down here eventually and Sutherland operated on him and I assisted. He's doing quite well. He'll probably survive.

And now I've had a haircut, and a couple of teeth filled, and bought some suspenders, and am going to have a bath, so I feel quite civilised again.

We're starting back at 7 a.m. tomorrow (we only got in at 6 this morning) but I may not have time to write before Sunday so shall post this down here.

I'm very sleepy, having had three nights up running, so this will be all this time.

Although it is 5 p.m., it is still much too hot to go out. It's about 75 in the shade. The mosquitoes are worse than awful. I've got some stuff that keeps them away fairly well but I hate their wicked little song round my ears all day. I'm glad to say I still retain the partial immunity I acquired so painfully last summer. The bites cause only small red lumps lasting for about 24–48 hours. But they itch abominably for an hour or two. Spring has almost turned into summer since the rain. Everything has turned green; the river banks are lovely. There are lots of violets and wild strawberry flowers out round my house and wild lily of the valley and a reddish flower like meadow rue are coming out. I am planting a bed of mignonette in the banking under my bedroom window.

I have got my house fenced in now, just about an acre of land round it. I've let Dan go loose in the hopes that he will cut and roll my "lawn" but all he has done so far is trample on the garden I dug the other day. Poor beast, the flies and mosquitoes worry him intolerably.

I am going to mount some more photos for you shortly. I have another 30 or 40.

When I was down in Peace River last week, Dr. Sutherland took me up to the new golf links. They were opened the week before by the Governor General, who played the opening round with Sutherland. I did the first three holes in about 50. I didn't keep score very carefully; but suddenly I've got bitten with the desire to be able to play. It's funny, isn't it, that when I've lived all my life within a few miles of some golf course I shouldn't have the slightest anxiety to learn until I'm nearly 100 miles from the nearest! However, I'm going to get a few clubs and practise. Perhaps if the school teacher or the preacher play we'll make a three hole course up here somewhere. That's how the Peace River course started. Dr. Sutherland and the parson made a 3 hole course for themselves.

A medical student in his 3rd year, who is also a theological student and is being trained as a medical missionary, has just come into the district for the summer to preach. He had supper with me last night. He's had a little more experience than the average 3rd year and seems very self-confident. I'm thinking of leaving him to it! It will save me a good deal of work if he can do some visits on horseback.

Brutus is very fit and still growing steadily. He has been promoted this week to the last-but-one hole of his collar! He is just over a year old, so probably won't grow so very much more.

He is trying to get cool just now, changing his position on the linoleum every few minutes. I wish you could see both my animals come trotting up whenever they hear the rattle of the bucket going down the well! I went out to get a jug full of water a while ago. Dan came up for a drink and was frightfully peeved when I wouldn't let him drink out of the well-bucket and he couldn't get his head into the jug.

He is much better for the restful time he's had these last two weeks. He was getting pretty tired.

I'm just going to start my visits – 5:30 p.m.

~: 12 *June 1930*

Dear Uncle John,

I was very glad to get your letter of May 18th. I had begun to wonder if you had forgotten me or if I owed you a letter. I do love to get your descriptions of the garden and the forest.

I can just imagine how lovely your garden looks. I remember it this time last year. It doesn't seem nearly a year to me. I find it difficult to realise that things are changing all the time I'm away. I hope the forest isn't being encroached on too much. I'm looking forward to many cycle rides with you from the Rising Sun into the forest next year. Horse rides, too, I hope.

There are enormous stretches of this north country very much like the New Forest. The trees are different but the whole effect is very like. The trails are much worse (what wouldn't we give for gravelled roads like those you consider hardly fit for a cycle?) and the birds and animals are less scared, but I shall feel very much at home riding horseback there. Except for the saddle. You know, I shall probably disgrace myself by falling off the first time the horse jumps. I've been riding a big man's stock saddle ever since I came out and an English "postage stamp" with little iron stirrups instead of the wide wood ones will be awfully difficult to get hold of.

~: ~

Suitable for the wilds, spring 1930.

Pause while I attire myself in rubber and moose hide from head to foot and go out and fetch in another armful of soaking wet wood to put to dry in the oven. It has been raining heavily and without a second's cessation for 12 hours now and, with the wind in this quarter, may easily continue for two days. It takes a good deal of wood when you've only a cookstove to keep the house warm.

I've also put my dinner on to cook. Cold turkey, creamed potatoes, green peas, banana jelly, fruit salad, rice pudding, coffee! That's a really luxurious dinner for this district, too. Most people are potato-less now, having planted all they had left. Potatoes are fetching £1 per sack just now, they're needed so badly for seed. The turkey was a present from a patient. They'd killed their turkey gobbler weighing 30 lbs and there were only two of them to eat it. I had supper there and they gave me a parcel just before I left, containing another plate. A very welcome present.

So far this year, gardens and crops are doing exceedingly well. The spring was a bit later than usual and very cold but that heavy rain (3 inches) came just when almost everyone had finished seeding. It has just been followed by a week of really hot weather and wheat planted two weeks ago is already 6 inches high!

We are already having summer here. The wild roses are coming out in thousands. The Canadian "bluebells" are out. They are really an Anchusa, big and brilliant blue. The things I thought were going to be lilies of the valley have turned out to be a tiny white starry lily, lovely things. So, although my big flower garden never got planted, I've still got lots of flowers out round my house.

The birds are thrilling. They are so easily seen. I know the voices of more Canadian birds already than I did of English birds. They haven't such beautiful songs but they are more vividly coloured. The red-headed woodpecker has a voice like a door swinging on a rusty hinges but he's amusing to watch and simply loves to make a noise. He'll rap on a hollow tree for hours just for fun, apparently, and you can hear him half a mile away! There are lots of hawks about and two eagles and there's a golden eagle nesting only a few miles up the valley, and wild geese and wild ducks nesting round all the sloughs. But we haven't got any cuckoos that say "cuckoo." (The Canadian variety say something else. I haven't discovered what yet.) The monotonous call of the white throat "Oh Canada Canada Canada" has the same sort of effect though.

I haven't been fishing yet. I hope to make time soon, though. There are a few fish in the river.

⌁ *13 June 1930*

The mail has just come in. Something must have happened to the English mail, for though I got a sackful of papers and letters, there wasn't a single one from England. Very disappointing. And I'd ordered two *sleeveless sand-coloured* over-blouses C.O.D. from Eaton's. They regret they've sold out of the particular ones I'd ordered and sent their nearest – long-sleeved, frilly, blue and red patterned voile affairs! Can't you see me riding round the country attired like that? They'd look so charming worn with breeches.

And the light had leaked into a film I sent to be developed and has completely ruined a good set. They're streaked right across.

So it's a very unsatisfactory mail day altogether.

For the last two days there has been a cold N.W. wind blowing. Yesterday, it poured with rain all day and today it has rained a little. So the roads are really bad again. There is a dance on tonight. I'm thinking of going, though I suppose it's foolish not to sleep when I have a chance. The district has continued to be pretty busy. I shall be glad of my holiday.

Brutus has disgraced himself today. For the first time in his life he took food off the table. To be sure, it was afternoon and he hadn't been fed all day (he's fed at noon when I'm at home, and in the evening when we're out all day) and I had started to eat a cake and left it on the edge of the table when I went to catch a man passing on the road and had forgotten all about it. Still, that doesn't excuse him. He's chained up outside now, very apologetic and sorry for himself when I go out.

He is still growing, in intelligence as well as well as size, and is a marvellous watch-dog. He's ridiculously affectionate, rubs himself against me like a cat (almost knocking me over in the process) and will sit for hours with his head resting on knees when I'm reading. I've always wanted a "one-man dog" and I've certainly achieved one. No-one could get him away from me unless they kept him tied up or took him a very long way away. He's a very good protection. I don't know what he'd do if any one attacked me – and I haven't found anyone foolhardy enough to try it even in fun – but I shouldn't like him to attack me. He's as tall as I am (when he stands on his hind legs, of course) and exceedingly powerful.

Canada is an awful place for vermin. There aren't any rats but oh, the *mice*. They're awful. My cellar is overrun with them, though I've trapped dozens. I can't keep anything there that isn't in tin boxes. They eat right through cartons and sacks. Flour. Rolled oats. Prunes.

Grape nuts. Apples. (They got into the box.) Butter. They are a frightful nuisance. In my living room, there are ants, the little black ones. They get in through the window screening, I think. I've just removed 6 of them who'd drowned in the honey in my little jam jar, got in through the hole in the lid where the spoon goes in. And the mosquitoes are terrible this year. I've had as many as 50 bites on one arm in one afternoon. Mercifully, they only bother me for an hour or so and fade completely in about 12 hours, if I don't scratch them. But they worry babies most dreadfully.

Do you remember my telling you about a Ukrainian woman named Kohut whose baby was born with extraordinary little fuss before I arrived there? They had no clothes to dress it in, so when I was down in Peace River I begged some and took them over. Mrs. Kohut was most awfully grateful. A couple of weeks ago, she and her husband got dysentery, not very badly luckily. They've recovered completely but when I called in last Monday I found her spoon-feeding the baby with a horrible-looking yellow fluid. Couldn't imagine what it was. After an awful lot of struggling (she speaks no English, practically), she managed to explain that the dysentery had stopped the breast milk completely. They had no money to buy canned milk, no cow. None of their neighbours had a cow, so she was feeding the child on raw egg. The child looked perfectly well and happy on it, too. I took over a can of dried milk next day and showed her how to make it up. But when you come to think of it, what else could she have done? It was just luck, too, that I happened to pass when she was feeding the child. She would never have tried to explain otherwise.

I spent a most interesting afternoon last Sunday, crouched on a steep hillside watching an eagle's nest. It was built in the fork of a poplar tree which grew lower down the bank and so was on a level with us.

I went with Bill Tyson. We didn't know that it was an eagle's nest, but thought it must be because it was over 2 feet in diameter and the four young birds were as big as hens, though still unfledged, and they had the true bird-of-prey beaks. So we waited hopefully, crouched in the bushes for the big bird to come home. I took a couple of snaps of the young ones and then sat with my camera open, waiting for the big bird. But when she arrived, I was so frightfully thrilled and excited at seeing a golden eagle only a few yards away that I quite forgot my camera and very nearly took a header down the bank. You've no idea how enormous they look close to and this one's wing-spread must have been six feet or more. My yelp of excitement startled her and she flew away. Lucky for us it was *away*. So I got no photo but I'm hoping to go over again soon. It isn't far away, just up the coulee to the south west.

I hope to goodness my camera is functioning all right again now. I think I'd better buy another before I go to the Rockies. This one has done marvellous service, 8 or 9 years. I had it before I went to University. If I get time tomorrow, I'll mount those photos and send them to you but I'll send this off when I go past the store tonight if I go to that dance. It's raining again!

~: 19 June 1930

This is a country! It never does anything by halves. It has rained almost continuously since Monday. The river is at least a foot higher now than it was when the ice broke and it is still rising steadily. Great trees of 100 feet long are floating down and any amount of smaller driftwood. Pieces of the bank keep falling in and it's still raining. The road out to Peace River is bad, but passable still. But Peace River is cut off entirely from the rest of the world. The telegraph wires have gone, the road is impassable and the railway track has washed out in four places. The Peace was 10 feet higher on Sunday than it was when the ice broke up and of course there is all this water to reach it now. The Second Battle is impassable except with a raft and I'm expecting a call across there any time now. It's a great life!

The Battle River sports which were to have been held on Monday and Tuesday next week have been postponed for a month, as half the people in the district couldn't get here and no outsiders in their right minds would tackle the Battle River Highway after all this rain. By the way, the B R Highway has been scheduled as a Provincial Highway (kept up by the Government and not by local taxes) and is to be part of the Sunshine Highway which, eventually, will run from the Arctic to the Gulf of Mexico. Loveseth told us this at a meeting last week. It's most amusing to be living on the main road to the north pole.

Things have been very quiet for the last week. I've had very little work and no visits since Sunday. I'd been feeling the need for a bit of rest but I'm quite fit and energetic again now. I played bridge the other night with the Bowries (telegraph operator and his wife) and the well-driller. It was good fun as they were none of them much beyond my standard and all of them played for fun. Most people in this country play for money, of course.

It's the Provincial Election today. I'm not at all sure whether I shall vote. I know all the candidates but very little about the politics of this country. It's all so mixed up with religion. All the Catholics vote Liberal. According to the Protestants and particularly those from Saskatchewan, the Catholics are trying to make Canada a Catholic country, importing Catholic emigrants and then insisting on them voting Liberal, so that they get into power, etc., etc. It is a certain fact that if you want a Provincial job you've got to be a Protestant.

Goodness knows when you'll get this letter. No mail is getting in or out from Peace River. I don't know how long it will take to repair the railway. I only hope they'll get it fixed before I go out for my holiday.

~: 23 June 1930

My dear Auntie and Uncle,
I wish you could see Brutus just now, lying down beside his dish of porridge, one eye on me and the other on his supper! It's still too hot for him but he is ravenously hungry and has been worrying at me for the last half hour. So, I've put it down for him but told him "it's mine"! Dirty trick, isn't it? But you've not been worried by a playful young elephant with muddy paws. I was trying to sew but he first of all dirtied the material with his feet and then tried to catch hold of the cotton and drove me almost frantic!

I was delighted to get another letter from you on Saturday, written on May 26th. The Tree of Heaven does sound a thrilling plant!!! I'm so glad it isn't something that I ought to have known. Your orchard must have been a marvellous sight. I have read in all the English papers how lovely the blossom has been this year. There are no wild apple, pear or cherry trees out here, and the district is too new for any to have been planted. But the wild strawberry, raspberry, saskatoon berry, gooseberry, black currant, and choke cherry all look very hopeful. There is a tremendous amount of wild strawberry about. It makes a sort of undergrowth everywhere and although it only came out about 2 weeks ago and is still flowering, we shall have strawberries ripe in about a week.

People pick hundreds of pounds of them for bottling and making jam. It is nothing unusual to hear of a woman picking and bottling 50 or 60 quarts of wild strawberries! It's no Saturday-afternoon-blackberrying-picnic out here. Unless the poorer people bottle wild fruit they will have none to eat for nearly 8 months of the year. Even dried fruit is too expensive for lots of them. So they get hundreds of quart glass sealers and bottle a moose early in the spring, which gives them their meat supply for the summer, and as they empty the jars they fill them with wild fruit, pickles and vegetables. Then they have the vegetables from their garden. If the man is anything like a shot they have occasional prairie chicken, duck, goose, grouse, deer and moose, so that living is possible on extraordinarily little money, considering the very high cost of groceries.

But you can see why the unfortunate British-working-man and his family come unstuck. By the time they've found out how to survive in this country, they're so starved and weary that they break windows or something so as to get to jail and be deported. It has taken me a year to learn all these things. If I'm not too busy to bottle fruit myself this summer I shall be able to live much more cheaply and very much more luxuriously next year.

It is very hot today. We've had three thunderstorms in the last 24 hours, and the mosquitoes are dreadful. I was outside just to get a pail of water and killed about half-a-dozen every time I slapped my hand down on my arm, they were so thick.

The screen on the window just beside me is humming with hundreds of them. My house is very well screened and I went all round with a hammer and a box of tacks the other day and fastened any doubtful places. But I get about 20 inside every time I open the door, so I spend lots of time catching them.

Brutus, having eaten his supper, is now trying to help me write! He can be a nuisance. He's very full of beans because work has been slack lately and he hasn't had more than a few miles exercise per day. You know, although he gets so much exercise, he's as keen as any city dog to go for a run. He gets wildly excited if he sees me change my shoes or start to pack my bag or write a note to put on the door. He jumps round Dan and licks his nose and nips his hind legs to make him go. And if that isn't enough to start us off at a gallop, he picks up a stick and raps him sharply. That always works!! He did it once when I was riding a borrowed horse, young and only recently broken. I thought I should never be able to pull up.

Dan is the foxiest old devil in the district. Everyone agrees. He's fat and in real good shape again. He has had a very slack 10 days and has run quite wild. I have been turning him out into Robertson's pasture with two other horses and hobbling him because he is so hard to catch. But the other day I'd left the hobbles in my barn and couldn't be bothered to get them so I just turned him loose in the pasture. On Friday, I wanted him (to go and see a kid who'd fallen from a beam and broken his arm) but when I went to get him he didn't intend to be caught, kicked up his heels, snorted very rudely and galloped off. I chased round for a bit and got him into a corner and thought I was going to catch him, but no, he just jumped the fence! (It's about 4 ft. 6 ins.) Well, to make a long story short, with the aid of two men I caught him eventually. It took exactly 1¼ hours! He's not going unhobbled again.

This letter seems to be nothing but Dan and Brutus. Sorry. There isn't anything else just now, things are very slack. The river is going down about a foot per day but is still higher than anyone has ever seen it.

~ *28 June 1930*

I was delighted to get three long letters from you by last night's mail – June 1st, June 8th and June 9th. And last Saturday I got the one written on May 25th, so I've done well lately.

The mail came up very late last night. (The roads are in a dreadful state, hardly fit for saddle horses, and in places the water is 4–5 feet deep over the road!) I called in at Bissette's at 10:30 p.m. on my way home and he was just starting to sort. He sorted one sack. It took till 11:20 p.m. and then he quit for the night. But I got 18 letters out of that sack and there are four more sacks to be sorted today so it seems I am in for a record mail! I got home at 11:45 p.m., having hobbled

Dan and turned him out in Jim Robertson's pasture. It started to rain again just as I opened the door and, as I turned round to close it, suddenly poured down with a great roar. The water looked absolutely an unbroken sheet. I've never seen anything like it. It was still raining when I got into bed and judging by the amount in the dog's pot and the bucket outside, we had 2 or 3 inches of rain during the night.

It really is a bit too much of a good thing. Lots of the crop is under water, the trails are almost impassable and the "casual water" is giving the mosquitoes the chance of their lives. They're really terrible. They get in your mouth and nose and behind your glasses. I have to skim them off the pail when I bring in water, and the well isn't 10 yards from the door!

Thanks for the patterns. I should think they will look exceedingly nice. I could never get cloth like that in Canada. Canadian woollen material seems to be a mixture of cotton and horse-hair by the feel of it and it wears very badly. I got some heavy breeches from the Hudson's Bay in February, cost me $6.75 (27/- approx.) They are in rags already. I only wear them under chaps. They've been worn hard, of course, but they shouldn't have gone so badly yet.

I've got some awfully good friends in this country. Although the trails are so bad and no one is travelling who can help it, I've just got a box of oranges, celery, cucumbers, tomatoes, bananas, etc. that I'd ordered from Peace River. I don't know how it got in. I've just fetched it the last two miles from a truck which was abandoned in a mud hole. They woke me this morning to tell me about it! It had done the last 4 miles in a truck. I don't know how it got to North Star. It had taken from Tuesday to Saturday to do 90 miles.

Poor Mr. Parker, the minister, went out nearly two weeks ago (with wife and young sister-in-law) to Peace River to buy some oddments, meaning to return next day, but got held up by that terrific rain. He wired in 5 days ago enquiring how the roads were, was told he wouldn't be able to get through with a car for at least another week, but started in spite of that. He's been on the trail 5 days and hasn't arrived yet!! The Whitemud is in flood, road 4–5 feet under water for half a mile. I can't say I like his chances of getting here. He'll have to go away out to Clear Hills to get across the Whitemud.

The case I was expecting across the Second Battle has come off without my assistance! They didn't even send for me and considering that there were people camping on either side of the river for *days* waiting to cross, I don't wonder they didn't try to get me. I have been in a blue funk about it for a couple of weeks. This river was higher than anyone had ever seen it, a thick milky grey colour (like the Aare), swirling along, sucking pieces of driftwood down into little whirlpools – altogether *most* unattractive to think of trying to swim a horse across.

Oh, did I tell you there will shortly be a road with a bridge crossing that creek I had to swim in? Old Plavin (who is in charge of the road work down there) suggests naming the bridge after me!!! Of course my little adventure is considered a huge joke.

Later

I went over and collected another lot of mail – 10 more parcels, letters, papers, etc.

I am going to have supper shortly. Have been trying to get at things all afternoon but odd patients kept dropping in and I pulled a tooth for one of the Hudson boys. It came out with a wallop and I hit my nose with my hand. I saw stars for a few minutes and then my nose started to bleed. I feel as though I've been hit with a club.

Later still

Two more patients and supper and now it is 8:30 p.m. and that's how my day goes.

My pastry is improving. I achieved some quite decent sausage rolls today (using canned sausages, of course). Did I tell you about the pastry that went wrong in the making? I don't think I did. I don't know what happened. Mrs. Waines thought I must have handled it too much, but anyway it was just like India rubber. You couldn't roll it out and could hardly cut it with a knife. But it made excellent dog biscuits!

I haven't half answered your letters now but will write again soon.

~: 8 July 1930

I was sorry to miss the mail this time but am writing this now and will send it out at the first opportunity. I did get in in time last night but, having had 2 nights out of bed, 55 miles on horseback in the last

24 hours and 2 maternity cases happening at once (three miles apart, 20 miles from home), I felt more than a little weary and quite unlike writing letters. Last week was pretty busy, long rides every day over bad trails.

I got your letter of June 15th on Friday.

There's a professor of Geology camped just outside my fence! I haven't met him yet but saw him on the trail tonight. He looks rather nice. I thought at first it was a homesteader trying to locate a quarter section but saw that the map was a full-sized one.

Then I heard who he was. I suppose he'll call in the morning, probably early. That means getting up early so as to get the chores done before breakfast.

So I'll stop now and put this ready to send out in case I do see anyone on the trail out tomorrow.

I'm very fit, except for indigestion, but that's only the result of irregular meals. I didn't get breakfast till 4 p.m. today.

~ 13 July 1930

Brutus has distemper very badly. I'm afraid he's dying. He's been bad since Monday and is getting steadily worse. He's had nothing to eat and drink at all for 48 hours. I can't even pour water into him. It's heartbreaking to see him.

I've had a terrible week, frightfully busy, very very hot, 80–90 in the shade, and the mosquitoes worse than you can imagine. I'm absolutely played out today. It's 4:30 p.m. now but still too hot to ride and I've 36 miles to cover in visits yet today. I didn't get back till 4 a.m., so couldn't get up early and start at 6 a.m. I've had to leave Brutus at home all the week and so have not been here to coax him to eat when he wasn't quite so weak.

If he dies, I don't know what I shall do. I can't imagine life here without him.

I'm due to leave next Saturday or Sunday for my holidays. I can't leave him. I suppose I shall have to stay up here. Just now I feel too utterly tired to care about going away anyhow. The heat is terrible.

˜ Monday July 21st – 6 p.m.
In train

I am on my way out to Edmonton for my holiday. I go on to the
Alpine Club at Jasper next Sunday. I'm glad to say Brutus is very
much better. He began to improve last Monday and for the last few
days I could hardly keep up with his appetite. He's desperately thin.
I've had to take up his collar 6 inches!

The heat is still terrific. Has been so for over two weeks now, 80–
90 in the shade. I left the Battle at 10 p.m. last night and got to Peace
River 4:30 a.m. It would have been frightfully hot in the daytime. I
slept till 10 a.m. and since then have had a haircut, bought a new
frock, stockings and gloves and so am looking quite respectable. I
had simply nothing to travel in. Clothes that were quite all right last
year and have been worn little since are hopeless now. My arms are
so much more muscular that when I bend them I split the seams! I'm
so much fatter, too, that I can hardly sit down in them and yet my
weight is now only just what it was when I landed in Quebec.

Mrs. Cameron (the nurse who is relieving me) came up on
Thursday night, bringing a young niece aged 18 to keep house for
her. They are charming people, and delighted with the place. The
river and the country is at its best just now and my hammock slung
between silver birch trees, half way down to the river really is the
most delightful place to laze. I slept out there Saturday night and
watched the mist creeping along the river and the moon and the
northern lights reflected mistily in the water. By 7:30 a.m., it was too
hot to sleep so I went fishing in my bathing costume. Caught nothing,
though. Then I had a swim, and sat on a rock up to my neck in water
and washed my hair, then back to the hammock, sun-bathed and
dried my hair and then up to breakfast. An ideal way of beginning
the day! I am nearly as brown as a half-breed. Even my legs are
beginning to brown. I have worn no stockings for weeks.

Crops in the Battle River Prairie are marvellous. The wheat has
headed out everywhere and if things go right, now, and there are
no hailstorms, frosts, etc., we should have a record crop. The whole
Peace River country is the same, but in the prairies – i.e. S. Alberta,
and S. Saskatchewan – the drought, wind and hail have ruined them
again. More and more the great wheat-growing belt of prairie is being
deserted and allowed to go back, while the farmers move northwards

to the Peace and N. Saskatchewan districts.

Battle River was the farthest north farming settlement in Alberta when I went in last year. Now Keg River, Fort Vermilion and even the Hay River country is beginning to be taken up. Fort Vermilion will undoubtedly have a rush next year as great as the Battle River rush of the last two years. At present, practically the whole population north of Battle River Prairie is breed and Cree, Beaver and Slave Indian – right up into the N.W.T. till the Esquimaux come in. They have been driven steadily northwards during the last 50 years and the movement is still going on.

Several half-breeds at Notikewin have sold out in the last few weeks. They will move north to where moose and deer and fur are still plentiful. They are not made for farming. It's too hard work.

This train service has been enormously improved since June. There are now 3 trains a week each way and this one leaves Peace River 4:30 p.m. and arrives in Edmonton at 9:15 a.m. Very different from the 6 p.m. to 6 p.m. we used to suffer from.

I am immensely thrilled about my alpine holiday. I was beginning to need a holiday, too. I was beginning to get bad-tempered and snappy when things didn't go right and I had three septic fingers, one after another, not bad ones but enough to be annoying.

I've just been talking to a man named Maloney. He's going over to England Sept. 1st to speak in a lot of places to try and encourage British emigration. He's an Orangeman and very full of anti-Catholicism and has been trying to rouse non-Catholic Canadians all over the West. This Catholic meddling with politics is undoubtedly very serious. If he's going to speak in Birmingham, I'll let you know. You might like to meet him. He's just gone to shave prior to taking me out to dinner! (We leave the train at McLennan and feed at the hotel.)

Perhaps I'd better go and wash and powder my nose!

~: *27 July 1930*
   In the train – 10:30 p.m.

I have just got into the train on my way to Jasper and the Alpine Club. I'm all togged up in breeches and hobnailed boots, am carrying a rucksack and, I flatter myself, looking "the complete mountaineer."

Honestly, I'm almost singing with excitement. I've met quite a lot of Alpine Club people already and met the president and some of the big bugs last night, and they are the most interesting people to talk to. I'm afraid I'm going to get bitten with mountaineering real badly!

I've bought a new camera, a real beauty, a lens about four times as fast as my old one and all sorts of gadgets from a rising front to a sky fitter. It cost lots of money but I had to have a new one and I felt I might as well spend a little extra and get a good one. The pictures are only the same size as my old one.

I've been in Edmonton 5 days and have spent $190!!! Have really run wild. You see, the sales were on!

The coat you had made is an enormous success. Both it and the breeches are far the most successful things the Town Mills have ever made for me. I have a little felt hat which matches the tweed, a sleeveless wool sweater which tones with it, biscuit-coloured shirts and the golf stockings you sent me at Xmas which are the same colour as the coat, so I really look *right*.

Have seen Dr. Bow and the minister this week. There has not been time to discuss salaries, they say, owing to the elections. (Provincial in June, Dominion tomorrow.) They will write me. But I don't think I shall come back home even if I don't get a dollar rise!! Honestly, I hate the thought of quitting. You see, there is no one to take my place. Canadian doctors of either sex just *will not go*. The only reasons Canadian men doctors are found in the wilds are drink, dope or incompetence – with, of course, a few brilliant exceptions like Dr. Sutherland in Peace River. Hence the English women they sent for. Of course, the salary is not large but in a year I've gained a reputation that I might never have got in a lifetime in England and, above all, the work is worth doing. I do feel I've earned my holiday.

Train will be going in a minute or two.

    ~: Canadian Alpine Club
    Maligne Lake Camp
    JASPER
    30 July 1930

This is the most marvellous place imaginable for camping out. It's at the south end of Maligne Lake, 50 miles from Jasper, on a little flat dotted with spruce trees, with the lake a deep greeny-blue in front and high capped mountains behind. The lake is fed by glacier streams and one can hear the roar of the falls on every side. I got here at 7:30 p.m. on Monday but my rummage bag and bedding didn't get here till midnight. Yesterday, I got up at 6 a.m. to go for a scramble up the "Thumb." (It's the nearest mountain, towers right over the camp). Mr. Moffet, the President, asked me if I'd like to go and I thought I was in for a nice easy climb to start with and said yes. When we lined up at 6:30 a.m. to start I discovered that there were six of us – the other five all climbers – and two Swiss guides!!! Well, it was obvious that they wouldn't be sending guides with the sort of scramble I'd been expecting but I didn't like to back out. So off I went.

It's only 9,200 feet high. It's the lowest peak there is in this region and is considered only a scramble by these folks. But they consider the Matterhorn only a *tourist* climb from the Swiss side.

For me, it felt like real mountaineering. We zigzagged across steep patches of sliding scree, negotiated a snow cornice, were roped up and climbed up a patch of almost smooth rock and then were pushed and pulled round a corner of rock with singularly awkward foot-holds and about 1,000 feet drop if you fell, and then did about ¼ mile up steep snow, a good bit steeper than a house roof, up steps made by the guide – and along a fairly *wide* snow edge (about 18 inches) with a drop to eternity on either side and finally achieved the top. I've never been in such a blue funk in all my life. We came down a different way, much more snow, and we all sat down and tobogganed down nearly 1,000 feet of it! A perfectly marvellous sensation till you come to thin snow and feel the rocks! I tore 6 holes in the seat of my breeches and my breeches got filled with snow, but it was great fun! It's taken 2½ hours to mend them this morning!

But wasn't I weary when I got to the bottom! My knees felt so weak they almost bent backwards and I'm horribly stiff today. That's why I'm staying around camp. I shall probably go for a scramble this afternoon.

In spite of my brown, I got badly sunburned yesterday when we were on the snow. I took lots of photos and so did several others of the party. We've probably 60 exposures between us.

The guides are two brothers Hans and Heinrich Fuhrer. I was awfully interested to hear that their father and their cousin Ulrich

Fuhrer were the guides who took Gertrude Bell up several first ascents in Switzerland.

By the way, ours was only the second ascent of the Thumb and the first one by that route, but that's because the mountaineers who've been here have been busy making first ascents of more exciting mountains, I suppose.

There are some awfully interesting people here.

Lunch time!

~: *Maligne Lake Camp*
Jasper
7 August 1930

I've been meaning to write every day this week but really I never had time. There was always something better to do! Today is only my second lazy day since I came and I've washed clothes and my hair and had a swim in the lake, and now it's 7 p.m.

I've done lots of climbing since I wrote to you and made my graduating climb, Mt. Charlton (10,500 ft.), on Monday.

Last Thursday, I did Llysyfran and Mary Vaux, the latter a first ascent, with Mr. Crawford of the 2nd Mt. Everest expedition, as guide. It was great, though I didn't enjoy it much at the time. The first few hours were really difficult rock work, chimneys and pinnacles, a crumbling knife edge with a horrible drop on either side, a long and tiring scree slope with cliffs at the bottom, etc. I was the only novice. It was very good training for me. Mr. Crawford is an awfully entertaining man, with the agility of a cat and nerves of steel. Odell, of the 3rd Everest expedition, is due in camp this week. There are quite a number of other celebrities too.

Monday we did Charlton. The first two parties who had climbed it earlier had taken the route over the glacier and up the snow to the col between Charlton and Unwin and then up snow and scree to the summit, a long and rather boring climb but perfectly easy. It was decided that that route was not suitable for graduation as there was only snow and ice, and no rock work. So it was decided that we must go up the N.E. ridge and face, a route which had never been tried. Six of us and the two Swiss guides went. We started climbing at 6 a.m. (after leaving camp at 5 a.m.) and got to within 1,000 ft. of the top in

4 hours. Then we could see what we were in for – almost 1,000 ft. of rock at an angle of 60 degrees or more, with a stretch of very steep snow in the middle. We were 5½ *hours* on that rock face. All the rock was rotten and broke away when you touched it. We had to climb one at a time while the man above hung on to the rope and that made us slow. The guides say they'd never again take more than one person on a rope.

Once I was left hanging by my fingers and the rope when my foothold, weighing about a ton, went crashing down about 6 inches away from the head of the man below. Another time, Mr. Weston, the last man on our rope, lost both hand and foot hold as he was coming up a narrow couloir filled with frozen snow. Luckily the rope was firmly held above.

We got to the top at 3:30 p.m. and shortly before we started down, Unwin staged a magnificent avalanche for our benefit. The fact that it finished up on the track that we had to take to get home didn't cheer me any but we had no trouble. There is an enormous glacier to cross coming down, much the biggest I've seen round here.

Unfortunately, we were trying to make time coming back so I had no time for photographs. I was just taking out my camera for one when the man in front suddenly poked his ice axe right through the snow and found we were on a snow bridge over a crevasse, so needless to say I didn't wait to take a photo.

I was much less tired after the 14 hours on Charlton than I'd been on any of the other trips – and really quite enjoyed it.

I am hoping to get in a badge climb soon.

I am leaving here next Tuesday, going out by train to Prince Rupert, by boat from there to Vancouver (it only takes two days) and by train from Vancouver to Edmonton.

I hope to have another two or three days in town before going back north.

I am sending you a few snaps. It will be some time before I can let you have the complete set, as I am arranging to exchange with some of the people here.

*British Columbia
In the train on the way to Prince Rupert
13 August 1930*

My dear Uncle and Auntie,

Your letter of July 11th was forwarded to me at Jasper.

I left the camp yesterday morning after a marvellous fortnight amongst the mountains. I have never enjoyed a holiday better. Now, I'm going west to the Pacific for a smell of the sea. I shall spend two days in a boat going down the coast from Prince Rupert to Vancouver.

We have just passed Mount Robson, had a marvellous view and are following down the Fraser River. We have just passed Mt. Stanley Baldwin. Now I ask you, what on earth has Stanley Baldwin done that a magnificent 10,000 ft. peak should be called after him? I don't mind Amery having mountains called after him. At least he was the first man to climb them, but I'm sure Baldwin never climbed his.

This is a *real* train. Everything from wireless to finger bowls at meals! I need hardly say that one pays for these comforts pretty heavily! It gives me quite a shock when I think how much this holiday is costing but, still, I've earned the money and I do like seeing the world. If I had had time I should have gone on down the coast to San Francisco and then back but I've got to get to Edmonton on Monday.

In spite of all the hard work I've done mountain climbing and all the pieces of my anatomy I've knocked off on various rocks, I've only managed to lose 4 lbs. in the last 2 weeks. I had hoped to lose 14 at least. But I am exceedingly fit and as brown as a breed.

The flowers in the alpine meadows would have delighted you. I have never seen such marvellous saxifrages and the forget-me-nots, pinks, anemones and heather on the high slopes above the timber were vivid beyond description.

The place being a national park, hunting is forbidden and the animals are exceedingly tame. Deer, moose and caribou tracks up the valley where we were camped were as thick as cattle trails, and the deer used to come round the tents in the early morning. The cook fed them with salt and got them very tame. I hope my snaps of them are more successful than that of the bear I stalked so carefully, who moved when I took it and just looks like a stump!

Mountain goats are also very common and their trails a great help when crossing scree but I only saw two in the distance all the time.

Please excuse the pencil. My pen is down in the cabin and I'm too lazy to go down again for it.

Well, the Pacific looks just the same as any other sea. Queen Charlotte Sound this morning was just about the same as a Channel crossing, a grey uneven swell that made the boat roll. But all the rest of the trip has been down the inside passage, mile after mile of calm sea between wooded hills and islands, with the coast range, rising to snow and glaciers, inland.

Different people have seen 4 whales today but I've missed every one. I'm very disappointed. We've passed the island where the sea-lions live but didn't see one.

This is quite a pleasant little boat and the food is excellent. There are a number of quite interesting people on board and also the two Doctors I met on the train, so I'm enjoying myself very much.

But for the different type of forest, the scenery is very like a magnified Falmouth harbour – delightful wooded inlets, little rocky islands and, last night, a marvellous sunset, very English-looking. I suppose the dampness in the atmosphere makes all the difference.

We are due to land in Vancouver tomorrow morning. If I have time I shall go to Victoria or Seattle. Then on Sunday I start back for Edmonton.

I did enjoy the camp. I feel I shall have to go next year, if only to renew several friendships. And I found myself in the train coming through the mountains yesterday, gazing at every peak with an eye to the best way of climbing it! So, if I stay out another year, I expect I shan't come to England till autumn and go to the Alpine Club first. Then I might perhaps get 6 months leave of absence and do a post-graduate course in London for 3 months.

But it's all in the air yet. I've spent about 3 months savings on this holiday!!

However, I've seen a bit more of the world. And there's always the work-house for my old age if I don't save enough to retire on! This wanderlust is an expensive disease and I've got a real bad attack.

Crops in S. Alberta, the prairie country, are bad again this year, but north of Edmonton they are good and in the Peace River country excellent.

By this time next week I shall be back in my own little shack, I suppose. It seems extraordinarily far off from here.

~ *Canadian National Railways*
En Route
18 August 1930

My dear Win,
I'm writing this in a very shaky train and hope you'll be able to read it. It's a really elegant train. I'm in a drawing room panelled in silver sycamore and ebony with imitation Lalique glass lamp shades, blue and silver chair covers and a radio. Then there is a barber and a bath and basins of green porcelain and a vibro-massage apparatus!!

Talk about ancient Romans!

Another three hours and my holiday will be over. Ah well, it's something not to have to face a city for another year, not to have to feel that I must take a last breath of fresh air and country smells, but to be going back to a house by the river, sleeping out in a hammock slung between birch trees on the bank, to a dog and a horse and swimming and riding and shooting and fishing.

Do you wonder I can't face coming back to England yet? It is grilling hot still. That rain I saw at Vancouver was apparently local. The drought and heat wave continue here, though. I expect they'll have had rain up north. I hope the roads will be dry. It seems donkeys' ages since I left, yet it's only a month and a day.

I had a lovely time in Vancouver. It's most awfully English. The lanes are narrow and winding and even the hedgerow trees are much the same. The big cedar woods are magnificent. Unfortunately, British Columbia has been suffering from drought and heat and there are great forest fires raging in many places. The air is hazy with smoke, which spoils the views. We were told that the smoke haze stretched from California to Alaska.

We saw several aeroplanes out looking for fires. The smoke drifts so far and there are such hundreds of miles of uninhabited country that it is difficult to find many of the fires.

I got home this afternoon after an adventurous trip. I drove nearly all the way (450 miles) and only succeeded in achieving one puncture, the destruction of one back spring and the accident known as "tearing the rear end out." I arrived into the village of North Star very triumphantly being towed at 3 miles per hour by a tractor!! (A man whom I had treated for frost-bitten feet last winter happened to come along with a tractor just after my breakdown.) But for these little mishaps it was most enjoyable trip! The country is at its most glorious. Crops in the north this year are all the farmers could ask and the sight of great stretches of red-gold grain between great forests is unforgettable.

I arrived home to find everything O.K. – house in apple-pie order. (Very different from February.)

The roads are enormously improved. The big Government grader is working on these river hills now and the trail from Grimshaw as far as the river is in fine shape.

By the way, we had a movie man in camp for a week, taking photos of climbs, camp scenes etc., so if you see a film of me washing stockings or greasing boots you won't be surprised.

The lakes are swarming with ducks and the prairie with chickens and partridges, so I'll be out shooting when I've any spare time.

I have had instructions to do school inspections. They're going to take a good deal of time.

I hear that Brutus is well. It will be a few days till I get him back. I shall be glad to see him. Old Dan looked at me with a fishy eye and condescended to run his nose against my shoulder but I think he was only removing a mosquito! He's an undemonstrative animal.

In Mother's letter she says she prefers even English climate to this. That's how I felt in June but the last 10 weeks I don't think we've had 10 hours rain or dull weather. The summer is really wonderful. My only objection is that it's so short. Another month, or perhaps less, till we get our first snow and only two months till the river freezes up! But while it lasts, the summer is *real* summer.

Now I must write some other letters. I'm still trying to engineer a 4-bed hospital up here. There seem to be chances.

~: *17 September 1930*

I expect you have been wondering what in the world has happened that I didn't write. I've been frightfully busy. I've had the Government Travelling Clinic here and, as I'm a Government Doctor, the Department economised and sent the Clinic in short of one Doctor. So I've been Clinic Doctor all day and done visits in the evenings. And there've been four confinements, so I've been up at nights too!! 24 hours a day I'm used to, but this really ought to be paid overtime. It's almost 36 hours a day! And my own work piling up ahead for weeks.

The Clinic leave tomorrow morning and I'm sending this out with them. I've enjoyed having them immensely. They're almost the same jolly crowd I was with last summer.

I've just got to bed and am deadly weary, so won't write more now.

I've lots to tell you all about a bandit hunt in Peace River and all the men rushing round with shot-guns. He was a Battle River homesteader who held up a bank and shot a policeman the night I got into town.

I've about 10 of your letters to answer!

~: *28 September 1930*

It seems ages since I wrote a proper unhurried letter to you and I have at least eight of yours unanswered. Things are only just beginning to straighten out after my holiday. When I went out in July, it was just summer, the grain just beginning to head out and the roads just getting over the effects of spring and the heavy rains in June. I came back to find half the grain cut, some of it almost ready for threshing, the raspberries almost over. And, a few days after my return, a sharp frost turned all the green to scarlet and gold. Then the Clinic came at 2 days notice and kept me awfully busy working and gossiping. They camped on the bank of the river in my yard. We've had nearly three weeks of cold rain and sleet, and a little very wet snow.

The work of the clinic was hindered horribly. We couldn't get round in cars, had to take teams and wagons. That part of the clinic who went to Ft. Vermilion had to come back to the Battle River Landing in an open boat in the rain and arrived tired and unshaven, with colds in their heads, a day late. We had arranged to do some 30 operations on the Monday, expecting them in on Sunday, and when the people arrived with their children after ploughing through miles of mud, we had to send them back and tell them to come again. Very unfortunate and disappointing. I've been wanting the clinic so badly. There was so much work that needed doing.

I had been asking for them again when I was out on holiday and so, when their work in the South of the Province was stopped by the outbreak of infantile paralysis, the Deputy Minister radioed Ft. Vermilion and wired to me and shot them all off north! Good man, Dr. Bow. There were at least 15 more children with bad tonsils that I know of, who should have been done. But still they had their chance and I can't help it that they didn't take it or couldn't get in. We did 30 operations altogether. I've got the two rheumatic fever children's tonsils out, thank goodness. I've been worried about them. I don't think either of their hearts is much damaged yet but they would have been. And then on Thursday I got the Health Educationalist sent out from the Department. (He finishes tonight and I shall send this letter with him.) He goes around giving lectures illustrated with moving pictures on various health subjects. They're very good pictures, and an excellent way of teaching the adults as well as the children. But arranging meetings and going round with him has taken time.

And with all these things I've also had quite a lot of work in the district, including a woman who was dragged a mile by a horse and pulled right across the 2nd Battle River and badly smashed up. She's doing splendidly but until a few days ago required daily dressings which actually took me 2½ hours to do!! Plus the journey of 12 miles each way with real bad roads. The population continues to increase by an average of one birth per week!

This weather is the limit. Cold and wet in the day and the temperature as low as 20° F at night. Twice last week I had to close my bedroom window at night and only four weeks ago I was sleeping out in my hammock. Did I tell you I'd a hammock slung between birch trees half way down the river bank? It's a lovely place to sleep. I used to lie and watch the great arch of the northern lights shimmering overhead and the moon reflected in the river and listen to the coyotes howling away to the west. Then, waken in the morning with the little grey squirrel twittering at me. Did I tell you there's this little squirrel and half the chipmunks in the country sharing my barn? Between horse-feed and dog-feed, they're getting fat! The squirrel is a cheeky little blighter and you should just hear him swear at Brutus! Brutus is very fit and getting fat again. He was still very bony when I came home.

Daniel is an old devil. He piled me off on Friday night. First time I've ever been thrown from a horse with a saddle. I've come off bareback sometimes. You see, he broke loose two weeks ago, got out of his halter apparently, and was finally found running with a bunch over at Ghost Keepers. I got him back last Wednesday and on Friday rode him across 2nd Battle and back, then tied him up and fed him in the village while I had supper and went to this Health Education meeting.

I went to get on him at 11 p.m. He was cold and anxious to get home and habitually starts as soon as I put my foot in the stirrup. So, as I'd two sacks to manage, I got John Robertson to hold his head. I was hardly on his back when he started to prance, stood on his hind legs two or three times and finally – failing to get rid of me that way – lay on his side and rolled on me!! No damage done, except to my temper! However, I left him there and came home by car, not wanting to risk a repetition down the road somewhere. It was pitch dark and raining a bit. And next morning when they went to feed him, he'd gone! Broken a brand new halter rope, if you please. But I got him back again today. He went back to the same bunch. Jove! I'll ride some of the spunk out of him next week! I've any amount of work waiting to be done. 30–40 miles a day to clear it off.

There's any amount of change taken place in this district lately. The highway is graded to within 2 miles of 2nd Battle now. The village now has Rousseau's store, Bissette's store, two eating houses (Mrs. Robertson running one and a Chinaman the other), the telegraph office, the bank (twice monthly) and a Ford garage. And the buildings are started for a druggist, a butcher, and a hardware store, and there's the Church, the manse, and the school house. And when I came last year there were two buildings only! Bissette's old store a mile away from here is being renovated and is to be the police barracks. Hayward and his wife are coming next week. It will be nice to have them for neighbours.

It is more than possible that I shall have the assistance of an English nurse this winter – not a Government nurse, a woman who came out this summer, having heard of the conditions in outlying districts. She's a trained midwife. The cash is the only trouble.

You see, the U.F.A. were going to build me a hospital this fall but this drop in the price of wheat makes it impossible. Do you at home realize what it means to the farmers out here? Do you realize that no matter how good his crop of oats a man living here is going to be *in debt* when he's had it thrashed and taken to Grimshaw? And if he's got a *good crop* of wheat he may make enough money from 10 acres to buy a sack of flour. It doesn't sound believable but it's a fact. There's going to be the most desperate need up here this winter. Starvation (unless they get Government relief) for many families, and the school inspections I did a fortnight ago revealed the startling fact that even now only ⅓ of the children are up to normal weight for age and height, and the ⅔ vary from 2 lbs. to 19 lbs. under weight.

I feel almost guilty when I feed the dog enough food to keep a child going, as well as his crackling shorts.

It makes me laugh to remember that I was still busy darning, washing and putting away my winter woollies in July, and had to start taking them out for wear again on the second or third day of September! I've been looking through some photographs, too, and find that I have to mount and send you some of dog teams and snow, the river breaking, snow melting, flood, etc. And here we are back to the snow already.

The proper time to take a holiday is February or March, and go to Honolulu or some place like that, and not spend the only snowless month of the year rushing up the snow slopes of a mountain!

I think you did miss a letter from me on holiday but I didn't keep any record, so cannot say. I met both Odell and Crawford. Odell is exceedingly attractive and both of them awfully interesting. I think they must be a little tired of Everest. Everyone kept asking them the same old questions but they answered all we asked and made it seem extraordinary vivid. I must read the *Epic of Everest** again when I come home.

I've been getting huge mails this last week or so and must have at least 50 letters to answer, so I'd better stop this soon. I've only answered two of your letters yet.

---

* Probably *The Epic of Mt. Everest* by Francis Edward Younghusband (London: Edward Arnold, 1926).

I regret to say that they were my nice new breeches that I wore out glissading. The seat is now a mass of careful darns. A patch for the seat and patches for the knees would be fine. I'll get Mrs. Waines to do the putting on. She's a great help; she has bottled some fruit and made some jam for me. She's doing my washing and mending. I'm really living the life of a lady these days. It costs a bit more but it's worth it. (Anyway, she'd starve this winter without the money she gets from me.)

I am enclosed a cutting from the Peace River Record about our bandit. I was in Peace River when Chornka shot Collisson and the day afterwards and the excitement was terrific. Everyone dashing round town with guns and revolvers, everything from shot-guns to 30-30's, the police all up in the air, doing nothing that I could see but rush up and down the street in a car with their guns in their hands and their eyes almost popping out of their heads! And on the Sunday morning when the fire bell began to ring the whole town rushed out. But it wasn't a fire – only the Mayor appealing to the people to get guns and go and hunt for the bandit, who'd been seen on the far side of the river that morning. I was afraid people would shoot each other in mistake for the bandit-but they didn't, luckily.

An Indian has just been in and says there's a foot of snow further north (30–40 miles). The wind is from the north now —— burr!

~ *29 September 1930*

My Dear Win,

You must have been wondering what on earth has happened to me. As you'll see when you get my letters from home, I've been fairly busy. One week, I had only two meals in my own house. Another week, I'd the clinic living with me. This last week, I've been home a good deal but have only had 3 meals (breakfasts) without visitors.

I've just been invited to go and live with the policeman and his wife, difficult to refuse but, much as I like them, I think I'd sooner live alone. Funny, but I've come to enjoy "baching" thoroughly. There's a kind of glorious independence, you know. And it would be awkward for them, meals at all hours but the right ones, disturbances about two nights per week on an average, dirty foreigners bleeding and vomiting about the place, and requiring to be accommodated for the night, etc.,

etc. But the thought of coming home always to a warm house, a fire, hot water. Lord! You can't think how tempting that is. Not to have to light a fire when your hands are almost frozen and you can't feel the matches, not to have to break the ice in the water to put in the kettle, not to get home at 3 a.m. to a house full of frozen food, dirty dishes, unmade bed when you've been out for 48 hours and are cold and tired, aching in every joint, wanting nothing but bed, hot water bottle, hot cocoa and cookies. Even now I can't make up my mind.

Canada is full of pests. I've just swatted two spiders on the wall. The flies are terrible. In spite of screened doors and windows, fly-papers, fly-tox and a fly swatter, there are still a few round all the time. The other night I killed 45 big moths, the dark brown wood moths, in the house! I only keep the mice checked with the aid of 7 traps. The catch averages 3 per night down the cellar and I don't see how they can get in, for the banking has been fixed again. Ants I have suffered from but am now mercifully free from. Bed bugs are about all I've missed, I think!

I emptied the well a few days ago. The water has not been fit to drink since my return. Mrs. Cameron spilt some milk in it. That always fouls the water very badly. But I found the rotting carcasses of 6 mice in the water I emptied out, so I think the lid must have been left open sometime!

The lights are brilliant tonight, great streamers of pale green and pink all over the sky. I think it will freeze hard. It's very cold now. Thank heaven I haven't any maternity cases due. I don't feel at all keen on a ride tonight. I haven't ridden Dan since I got piled and he's still pretty wild.

Now I'm going to bed. I'm getting chilly.

~ *McNamara Hotel*
PEACE RIVER
3 October 1930

I was just remarking at lunch time today that I hadn't a single visit to do and things really were slacking off nicely, when an old half-breed came in and wanted me to go and see his daughter. And here I am, down in Peace River, only three hours on the way! That's a record for bringing out a patient. Usually they wait till the roads are at their worst before springing acute appendicitis.

I expect to go back tomorrow morning.

The weather is just perfect again, Indian summer, really warm in the daytime and the whole country is vivid with crimson and gold. Even the New Forest cannot beat it. Threshing is in full swing all over the district.

There really doesn't seem to be any news. I am well and so are Brutus and Dan, judging by their appetites.

~: 7 *October 1930*

My dear Uncle and Auntie,
This is a very belated reply to your letter of July 29th.

It is 5:50 p.m. and already I have had to light the lamp. A north east wind is howling round the house. It is bitterly cold, blue-grey snow clouds are scudding past and occasionally spitting a vicious flurry of snow. In other words, it's a beast of a day! I'm crouching over the stove, nursing the beginnings of a cold in the head and a really wicked temper. I ought to be thanking heaven that I've no visits to do and that I haven't been called to an emergency, I know, for that is one blessing. But oh my goodness, what a country! The wind last night and today has stripped all the trees. The edges of the river began to freeze last night and anything drearier it would be difficult to imagine. Even Brutus seems to feel it. He keeps coming and bothering to be talked to and patted. He's interrupted this letter three times already! He comes and knocks the pad away, puts his head against my shoulder and sighs very soulfully down my neck.

He is really very fit again now – almost too fat but full of beans – and his coat is thick and sleek again. He simply loves riding in a car. I've been driving a bit lately. I had a car lent me for a month. It was taken back yesterday. Last week was the only time the roads were fit for me to use it, though. He loves *speed* and when I stop (whether voluntarily or in a mud hole), he whimpers and howls and barks till I get started again! Even when I get out to open the gate, he always has to get back in again with me to drive up to the house. He won't miss 10 yards of his ride for anything!

I have started redecorating my living room. In other words, whitewashing the ceiling, repapering and painting door and windows. Then I'm going to alter the positions of all my furniture. Today I've painted door and window frames. Tomorrow I want to do the ceiling. That should have been done first, I know, but I had to get the stuff from the village and an 8 mile ride didn't appeal to me this weather. I hope it's warm tomorrow.

Oh drat the dog! He looks so frightfully injured when I tell him for goodness sake to lie down and stop bothering me.

I've been reading J.L. Garvin in the Observer on Free Trade, Empire preference, etc. and unemployment. Interesting but horribly unconvincing. I must say I can't see how this Empire business is going to work. It seems to me that as long as wages are kept at an artificial level by Trades Unions and labour doesn't follow the ordinary laws of supply and demand, then there must be a vast unemployment.

Take wheat. The price paid to the farmers here is ridiculous, 60 cents a bushel. However, there's a big supply left from last year and this is the result. But flour is still high – $4 per 100 lbs. now. It was $5 till last week. And the entire crop from 10 acres will only buy 2 sacks of flour. All the rest of the money goes to those who thresh it, haul it, sell it, mill it, sell it and haul it back again and the largest proportion goes to pay the labour, not the profits to middlemen, etc. There are hundreds of men unemployed in Alberta, yet the employers have to pay a given minimum wage determined by unions, with the result that the initial cost of wheat has no influence hardly on the eventual cost of flour and hundreds more people up here are going to be forced to the dole this winter.

It's all very puzzling to me. After all, a few men are getting good wages and are keeping the cost of food high. If lower wages were paid, more men could be employed and the cost of food lowered so that even with less wages they could buy almost as much.

Enormous sums are going to be spent on relief work in Alberta this winter, with the idea of providing *work* and not doles, but we are frightfully handicapped by the climate. From freeze-up, about the middle or end of October here, till the end of April, road and bridge building is almost impossible. So, badly as we need them, nothing but preliminary clearing can be done and much of that has been done as relief work already. During the summer, all the men are too busy on their farms to do much road work. Even though wages are good, few men can spare more than a few weeks. That money has been spent already in most cases and now there is no money, a crop that it hardly pays to cut and thresh (oats cost 9 cents per bushel to thresh, and 20 cents per bushel to haul to the elevator in Grimshaw, where the price is 10 cents!!!) and it is too late to start the road work. Goodness knows what will happen this winter.

I hope this isn't very muddled. My head is full of cold.

∾ 8 October 1930

I got back from Peace River on Saturday afternoon, just before the weather changed for the worse. We have had a little snow up here but both to the north and south they have had very heavy falls. George Robertson brought some feed for Dan this afternoon and said it took 4 hours to do the 30 miles from Grimshaw to the Whitemud in a car yesterday because of the snow. And it is over a foot deep further north.

I was certainly glad that I'd taken my patient out and not waited, hoping she'd settle down. This really is a beastly autumn. It is over a month now since the grain was ready to thresh and since then it has been soaked and dried and soaked and snowed on and frozen till some has sprouted, some is ruined and all is discoloured and the grade lowered considerably. It is hard on the men who have worked so desperately.

The mail will be in tomorrow or Friday and I find I've still several letters of yours unanswered. You must get fed up and wonder if I don't read them properly. I assure you I do, 2 or 3 times always, but my letters to you have been written at odd moments and in great haste for the last few weeks and I haven't even stopped to open my case and take out the letters to answer.

Yes, I'm an active member of the Alpine Club, all right. That was the point of that particular climb. Though only just two months, it seems an amazingly long while ago. I still haven't got a quarter of the photos I arranged about. So far I've only about 80 and if other people's were as good as mine there should be at least another 120. But the people who took them are scattered over Canada and the States and it will take quite a long time. The man who has my negatives now is away north, much farther off the map than I am. He had no intention of going when I met him in Jasper. I hope he won't keep them too long. I want to send them on to someone else. I also want his negatives. He was behind me on the same rope the first day I ever climbed and took about 50 snaps that day.

I read the crits. of the Brownings of Wimpole St.* You are lucky to have seen it. I shall treat myself to a perfect orgy of plays when I come over. I haven't seen a play since I left. They don't have them in the west except as a very rare treat. At least, there's not been one in Edmonton any night I've been there, nor in Vancouver. The Talkies have an absolute monopoly and in fact they have bought up what theatres there were so as to prevent competition.

You know Brutus is very funny, when I go away and leave him for Peace River or a long trip or on holiday. He howls and howls when I go and his voice is singularly like a fog horn, so it's a good thing I've no close neighbours. But when I come back, he behaves as though I'd been punishing him! He comes crawling up, wagging his tail and looking most abject, begging forgiveness, and not until I've patted him and talked to him and assured him that he's a good dog for about 5 minutes will he show any signs of joy.

Then he races round and round in circles and goes crazy with excitement. But he always seems to regard my going away as a punishment. When I came back from my holiday, he wouldn't move a step towards me. He just stayed and cringed, the most pathetic looking specimen! Then, once he decided he was forgiven, he was absolutely uncontrollable for about two days. He's a funny hound but *some* watch dog. I'd hate to annoy him.

Thanks for Mr. Stewart Smith's advice re: his barking at visitors. The difficulty is this, I *want* him to bark but

1   only at people who come inside the gate, not at everyone who passes on the trail

2   only when I'm at home

3   I don't want him to move towards them threateningly as he does sometimes, and

4   I want him to stop as soon as I tell him it's all right.

At present he barks but sometimes scares people badly by advancing with a really menacing growl, hairs standing up along his back. And I

* Probably "Barretts of Wimpole Street," a play by Rudolf Besier.

know how I feel myself when I've had to pass huskies of about his size to get into a patient's house. I'd sooner *not*.

Then he regards it his duty to guard *any* house or place I'm in. He will stay outside the church if I'm inside but he lies on the top step and refuses to allow anyone to pass!!! The same at meetings. So I have to tie him up or shut him in a barn or a car.

If I go anywhere to supper or bridge, he'll stay outside but barks at everyone who passes (a nuisance in the village). But his bark is very useful and his reputation even more so. I've never had any trouble with stray half-breeds or foreigners. I should say that, as long as I've got him, I never shall have any trouble. They all know him and marvel at his understanding and obedience.

He's in great shape again and his coat shines in the sun and his eyes are bright. He's a joy to look at. Dan has his winter coat already (and a jolly good job, too, this weather) and looks furry. He's quite tame again. His bad behaviour two weeks ago was not repeated but, of course, *everyone* knows I came off. It's difficult to see how I could have stayed on considering that the beast came down on me. Still, it's regarded as a great joke. My only consolation is that he threw Bill Tyson once last winter.

There's no news. Things are pretty slack, thank goodness.

~ *16 October 1930*

Your long letter of September 21st arrived here October 9th. Thanks very much. I think I am well-fixed for woollens this winter and, as for blankets, I've two pairs of Hudson's Bay Trapper's blankets (weighing 12 and 16 lbs. per pair), three ordinary white blankets, flannelette sheets, an eiderdown, my travelling rug and a big imitation Buffalo robe that must weigh 25 lbs., so I shall be warm enough in bed! (Of course, I only use about half of those.)

You will be glad to know that I've got a nurse coming up here shortly. Not a Government one, unfortunately. As I told you before, they can't afford to send one. This woman is an English woman, a trained midwife, middle-aged and of independent means, who is just out from England having heard of the appallingly high maternal mortality of outlying parts of Canada. The Department can't give her a job because they'd cause an uproar amongst the Canadian nurses.

But when I was in town, Miss Conlin mentioned her unofficially and I've been corresponding with her and she's coming up to try it out. She sounds the right sort. I enclose the last page of her last letter.

> I am learning to ride here, also to shoot, and having
> a pleasant time. I will wait to hear from you that you
> are expecting me, and would like about a week's notice
> to say goodbye and pack up. I would like to bring
> my portable wireless set. Need I bring a revolver or
> firearms of any sort? People here tell me I shall have to
> travel to you by dog sleigh and be chased by wolves. I
> have no means of knowing whether they know what
> they are talking about.

You see, even Canadians 500 miles away (she is at Alix, Alberta) don't know much about this part of the world. Wolves indeed! There hasn't been one within 30 miles that I know of, worse luck. This place is getting too civilised for me.

Winter has come already. The temperature is wandering down to zero at night now and doesn't get much above 15° or 20° in the daytime. We've had strong north winds and blizzards now for nearly a week.

The river is nearly frozen up. It's becoming difficult to break through it to water Dan. This must be quite a month sooner than last year but I suppose it was too much to hope for another fall like last year's.

One or more of my letters to you have gone astray, I think. I kept no record while on holiday, unfortunately. I told you all about driving up here. The car belonged to a man who lives north of here and was lent to me. It's an oldish (1928) Chevrolet but don't imagine the mishaps were entirely due to age. My driving might have had something to do with it!! Also, you don't realise, even though I must spend half my letters telling you about them, what these roads are like. Major accidents to cars' internals are much more common than mere punctures. Hayward was telling me the other day that the police car had had 9 new rear ends in 2 months!! I've been into the ditch lots of times (only once when driving myself) but never when there's been much damage done. As for springs, well I told you I think that it was becoming a joke at the garage that every time I went out in a car a spring broke! But it's a fact that I've been in 7 different cars since June when a spring has been broken. The average life of a car out here is about 3 years. I may have the old Chev. again for a month in November but I am afraid the snow will make it almost useless.

Thanks for the farming article but don't you believe the Fort Vermilion story. "The temperature falls as low as 110° below freezing point in winter" is perhaps not a lie, but it certainly gives a wrong impression.

Once the temperature in Fort Vermilion went down to 72° below zero (i.e. 104° below freezing point), at which point the thermometer gave it up and broke! That was a very famous winter, when for 5 or 6 weeks the highest temperature was -22° F and it went down to -50° at nights. But as a general rule, Ft.Vermilion's temperature is much the same as here and 50° to 60° below zero is the lowest. And that not for a long time. Last winter we never had it lower than -50° as far as I remember, but we had a winter of unusually steady cold without the chinook winds that usually cause a thaw for a day or so.

It's funny to think that only 6 or 7 weeks ago I was having to keep things down the cellar to keep them cool and now I'm having to keep them there to keep them *warm*! I left the milk up in my living room last night and it was frozen solid this morning! I'm not bothering to keep the heater on at night yet you see.

I am enclosing a report of some speeches made at Ottawa last year that I think may interest you. They describe much more clearly than I can in letters the importance of the railway, Government clearance schemes and so on to this district. Of course personally I'd be in favour of stopping all further aided immigration to Canada and I do think the importation of central Europeans ought to be drastically restricted. I can't see the point of raising yet more wheat when half last year's crop is still unsold.

I have been busy the last few days in papering and painting my living room. You'd hardly recognise it. (Not that you would have done before, of course!) The walls are papered blue, the ceiling distempered a deep cream. I've also distempered a 2 ft. frieze in cream and I've a narrow black picture moulding. The door and window frames I've stained a very dark brown. I've moved all the furniture and cupboards and the whole effect is just fine.

Thanks very much for the magazines. I am always delighted to get them.

~: *October 17th*

Received your letter of Sept. 28th, today. I'm just into a spot of bother – Coroner's inquest. An infant aged 9 weeks (born when I was away) died suddenly yesterday afternoon. As far as they knew, so the father told me, the child had been *doing well* and there was nothing to suggest it was ill. I go out and view the body and discover a wasted little corpse weighing just barely 5 lbs. and I have Mrs. Cameron's record that it weighed 6 lbs. at birth! It had several large sores and I found traces of green vomit on the clothes. 'Fraid they're going to get into trouble. They only live 4½ miles from me and have neighbours who could have brought a message. I'm sure that child would have lived if it had been treated early enough.

~: *23 October 1930*

I have been exceedingly busy since I last wrote – babies to the north and babies to the south, to say nothing of twins to the southwest! It's a great life. The birthrate up here is about 50.

I had a telegram from Miss Francis (the nurse) this afternoon. She will arrive in Grimshaw, Tuesday morning. I shall be glad when she gets here. In all probability, the immediate effect will be a sudden lull and she will wonder what on earth I do to earn my wages! But there was very nearly a tragedy here on Monday. A young Ukrainian woman and her husband moved into their homestead 7 miles east of me last week. They came in a wagon over bad roads and it was bitterly cold. The woman was pregnant, due at the end of January. She did not feel very well when they arrived but told her husband she would be all right. He went back to Grimshaw to fetch the stock, leaving her alone and the nearest house a mile away. Her neighbours, a couple of young Ukrainian boys, lent her pans for baking bread and as she had not returned them, one of them walked over on Monday to take her a prairie chicken and get the pans. He found her in an icy cold house with no fire, below zero outside, lying in bed desperately ill. He lit the fire, then ran home and got his pal to come for me while he went back.

Young Misura ran most of the way (all the horses in the neighbourhood were out taking grain to Grimshaw) and got to my house about half an hour after I'd started on a 30 mile round of visits! He didn't know what to do and finally left a message with

Mrs. Waines and went back. Mrs. Waines waited up for me till nearly midnight but I collected a lot of work on the way and got home much later than I'd expected. In the morning, she came dashing up and told me about the case, so I got ready to dash off and just as I was saddling Dan, Misura came along. The baby had been born, dead of course, the previous day. The woman is doing all right, though she had a serious haemorrhage from all appearances. She is lying in bed in a log and mud cabin a mile from anywhere, her nearest neighbours a mile away, and no white woman within 5 miles, so the boys are having to go over and cook for her and look after her!

There is no floor, only mud – the only furniture a bed, a stove, no chairs or tables and they've no money. They brought potatoes in with them and they got frozen on the way and someone, may he rot in Hades, had sold them those for $2 a sack when the price is $1 or less. It's wicked the way the unfortunate foreigner is tricked in this country.

I guess I'll have to rustle some grub for them from some place. She's a nice clean little woman, doing her best to learn English (she's only been out a few months) and absolutely heart-broken about the baby. But isn't it a mercy she didn't die alone out there? She might easily have frozen to death. There were 4 men frozen to death in a car last week, in Saskatchewan, I think it was.

There is no news – oh! except that Brutus bit a visitor this morning! Not much, luckily. He has done worse to me in play. I was still in bed (9 a.m.) as I'd not got home till 2:30 a.m. from a case 20 miles away. It's 10:30 now and I'd been wondering why I felt so sleepy. I'd forgotten I was out last night till I wrote it down.

⁓ 27 October 1930

This is just a hasty note which I hope to post in Peace River tomorrow when I go out to fetch Miss Francis (the nurse). The last time I went out with George Robertson we ran into the ditch twice but I trust we shall make it all right this time. Life continues to be hectic. Poor old Dan has worked so hard the last 10 days he's getting positively knock-kneed, and I'm getting bow-legged! Glad to say Mrs. Paahioda (the woman I told you of who had the bad miscarriage last week) is doing well. My latest excitement was a half-breed babe of 2 who drank some lamp oil this afternoon! Doesn't seem much the worse for it, either.

I intend to run away and leave them to it on Friday and go down to Davidsons' (20 miles east on the Peace) for a moose hunt. The season opens on Nov. 1st, so I shall be right there.

As I've never shot anything larger than a duck or handled anything bigger than a shot-gun, I'm really quite excited about it. Hall Reber, an old bachelor and a good hunter, is going down with me and is lending me his 38.55 and Mrs. Davidson told me there were 13 guns in their house and I could take my choice. They saw 15 moose at different times from their own shack last week, so with any luck I ought to get a shot at one. Even if I get nothing but a bruised shoulder I'll have had my moose hunt! I only hope some silly chump doesn't decide to go and break his neck or chop his leg on Thursday. I'll be awfully tempted to ship him out to hospital if it interferes with my moose hunt.

~: 4 November 1930

Well I had my moose-hunt and, though I didn't shoot a moose, I enjoyed it thoroughly and am off again just as soon as I can wangle a weekend. Big-game hunting – what ho! That's another of my life's ambitions realised! But like mountaineering, it's much more fun to have done than to do!

I got back Sunday night and yesterday we were all three almost too tired to move. Poor old Dan could hardly stand, Brutus just lay where he fell and was almost too tired to get up and eat, and I couldn't find a muscle anywhere that didn't ache! On Friday, Hall Reber and I set off for Davidsons,' about 20 miles away by the trail and 25 or more the way we went across country. We ploughed across miles of sloughs, the ice thick enough to hold but very slippery for the horses, and then through miles of virgin forest – very, very hard going. In places, there had been forest fires enough to kill the trees without burning them much and the wind had blown these dead trees down, criss-cross, till they were piled breast high and we picked our way through these (on horse back) going about 500 yards per hour.

Reber had just remarked that that was a favourite sort of place for moose because they could hear you coming and I'd said "well we've certainly warned every moose within 5 miles of our coming," when a big cow moose got up about 75 yards away!! Reber tried to get off his horse but got hung up on a branch for a second, by which time the moose had started to move. Although the beast was within shooting distance for 5 minutes at least, we never got a shot because we could only hear her and couldn't get a glimpse of her through the thick bush. Brutus chased her for 10 minutes or more in a big half circle around us. I did wish I'd got him trained to chase animals towards us. He also had a marvellous run after a deer that we never saw but only heard as it jumped away.

Saturday, Reber, Mr. Davidson, Thos. Borton and myself went hunting on foot down the Peace and never saw a thing except rabbits, though there were very fresh tracks of moose, bear, deer, and lots of wolves. There's a pack of wolves hunting down the river only a mile or so from Davidsons.' Mr. Borton heard them howling in the daytime last week while he was cleaning a deer he'd just killed.

Sunday, Reber and I rode back home, taking a different route through very heavy timber and then across the biggest muskeg I've ever seen. Old Dan sank nearly out of sight and I had the surprising experience of suddenly finding myself almost sitting on the moss, with only the head and shoulders of my horse sticking out above the ground!!! *Most* unpleasant. I've never had my horse in further than the saddle before. I had to get off and lead him for the next half mile, testing the moss all the way and going in up to the knees sometimes even then. I was so busy doing that that I never thought of getting Reber to go ahead so's I could get a photograph of a horse sinking in a muskeg, which is a pity. I'd have liked one because no-one who hasn't tried it will believe me, I know!

~ *Monday Nov. 10th*

I am sorry to say I've been much too busy to finish this letter. I got called away while writing and have been almost run off my feet ever since.

I received the cake and the stuff for my breeches and your letters of Oct. 15th and 19th last mail. Thank you very much for all of them.

I've got an enormous pile of letters to answer. I've written to nobody but you for 3 weeks now. Even a letter from the Minister of Health requesting a reply at my earliest convenience has been waiting 10 days!! I am hoping to polish off most of the urgent ones tomorrow.

In spite of Miss Francis, I'm still as busy as ever and people are still coming into the district.

Miss Francis has been here nearly 2 weeks now, but I don't want to say too much about her just yet. She's better than nothing but is very *very* English (= very very helpless in this country). She is fairly well-to-do, having a "small income" (£500 a year). She brought 7 trunks and suitcases, a portable radio, a typewriter and golf clubs, and owns more clothes than ever I hope to. She has travelled a good deal in Europe and also spent a holiday in India 2 years ago with a brother-in-law who is a doctor (R.A.M.C.).* She talks with a London-Oxford accent which sounds dreadfully affected to the Canadians and has never done any housework of any sort. I was pretty helpless myself when I came out but I did know how to wash up! She won't do a bit for the sort of job I wanted her. The first case I wanted her for I took her to see last night, a woman whose 6th is due in 3 weeks time, whose husband is out on the trapline and who has no woman living near who could help her. She lives 9 miles from me over a rough trail and heaven knows what the roads will be like at that time. But, as Miss Francis pointed out to her, in England a nurse is not expected to cook or do housework. So, she really couldn't offer to look after the house and family because she's never done it and doesn't know how and in any case she'd need a place to sleep. She couldn't stay in that house. (It's a one roomed house, very small, and they sleep in bunks.)

Well, well. If it isn't beneath my dignity as a doctor to turn in and scrub the floor or feed the pigs, I'm *damned* if I see why it should be beyond hers as a nurse to wash and feed 5 young children.

As regards sleeping in the house, I agree it would be a crowd. Still, I've had to do it and the house hasn't always been as clean as that one. And as for not being able to manage the cooking – well, there's not such an enormous amount to cook in that house that she couldn't learn to do it in 3 weeks. Bread, potatoes, carrots and milk and possibly prunes are about all they're likely to have. But I hope she'll improve. She could be such an enormous help in that sort of case. If she can't help in the house she won't be much use because, though it is very delightful for me to have a trained midwife to take around and she has given two most excellent anaesthetics for me last week,

* Royal Army Medical Corps.

yet I've managed alone for so long now that I don't find it a terrible hardship to do everything myself.

The long dark nights are here now. It gets dark about 5:30 p.m. and is not light again till 8 a.m. but it has not been very cold just lately. Tonight it is threatening snow but during the last hours a terrific gale has come up and is howling round the house. The door flies open unless I keep it bolted and the windows are rattling. I'm hoping for an uninterrupted night in bed. I'm not a bit keen on travelling in this weather.

~: *13 November 1930*

At last I have made time to mount these photos for you. Sorry I've been so slow. It seems ridiculous to be sending photos of dog teams and snow now, when the river is frozen up again and snow on the ground and yet it's only 6 months since they were taken. I haven't touched my summer holiday ones yet and haven't collected nearly all that I've been promised but you'll perhaps get these before next summer! You may find a good many of these uninteresting as you don't know the people but I want them for my own record so they've all got to go together. I'm very proud of my free enlargement of old lady Auger.

It's 15° below zero tonight. I must go out and get some more wood in shortly. It was 10° above this morning, so I didn't fill the box. I got my storm door fixed this morning but little dreamed how soon I'd need it.

I've been busy cutting up grapefruit to make marmalade this evening. Mrs. Waines came up to supper (I had a present of venison and wanted help in eating it!) and she is instructing me how to do it. I hope it turns out well.

The mail came in tonight but I don't know how I'm going to get it tomorrow. It's too cold to ride and in any case poor old Dan isn't fit. I've just simply worn him out since I came back from my holiday and Hayward told me he wasn't fit to ride any more. I doubt very much whether I could ever get the car started. (I got the old Chev. back this week, to use as long as I can during the winter. Very nice of him to lend it me but I fear it won't be much use as I'm an absolute dud at cranking a car and it gets too cold to start with the starter.)

There is really no news, as it's only a few days since I wrote and things have been quite quiet since then.

~: *The Corona Hotel*
EDMONTON
22 *November 1930*

I am busy getting my teeth attended to. It seems ridiculous to have to come 450 miles to see a dentist, doesn't it? That's just 4 times as far as Dudley to London! But the one who filled two teeth for me after my holiday didn't do them properly so I got abscesses under the roots, and that's what's been making me so tired and bad-tempered lately. I am trying to get done quickly so I can get back north. I've been to the dentist 4 times in the last 2½ days! It's going to cost an awful lot of money.

It is very warm here compared with Notikewin, and today we've had a chinook. That is a very warm southwest wind that comes in from the Pacific sometimes in the winter. This was a terrific gale and blew the dust up so thick it was like a fog. It blew in several plate glass windows in the shops, blew a lot of advertisement boardings down and damaged an electric cable somewhere so this hotel and a block of houses were without electric light for over two hours this evening.

That wretched wind is starting up again, shall have to close my window.

~: *Corona Hotel*
EDMONTON
27 *November 1930*

You will be glad to hear that I'm getting assistance – a Public Health Nurse – for the outlying S.E. part of my district for 4 months of the winter. She went north on yesterday's train. I shall follow her as soon as my dentist has finished with me, a few days yet. So with both Miss Little and Miss Francis I should have an easier life this winter.

Meanwhile I've had a lovely week. I went up in a plane on Sunday, only a short ride but very enjoyable. Try it if you get the chance. I'm sure you'd love it. I didn't feel a bit nervous. Why I should feel perfectly safe 200 ft. above the ground in an aeroplane and be in a blind funk if that far above the level climbing on solid rock, I can't imagine, but it doesn't seem unsafe at all. You know there is a commercial service now between Peace River and Edmonton. I had hoped to come out that way but the wing had been damaged on the flight before so the service was not running when I wanted it and I can't go back that way because I can't wait. The service is only once a week, on a Friday. I'll have to find a patient to bring out sometime this winter.

The scheme of living with the Haywards appealed to me enormously. They're a delightful couple and have a really excellent wireless set and a ripping Alsatian pup. But, after much consideration, I found it absolutely unworkable owing to the plan of their house. You see, I couldn't live there and see patients at my house a mile away. It meant moving all my stuff over and seeing patients at Haywards. And if I had his two top rooms then all my cases had to walk through his dining room and living room to get to the stairs, quite hopeless obviously. Also Hayward is a bit unreasonable. I told him what a disturbed sort of existence I led, odd people coming in at all sorts of hours, and all he could suggest was that I ought to refuse to see them except at given hours. Dash it all, when it has taken a man from 18 hours to 10 days to get to you, you can't say you won't see him till next day. Oh, I shall get on all right. I know more about how to manage this winter.

It's snowing off and on and getting colder. It was exceedingly warm here over the weekend, and a great change after Notikewin.

~: 21 December 1930

It's very sad but I seem to owe you four letters. I had not realised it was so long since I wrote. However, I have your letters of Nov. 9th, 16th, 23rd and 30th; also the magazines, Christmas pudding, cake, mincemeat, candy, etc. Thank you very much indeed for them. I should have a really swell time this Christmas, if food counts for everything. Everything you sent was undamaged, I am glad to say – also the tins of cake, biscuits, etc. that I received from 4 other people in England. But the tins were very much dented and a good deal of Canadian mail very badly smashed up. I am having to return some surgical instruments that are smashed beyond repair.

I have been very busy since my return from Edmonton and landed into a police case which took up a good deal of my time and will probably necessitate my appearance in Edmonton in April, as it has been referred to a higher court.

After Jan. 1st, we are to have two mails weekly. You can imagine how joyful I am. This weekly service is very inconvenient. It seems a very very long time since we were thankful for mail twice a month. Fort Vermilion's air mail service is an awful washout so far. The first plane has not yet started. (They've had no mail since the beginning of October, officially.) Louis Bourassa went through here two days ago taking mail in by sleigh, again. You see, the weather is unbelievably mild and we keep having chinooks. The Peace isn't safely frozen over. It was better in the middle of October than now. There is snow in Ft. Vermilion – necessitating skis for landing – a little snow at Carcajou and practically no snow at Peace River or Edmonton, so that wheels are required for taking-off. Very awkward.

I told you I'd bought skis for myself, did I? I haven't had a chance to try them out yet.

I found Brutus in a bad way when I came home, thin as a rake. He'd spent all the time looking for me, chasing up and down the roads from Waines' to the Policeman's, the village, Robertsons' and back home again, then down to Tysons' to Dan and back to Waines.' Everyone gave him scraps and tried to keep him but couldn't. He refused to eat his ordinary food that Mrs. Waines prepared for him. However, he's all right now, must have put on 15 lbs. since I got home.

Miss Little, Government nurse, is now settled at Ashworths', 20 miles S.E., and is taking charge of the southern ⅓ of the district. This leaves me the other ⅔ to look after entirely and she calls me in as consultant in difficult cases in her district. Miss Francis is having a log house built just across the bridge by that group of spruce trees. She is an interesting individual – very – but has started by putting her foot into things up here. I don't know how she will get on.

Brutus has just started a real barking fit. I don't know what at. He lay and growled and barked for 10 minutes in the house and no-one came, so I let him out to see if someone (cow or stray horse) was prowling round. He's still growling furiously but I can't see or hear anything. I'd hate to have to pass that dog at night. I'm glad he's mine and not one of my patients' dogs.

Thank you so much for the cable. It arrived here at 5:48 p.m., Dec. 24th. When did you send it? (They don't mark that in Canadian telegrams.) It was so nice to get it.

I wonder if you had as enjoyable a time as I did yesterday? You certainly didn't have a better dinner. I've actually discovered a rival to Mother where turkey cooking is concerned. Unless perhaps it was the contrast after a couple of weeks of my own cooking. I went out to the Davidsons,' where I went moose hunting this fall. There were 12 of us, 8 adults and 4 children, and we cleaned up two (total weight 18 lbs.) turkeys at one meal. There wasn't enough left to make a sandwich. We also ate a plum pudding, a whole Xmas cake, a small bucket full of ice cream and a quart of bottled strawberries.

This was midday dinner. We didn't begin to think of food again till 11 p.m. and then had tea and cake. I started to learn cribbage and backgammon and we also played bridge. The wireless was working perfectly and we stayed up till 2:30 a.m. listening to San Francisco, Salt Lake City and Chicago.

I came back this evening and have just finished reading my mail. Dozens of Xmas cards from people whose existence I'd almost forgotten, including 3 from people I just met on the train or boat in the summer. Canadians are funny about cards. I sent off dozens this year knowing how keen they are on them but I seem to have missed an awful lot out.

I wish Mother was going to be here tomorrow, my birthday. I'm having a party. No-one very much, just Jack Hayward and his wife, Slim Jackson and his wife, Mrs. Robertson and Jim, and Dora —— (who is staying at Hayward's as company for Mrs. H.) but it will be the first time I've had people to a formal meal and cooked it myself. (Mrs. Waines usually does anything more difficult than potatoes and Ted carries it up when it's cooked.)

By Jove! That was a narrow squeak, I'd forgotten to fetch in the chickens. They're frozen, of course, hanging outside and have to be brought in tonight to thaw slowly.

~: ~

That's that. It's a good job I've got the pup well-trained. Otherwise, it would be difficult to have him in the house with meat thawing on the table.

I had a "bridge party" Xmas eve – 3 bachelors and me. Great fun, though I was 600 down, but that was almost entirely the result of a 5 spades doubled which our opponents made.

I have had a present of 4 white muskrat skins. I want to send them to be tanned and made into a cap. White muskrats are very rare, albinos of course, and four perfect skins must have taken years to collect. It will be a unique cap. It will have to be made with flaps, of course, so I can't even wear it in England without all the boys in the street running after me. All my really interesting clothes – beaded moccasins and gloves, leather chaps, moose-hide coat, etc. – are only suitable for the wilds. I should hate to leave them behind, yet it would be foolish to cart them to England.

I am enclosing a scrap of the Peace River Record. I don't think I had time to tell you that I went over the new hospital on an official tour of inspection by the "Powers that Be" before the opening. I think I've described the old place to you so you'll realise what a marvellous change this will be. Dr. Sutherland is simply thrilled.

You will be interested I think to see how recently Peace River, my nearest *town*, was only a trading post without a Doctor or nurse for a 100 miles. Also note the average of nearly 17 patients per day in a "*fairly* well-equipped" 10 bed hospital. The entire hospital is run by 3 nurses, 2 day and one night. They also (1) manage the X-ray work, (2) do all the office work and accounts, (3) act as theatre sister, assistant and (if necessary) anaesthetist if only one doctor is available, and (4) order the food supply, arrange kitchen and laundry work, etc. in a hospital without baths or any inside sanitary accommodation. And yet think of the results they've had on the cases I've taken down, all of them bad cases too. No deaths, no failures, except one fracture which was an ugly thing when first done and I had to send it back to be plated. The result is ugly but the function is fairly good and improving steadily and he might easily have gone to Edmonton and had a worse result.

Now I must go to bed. I've had two late nights, 3 a.m. each time.

⌁ 2 January 1931

My best wishes for a Happy New Year. They'll be late arriving, I'm afraid, but I forgot about it in the middle of December.

I am trying to clear off some of my correspondence, an awful task. I just don't know where to begin, so here I am, starting with the only people to whom I don't owe a letter! But really people are unreasonable. I wish they could see my writing case, overflowing with unanswered letters, and my desk with Government reports, etc. They read half a dozen of my letters during the year, written to you, write to me once and then wonder why I don't reply within two weeks! I still owe letters since before I came out to Canada.

However, I've started well by mounting the remainder of my 1930 snaps and am sending them herewith. There aren't many but I don't want to accumulate them like I did all summer. I lost so many. I used to show them to interested people who called in and unless I checked them over afterwards they diminished steadily! I caught one Government Official sneaking two of the most interesting! I had mentioned the fact that I had not taken them, as he wanted to borrow the negatives.

I am rather pleased with the last 4. My portrait attachment seems to be working well with my new camera. The two of Brutus sitting on the doorstep are very typical. He sits there for hours watching, and growling if anyone goes past on the trail. I have just put 12 dozen eggs down in waterglass. Now I think I really am all set till June. I could certainly stand a 4 months' siege without discomfort. The mice are my greatest trouble. I'm working a regular trap line (9 traps) down the cellar. They're into potatoes and carrots and Quaker Oats and dog feed and biscuits and are even removing the papers off tinned fruit and vegetables.

Mother's plum pudding was simply delicious and greatly enjoyed by a collection of people who hadn't even eaten a real English plum-pudding. I have had 4 parties during the last week, all very successful, and I've been out every other day. I shall be glad to get to bed early tonight. This succession of 2:30 and 3:30 a.m.'s doesn't suit me; afraid I'm getting middle-aged.

I was amused at the picture of snow in Oxfordshire. It's lots more than we have. Our winter hasn't begun yet. December was as warm as England (never below zero) and much more delightful.

I have decided to mount what holiday photos I have, about 150, and send them to you, and then send on the others as I get them. You see, the man to whom I lent my negatives hasn't returned them yet. So, I can't send mine to other people. There are three more lots I hope to get. However, I've started losing what I have, so I think mounting them must be my next work.

~: *8 January 1931*

I have been quite busy this week, a great change. I did very little but dentistry the previous two weeks.

I was unlucky on Sunday, was at Jack Hayward's (the policeman) birthday party and got called away about an hour after I arrived, but that's the only bad luck all Xmas. I am expecting to be pretty hard at it during the rest of the month. I've been to two maternity cases this week and 5 more are due before the end of the month.

The weather continues to be simply marvellous. Still no snow, bright sunny days and brilliant moonlit nights, temperature around zero at night and up to 15 in the daytime. Sleighing is atrocious but all the roads are open to cars and I'm using the old Chev. quite a bit. I had an exciting trip in a buggy behind an unshod team on Monday. The highway is a shining stretch of ice and those poor horses skidded all over the place.

The house is very much warmer since last winter. I took the window frames off when I papered my living room and took the paper to the edge of the window and that has eliminated many draughts. The storm door fits well, too, so I don't get that awful draught under the door, and the total result is startling. Last night I had Frank Close and his father to supper and, although I had two windows wide open and only the cook stove on (and not the heater) and the outside temperature was zero, we had to have the door wide open for half an hour because the room was too hot!!!

Frank Close has built me a very nice dresser. The lower half holds all my pots, pans, cleaning things, bucket and oddments, and the top has three shelves and takes crockery, bread, tea, coffee, flour, sugar, etc. It is an enormous improvement. When I have stained and varnished it and varnished my wood box I think I shall have done with altering my living room and can start on my bedroom (papering, painting etc.). I do love having a house of my own and doing my own decorating! I'm going to try to take some photos of the interior to send you.

Brutus is a faithless hound. He went off on Sunday afternoon, just before I went to Haywards'. I suppose he came home and found me gone and tried to track the car. Anyhow, Bill Whiddon saw him heading east, about 3 miles away and says he was going full speed down the trail! I was awfully worried when he hadn't returned last night, 3 days and nights, and he'd never been away like that before; I thought of the wolves on that trail and the big traps for wolf, lynx, coyote and fox that he might be caught in and was thoroughly worried about him. I couldn't sleep properly, kept thinking I heard him outside whining to come in, and altogether got myself into an awful state. But last night, just before supper, in he trots, looking frightfully pleased with himself, wagging his great tail and asking for something to eat! Wretched beast! But I am glad to have him back. He's pretty good protection apart from being good company.

I'm still not much farther ahead with answering letters, so I won't spend any more time on this. There's no news anyway.

~: 16 January 1931

Thank you ever so much for your two letters (Dec. 21st and 28th).

There's lots and lots to tell you, but no time. It is 12:15 a.m. right now and I'm going out to Peace River in the morning. (Incidentally, I only came back from there yesterday, after taking a patient out in a young blizzard.) And I've had 4 nights either partially or wholly out at cases in the last 6 days, so I'm thinking of going to bed.

I'm very fit indeed. This spell of work has made me feel much better. I was very much bothered by a piece of bone working out where I'd had a tooth removed in Edmonton but it has come away at last and the gum is healing up.

I've *heaps* of letters to answer – literally – and more coming every mail. Absolutely no time for answering them. If you hear complaints from my relatives that I haven't yet acknowledged parcels do please apologise.

Uncle Albert sent me a ripping riding crop. See old Dan buck if he feels that! I tried to strike terror into Brutus with it but he only thinks of sticks for playing with. I always go for him with a rope end when he requires punishment, consequently he took no notice when I warned him that I should use it on him.

Miss Francis's house is nearly finished. She will be living there before another month, I hope. I must say I like her more every time I see her. She's got a very well-developed sense of humour and plays a very good hand of bridge.

~ *24 January 1931*

Winter at last. Quite a lot of snow, 14 below zero, and a pleasant N.E. wind that almost cuts your head off! But gloriously bright and sunny. I tried my skis out yesterday and intend to take this letter across to Haywards' on skis today. It's great fun.

I have had less time than ever this week, as I have played bridge every night. I haven't been out at cases. The population continues to increase by one or two per week!

My nearest Doctor to the north, Hamman at Fort Vermilion, is out on sick leave, so there is no Doctor between here and Resolution at present! I got the following telegram the other day

> "Fort Vermilion Alta Jan 19/31
> Dr. Percy
> Notikewin Alta.
>
> Mrs. Gibbons, Leon River sixty miles southeast of here sends word "her husband has had pneumonia and his heart is bad". Can you prescribe something that nurse at R.C. Mission might put up. Have admittance to Dr. Hamman's house in case nurse needs anything from there. Please answer.
>
> R.D. Collier."

I sent back instructions but the difficulties of making a correct diagnosis on that information and then of prescribing something that can be dispensed by a nun are pretty considerable! However, I hope he'll recover.

Mrs. Cole (you remember I stayed with her at Wanham in Feb. 1930) has been sent in to Ft. Vermilion by the Dept. I met her in Grimshaw last Saturday and motored her up to the Third Battle, as roads were excellent. This saved her 100 miles but her last 200 miles have to be made in a caboose. She should arrive in Fort Vermilion today. We have had blizzards and below zero weather ever since she left, so I am afraid it was no joy ride.

I was simply green with envy, of course. I'd have been only too delighted to go up myself and leave my cases to Mrs. Cole! I told her that if she got half a chance to send for me to a case I'd be simply thrilled! But I fear I shan't have the chance. The trip couldn't be done over the trail in less than 3 days (and that by getting relays of teams arranged) and most cases would be dead before then. Still, there's just a hope!

If Hamman should stay out for good I should certainly apply for the job. It's mainly Indian work, of course, but for a year or so it would be great.

I'm having lots of thrills, the most interesting run of cases and lots of police work. I haven't time to tell you, though, if I'm to get this to Haywards' in time to catch him before going to town.

~: The Interviews

Coming home from a trip to the city.

ᔗ Note on Transcripts

These interviews were conducted over a two-day period in April 1994 and were used in small part in writing the introduction to the first edition. They had a larger purpose, however, and that is why it is important to reproduce them here. Dr. Jackson once complained to me that in anything written on her life, there was precious little content on medicine. So, for three hours, I asked her questions with that specific focus and she provided a description of her practice that exists nowhere else. I later sent the tape to the Provincial Archives of Alberta where they may be found under Access #94-149. Anyone who accesses them however should be warned that this is not the professional sort of interview we were held to by the NFB director, where we had to make sure I shut up and she provided as long a sound bite as possible. In these far more informal interviews, made on a small recorder, there is much laughing and rambling. There is also the fact that Mary is aware she is chatting with someone who knows her well and therefore makes less attempt to articulate. Andrea MacRae, who transcribed the tapes, often could not make out certain words or phrases and I often had to replay sections myself several times before I could be sure. Where I could not be sure, I did the best I could. Indeed, I have Mary to thank for the opportunity to learn one more thing: the many judgment calls that need to be made in converting recorded material to print. One thing to note particularly is that the convention of three dots here covers any of three things: Mary has paused, Mary has switched topic in midsentence, Mary has said something I cannot entirely make out.

Why reproduce these tapes? Aside from Mary's request that something "medical" appear in print, the conversations provide a perfect counterpoint to the young woman of 25 who wrote the letters. At 89, she is funny and she is intelligent. And she certainly is feisty! The careful reader will notice an ongoing sub-conversation between us about not being able to lay her hands on certain papers. The second reason I had made this particular trip was to inquire about preserving other papers of hers, in particular her medical records. We had had this conversation over the phone a number of times and she had been evasive, in her typical way not wanting to give me a direct no but not being convinced by my arguments either. I live with the guilt that it was quite likely my pressing of the issue by arranging to arrive once again on her doorstep that led her to make a huge bonfire of an irreplaceable archive of frontier medical information.

One thing some reviewers criticized me for in the first edition was the fact that I spent a great deal of space analyzing Mary's life, providing historical context and describing my own exploratory journey north, rather than letting the letters just speak for themselves. While I still doubt that anything I did managed to place a bushel over Mary's light, I have taken this to heart. You will however notice my appalling tendency to try to sum her up, usually prefaced by the fateful word, "So." Thankfully, she paid absolutely no attention to this and continually put me in my place. Pretty much, the reader is free to make of this what she or he will.

The medical material here includes a number of aspects of her lifelong practice. There is her work among the Metis, the immigrant Mennonite population, the rabies epidemic and reference to some of her most unusual cases. Of great interest to me was reference to her training in the slums of Birmingham. Of note is her particular pride in her dogged commitment to diagnosis and her determination to do whatever lab work she could. Of great worth is the lesson she provides in how to live a life with commitment and joy.

The tapes were used by permission of the Provincial Archives of Alberta. Access No. PR.1994.149/1-3.

Mary Percy Jackson
First Interview
18/04/94

J:~ Janice Dickin
M:~ *Mary Percy Jackson*

J:~ This is Janice Dickin. I am in Keg River, Alberta talking to Dr. Mary Percy Jackson and it is the 18th of April 1994. Dr. Jackson I would like to ask you about your Mennonite patients which you've had over the years.

M:~ *Mennonite patients, they're on the East side of the Peace River. The first ones who came to the country settled in Carcajou in the 1930s, 1932 I think was the earliest, and then there wasn't enough land there and they moved on down to the area south of Fort Vermilion which was known as La Crete where there was a good deal of Metis settlement from way back but also a considerable amount of open land and they filed on what available land there was and bought from the Metis people some of their homesteads and gradually built up from a few families.*

There are now three or four thousand people there but at the time that I was dealing with them, in the 1950s and 60s, there were two or three thousand and I was a hundred miles away from most of them. So, I wasn't paying house calls but they came over to see me. Through the late 1950s they had a very good government nurse there who was married to one of the school teachers and we, we treated patients. We saw them between us. I could see them here once and she could follow them up at La Crete but they were a people who believed that illness was God's judgment for something that they had done. They were not used to going to doctors.

They were an extremely fertile population. They had a very high birthrate, and the more children you had, the more likely you were to go straight to Heaven when you died. And they were busy building up farms so that they, they spent a minimal amount of money on the houses. They built log houses, mainly, and they were small houses for the number of children who were in them, so that epidemic disease would go through a family of 12 children and their neighbors. Polio, in the 1950s, before there was any vaccine, and strep throat, pneumonia, so on. They, they considered that the illness was an act of God and they didn't rush for a doctor and, as I say, I was a hundred miles away from most of them.

They had a doctor at Fort Vermilion but the pregnant women didn't like him. He was a retired surgeon who was practicing there and didn't, wasn't, interested in obstetrics. They had a midwife, not a trained midwife but an experience midwife, who used to send her pregnant patients over to me and if I said everything was okay, she'd figure it was okay to look after them in their homes. She had, I know, a hundred and fifty successful deliveries with no problems right after that, which is experience, and how!

J:~ She was part of the Mennonite community, then.

M:~ *She was a Mennonite woman, yes. And she also laid out the dead. It seemed to be a rather dangerous…*

J:~ *…combination!…*

M:~ *Yes, but she was very well liked by the women there and I didn't know her but it put me in an awkward position because if I said the woman was alright, she could say that if anything went wrong that it was my fault that I hadn't spotted it, whatever was going wrong.*

And I was trying to do blood tests for, the testing for the RH factor, you see, and to try to persuade – as I did one Mennonite woman – that she shouldn't have any more children. This is before the drug was made available that you give to prevent the RH negative woman from developing antibodies that might harm the baby. But anyway I was busy trying to do proper prenatal care on women whose deliveries were done by an untrained, experience midwife. This was sticking your neck right out, but if I hadn't done the prenatal she would have continued to do the deliveries anyway. She figured that, if I said things were alright, this made it legitimate for her to go ahead. I did several external versions on women whose babies were in the breech position. And so, having turned the baby, the woman goes back a hundred miles and I don't see her again! You always have to watch very carefully that the baby doesn't turn back to breech. None of them did but it was by the Grace of God, not because the midwife or I had any knowledge of what was going on.

J:~ So she wouldn't necessarily know how to do it.

M:~ *She wouldn't have known, she wouldn't have known that it had gone back to a breech! At least I don't think she would have done. But the Mennonite women had had enough breech births, enough disasters in the community history, that they were ecstatic to find somebody who'd turned the baby and they wouldn't have another breech. And (laughs) this is another of the things I wouldn't have been allowed to do, if I had been in civilization! They would have had to go to an expert obstetrician! And, then, they often didn't turn the babies. They did caesareans, you see. It's very difficult to know why some pregnancies result in breech. My son was in a breech position and I couldn't turn him, tried very hard. I mean, from the first time I could feel the position he was in, I knew it was a breech and no way could I get him to turn.*

J:~ Frank delivered that baby.

M:~ *Frank delivered that baby.*

J:~ And was there a problem?

M:~ *His arms were down between his knees. To turn them you keep tapping them on the back of the head until they finally flip over and then the head is down where it belongs. You give it a little push so it sort of stays down and in a few minutes the uterus adapts to the new position and everything's fine, in theory. I had one breech that turned back again when I was in Battle River in 1930. But most of the breeches that I've turned – all the breeches that I've turned, that I've succeeded in turning, stayed, except that one woman in Battle River. But the Mennonite problem was that to do proper pre-natal care was something that was totally outside their, their culture. I mean, if I wanted to stick needles in them and get blood out of them, well they didn't know why. You couldn't really explain to them and if you tried to give them advice on diet or anything else a lot of it fell on deaf ears.*

J:~ What about hands on? I mean, I know from somebody I've talked to that a doctor dealing with Hutterite women was, could not touch the women.

M:~ *If they came over to me they were going to get what I thought was proper treatment!*

But it was the same with the Indians. If I wanted to wear the white gown and the mask when I was delivering them, well that was my mumbo jumbo and it didn't make any sense and the moment that I'd left the house they would take my clean sheets off the bed and go back to a deer hide, hair side up. But the Mennonites are a people whose culture has changed dramatically over the last 50 years. They are now, I think, getting medical care much more enthusiastically than they used to.

J:~ What about limitation of family size? Are they having smaller families?

M:~ *No, no. The larger the family, the more certain you were to go to Heaven.*

J:~ But even now they're still having large families?

M:~ *Well this I don't know about because I don't have any patients. I might be in casual contact with patients who come and visit me but I can't very well ask. It might be entirely the wrong thing to ask them whether anybody's using birth control or not. But I've taught a good many women when the pill came to be financially possible, in about 1960 I think it was. A number of them started taking the pill, some of them without the knowledge of their husband, which I disapproved of strongly! But most women didn't want to limit their families. And of course the more men you had to work on the farm, the better. This was really primitive farming then.*

Now the Mennonites use big machinery, just like anybody else, but I used to have parents who would come to me as soon as a boy was 14, wanting me to give them a chit that this boy was needed at home. The traditional excuse was that father had a bad heart and needed his son's help on the farm. And this would enable the school board to let the kid out.

J:~ What was your reaction to that? Obviously you value education.

M:~ *What actually happened was the school built this big shop in which they could repair their own tractors. And it suddenly became very important that the son should stay in school into high school to learn farm engineering.*

J:~ Which they couldn't learn from their fathers.

M:~ *They couldn't learn from fathers who were still thinking in terms of horses. But, seeing what tractors could do and what combines could do, father hadn't the least idea how to repair them, didn't know what had gone wrong. But son, who had taken a tractor down completely*

through the winter and built it all up again! And I mean, it was....
It's a pity you can't see that school! It's a superlatively good shop, there
isn't anything in the North Peace River as good. They had all the
equipment, all the machinery. They learned everything and I mean it
revolutionized education for the Mennonite boy. In a matter of two or
three years it suddenly became a different, a different value.

J:~ I was just wondering what it would do to medical statistics, too, if
you'd been filling out forms saying these men all had bad hearts
and suddenly when there is no excuse to get the boy out of school,
the men didn't have bad hearts!

M:~ *No, because I was on the school board as well as being a doctor.*

J:~ Ah, so you weren't going to oblige.

M:~ *This made it particularly tricky. Because the school inspector*
obviously figured that these boys should stay in school and I figured
that they might learn on the farm, hands on agriculture as it couldn't
be taught by anybody in school who didn't know it to teach it. Oh well,
we worked out a deal with some of them. Then, after the teacher got
this very good library built up and allowed the kids to come into the
library at ten past 12 and they could read like mad all through lunch
hour. If they'd eaten their sandwiches in the first ten minutes, they
were free to go and read books. But their parents took a very dim
view of girls getting an education. They might be wasting their time
reading when they should have been doing whatever.

J:~ So a very traditional view.

M:~ *I mean, this was, the Mennonites were living as their ancestors*
had lived for a very long time. I mean, the way that they struggled
through the first year or two in Carcajou was absolutely basic, third
world existence, really. Still, they survived and had all these children.
There was the one that died. One of the very few stillbirths of my life
was a Mennonite women who came up to the outpost hospital from
Carcajou to have her first baby. Perfectly normal pregnancy, perfectly
normal baby, perfectly normal delivery except that the baby was dead
because the cord was only about so long. It had drawn the placenta...

J:~ Drawn the placenta?

M:~ *The baby bled to death. Possibly in this day and age, if she'd been in a*
hospital they might have spotted that something was going wrong and
done a caesarean, an emergency caesarean. I don't know, but I was
heart broken but it wasn't anything that I could have prevented.

J:~ Or foreseen.

M:~ *No, or foreseen but when the head was coming down, had I been listening to the fetal heart, I might have realized that something dreadful was going wrong. But I couldn't have accelerated the delivery. I think it was an eight pound first baby. I mean, the delivery was going normally enough. There was no reason to drag the baby out with forceps or something. There wasn't anything that I could have done but I was very cut up about it.*

J:~ Well, it couldn't have been that unusual for them to be losing babies, either, could it? With that size of family?

M:~ *I don't know. One year, I delivered three post menopausal women, or at least prenataled three. One I sent out to the city, a women having her 17th child. It seemed to me this was a high risk pregnancy, but she was perfectly normal. I insisted that she go to Edmonton to have the baby where she had a perfectly normal, simple delivery, no problems at all.*

J:~ So post-menopausal, you mean she'd stopped menstruating?

M:~ *If a women has stopped menstruating for more than a year before the baby was born and the woman is over 45, you can assume that she had stopped and this was sort of the odd egg that she had produced.*

J:~ Well, what happens then? Isn't the menstruation the lining in the uterus coming out? Would her uterus have made the lining then to accept the, accept the baby?

M:~ *Yes, and she hadn't menstruated but the lining was still there, and when she happened to ovulate, she got a pregnancy started. I've had several women who have come quite convinced that they were menopausal and have turned out to be pregnant. But to get three in one year was a bit startling. And they were all Mennonite. But they all did alright. But the interesting thing about the 17th was that the baby had patent urachus.*

J:~ What is that?

M:~ *The bladder of the fetus has a long sort of tube coming out of the top of it because of course the urine forms part of the, part of the waters) and this closes off at the umbilicus when the baby's born and this one didn't. And they sent this baby home from the University Hospital with a leaking discharge at its umbilicus and sent it home on penicillin. And I mean, here was a patent urachus and of course I was ecstatic to be able to send this back to the University Hospital and suggest that the child required immediate surgery.*

J:~ You were the, you were the superior diagnostician here.

M:~ *It's just one of these odd things that makes medicine so exciting because I mean I possibly could have — if it hadn't been possible in those days to get out to Hospital, which it was — I could possibly have repaired it right here and now. But in the end it would have been malpractice. Once you could get the child out to the hospital, you should do. But I always wondered what they, what was said when they got my note and this baby that they'd sent home already with ...*

J:~ (laughing) and there you'd got it back!

M:~ *The sort of glee at having spotted something they'd missed! I think this is the...as I say, I don't know whether it was a woman or a man who'd missed it but somebody had missed something that I had spotted and here was I a lone, lorn female up in the North who wasn't expected to know anything anyway!*

J:~ Actually, after one of the readings of your letters that I gave in Calgary, a young woman doctor, younger than I, came up and said that she knew about you from medical school because you were considered a superlative diagnostician. So, were you ever invited down to speak to medical students?

M:~ *Not until I was a geriatrician, if you can call it that. And then that wasn't to medical students, that was to people doing geriatrics.*

M:~ *I mean, this was part of the, they'd call it the challenge these days, I suppose. This was part of what made medicine so exciting because you never knew what you were going to see. You got up in the morning and you had no idea what, where you might be by night or what you might have seen. And you might see a whole list of totally uninteresting, routine cases but you were on your toes because you might see something that was quite, quite exciting. Of course I had been keen enough on obstetrics that I was doing state of the art in pre-natal care as far as I could. I wanted to be as good a doctor as I could. I used to go down to refresher courses and things whenever I could get out which depended of course on the state of the, of the trail to Battle River.*

   But there wouldn't have been any satisfaction in practicing if I hadn't done my damnedest. And there was an enormous satisfaction, as I say, in spotting something that was so unexpected, so absolutely... It was the nurse at the Paddle who spotted the woman with cancer of the brain, brought her over one evening after supper and said, you know, I think this woman's got a tumor in her brain. This woman

had tripped over her own door step several times and when she was
brought to me, she had been pouring tea into her cup and she had
missed the cup. She had been complaining of headaches and the nurse
brought her over and thought that this could be cancer of the brain,
and I did a very vigorous check of her nervous system and thought, by
God, she could be right! This could be!

J:~ laughs

M:~ *So I sent her out. I've forgotten the man's name now, a neurosurgeon,*
and to my horror and disgust, he sent her back in about a week's time
or less than a week's time and said he thought it was all in her head,
or words to that effect.

J:~ So he didn't agree with the diagnosis.

M:~ *No, he didn't agree with the diagnosis.*

J:~ ... of the two females from the North.

M:~ *And he hadn't, to my way of thinking, done an adequate investigation.*
But he thought that she should see a psychiatrist or words to that effect.
So I, I sent her out to a psychiatrist who, having checked her over, sent
her back to the original neurosurgeon and told him where to look for
the tumor.

J:~ So, the psychiatrist knew more than you, so far as the
neurosurgeon was concerned.

M:~ *So, she had a tumor removed successfully and is still alive. She's in*
Manning.

J:~ Was she all, alright then? So they got all the tumor?

M:~ *Year after year she had to come to me and I'd check the bur holes in*
her skull. You see, to make sure that there was no pressure building
and check over her nervous system to see if it wasn't any recurrence.
And then her sister had successful surgery, for cancer of the brain,
after she'd left Paddle Prairie.

J:~ Is this a genetic sort of thing?

M:~ *I don't know. Both these women, as far as I know, are still alive. They*
must be well on in their 80s.

J:~ It's interesting, the diagnosis. I was thinking, I have a friend who
is a vet. She deals with patients who can't say "I hurt here, or I do
this" so it's a lot of looking into eyes and trying to figure things
out. It seems to me that you dealt with so many people who
didn't even speak English or through translators. Do you feel that
your job was somewhat like a vet's in that way?

M:~ *Oh yes, absolutely. A lot of the people, I couldn't talk to. I could read some German, but I couldn't understand the German that the Mennonites were talking and my efforts to try to learn to talk Cree from Frank didn't get very far. And I would get an interpreter.*

J:~ But you must sometimes have just had to go with what your fingers told you about the body.

M:~ *I mean, sometimes it was by guess and by God! You did what seemed to be the right thing to do. But it was a bit like veterinary medicine in that way. You couldn't ask a patient, you had to figure out what it must be or what it logically had to be. Of course, the population here were rapidly learning English. Much more successful at it than I was at learning Cree. And Emma MacDonald, my next door neighbor, she was...*

J:~ next door neighbor. You make it sound like it was next door!

M:~ *yes, well, half a mile.*

J:~ half a mile, yes.

M:~ *Her father was the first member of parliament for the Peace River country back in 1905 and Emma was his daughter and my good friend. She's the Godmother of two of my grandchildren. Patricia is one and Deedee is the other. And Emma was really fluently bilingual. I mean she was really well educated in English and her mother had been Cree. She grew up with both languages and was extremely useful as an interpreter because she could make them understand what I was talking about and make me understand what they were talking about. It was a great help.*

J:~ So you could always call on her.

M:~ *So, she would rally around and tell me what not to do on occasion. But the Mennonites, most of the men talked some English, but the women much less.*

J:~ Did you deal much with Mennonite men's health problems or was it mostly the prenatal?

M:~ *Oh, I did deal with some of them. Most of the men didn't have much in the way of problems until they were old. And then they were old and arthritic and they had bad hearts but I had some of the Mennonites with leaking heart valves. Most of them were women. I was going to try to find that article for you last night. I went to bed and forgot about it. I went to bed with the "Immortal Hour" sort of singing in my head.*

J:~ (laughs)

M:~ *I forgot all about it or else I could have looked for it this morning. I've got it on file.*

This was from medical students that they sent up here and I chivvied them over to the Paddle to go and listen to more leaking heart valves than they ever would find in their whole working lives.

J:~ So, this is a laboratory of leaking heart valves.

M:~ *Henri Chateney got in touch with these fellows. I'd totally lost them. I'd forgotten their names even, but I found this article for him, so he looked up these fellows and told me where they were practicing but I didn't put it down, so I've forgotten it.*

J:~ Was this an article that you wrote?

M:~ *No, they wrote.*

J:~ They wrote. Oh, I would be interested in seeing that.

M:~ *This was their – I don't remember how long they were here – a month or two anyway.*

[pause while tape is turned over]

M:~ *The dental student had done a lot of dentistry and he was appalled at the situation I introduced him to among the Mennonite community. They had an amateur dentist who was making false teeth as well at La Crete and was pulling teeth left and right with dirty forceps. They had to have somebody to pull their aching teeth and he had a pair of forceps and he pulled their aching teeth! If he had sterilized the forceps between times it still would have been a pity because he would leave roots and things but the infection that he spread into the blood of people who already had damaged heart valves was disastrous. This one girl should have died but she didn't. She was very lucky,*

J:~ What year was the strep throat epidemic?

M:~ *I don't remember. In the '50s sometime. I've got it all down somewhere. If I knew where the papers were, I'd find them. If I didn't destroy them along with a lot of others. Could have been the ones that went. A person piles up…I mean, I've got drawers full of papers. I daren't take them all out because you'll never get them all back in again. So when they get too tight, then I take a bunch upstairs which is where I figured I was going to find the rabies but some of it was still* downstairs. It hadn't been moved upstairs because it was when we were writing the rabies thing for the Keg River book. That was why some of these things were downstairs. I couldn't think why.

J:~ Just as well. They got saved this way.

M:~ *Well, I didn't remember why I'd had them on the desk amongst all the rest of the clutter and that was why. But the strep throat epidemic produced a record amount of rheumatic carditis with a lot of damaged heart valves. Of course when I was a medical student we saw lots, and we didn't have a clue that there was any connection between streptococcal sore throats and rheumatic fever. People would get rheumatic fever when you knew what it was doing to their hearts because we could hear that and see it post mortem in a great many of them, too, but all we could do for them then was to keep them in bed month after month, hoping to get a minimal amount of damage to the heart by keeping the strain off the heart. You'd have children in bed for a couple of years*

J:~ But what is the connection? I know that the rheumatic fever is a reaction to the strep but what amount of time would there be between the strep throat and the fever?

M:~ *I don't know because I didn't see that end of it. But I knew that at the same time I was getting a lot of strep throats in the Metis community at Paddle Prairie and I was treating them vigorously with penicillin. And that I had two or three kids in bed with rheumatic heart disease who did very well except that one of the boys still can't get insurance. He can't get life insurance because of his leaking heart valve but he doesn't require surgery. I think he's very prosperous. I haven't seen him in years.*

J:~ So, is there anything else unusual about dealing with the Mennonite community?

M:~ *Oh, I could talk about the Mennonites for days because I saw such a lot of excitement.*

J:~ What about nutritionally? Has their nutrition changed much? They're very thrifty so I imagine they...

M:~ *I don't know because I haven't been seeing them. I haven't been practicing for so long. I retired in the '70s, you see, in '74. It's now twenty years and I have no idea what state they're in now, unless they happen to come over and visit. And then it's so interesting to hear what's happened after I stopped seeing them.*

J:~ What about dealing with them at the time? Did they have any nutritional diseases?

M:~ *Oh, good heavens. Their nutrition was appalling! They'd come in with children they'd want me to pull out all the teeth in their head because the teeth were all rotten.*

They were living on a high carbohydrate diet. They grew very good gardens but if they could sell their corn in Yellowknife for cash money towards breaking up more, or clearing more land or building more of their barns or increasing their house or something! They didn't realize that they were depriving their own children. They were getting good homemade bread and good homemade butter or cream and good homemade jam but this was a darn poor diet to be growing on. I mean, their teeth showed that. And they were very anemic, a lot of them.

The rapidly repeated pregnancies produced babies that were anemic when they were born, mothers that were anemic when they got pregnant! It's routine, I don't know whether it still is, but it was routine at that time to give your newborn little pigs a shot of iron. I was giving a lot of the Mennonite babies a shot of iron and I told one of the fathers who had had his young baby there that the reason I've got to give your baby a shot of iron is because your wife never had a chance to build up her blood after she had the last baby before she got pregnant with this one. Not exactly criticizing, but explaining why this unfortunate woman hadn't been able to give her baby enough blood before it was born. It was short of iron because she was short of iron, and she was short because she hadn't had any interval, you see. I said, "you give all your little pigs iron, don't you?" And "oh, yes," he said. I said "well, an awful lot of the human babies that are born need iron if their mothers haven't had long enough between pregnancies." I sort of figured that the idea might soak in after a while, you know, the ripples would spread. And people talk a lot, discuss things and to fathers who were doing the best for their little pigs, it was a new idea that their children might be just as vulnerable to iron deficiency.

J:~ That you would be in the business of raising children just as you would be in the business of raising pigs.

M:~ *Well, I mean they didn't… of course, big families were the routine, I mean, amongst people other than Mennonites. You get the Canada Year Book for the 1920s or so and see how many families of 12 or more* children there were and then see how many children were born to women over the age of 40.

J:~ What about Native women of that time? Were they having comparably sized families?

M:~ *Yes, they were having comparable sized families, but the children were dying of TB. The biggest number in any family when I came here to Keg River was five and there wasn't a woman whose completed family had been less than 10 and most of them had been a lot more.*

J:~ So they had been losing half their children.

M:~ *They'd been losing more than half their children.*

J:~ And at what age would the children tend to die?

M:~ *Of course, the babies were getting tubercular meningitis and dying and the older children were getting TB and the teenagers were dying of TB. A lot of the older people didn't get TB. I always wondered whether it was that the old people didn't meet TB until they were full grown adults and they just didn't, were not as susceptible, but they might well have had inactive TB that had spread to their children and their children's children. Whole families were dying of it. It was absolutely heart breaking.*

J:~ They must have just seen this as a will of whatever, then. It must have been hard to counteract in terms of…

M:~ *They knew that when somebody started coughing blood that they were going to be dead fairly soon!*

J:~ What about getting them to quarantine themselves or to do what we do and just put them to bed for two years?

M:~ *These people didn't know anything about germs, anything about infection. They didn't even realize that they were spreading it from one to another. They only knew that one child after another, one teenager after another, was starting to cough blood and dying. But they had no idea of why.*

J:~ What was their explanation then?

M:~ *This was something that just happened. This is what made it so darn interesting! They didn't realize that if you kept a wound clean it was going to heal much better than if it was dirty. They didn't know that it was vital to keep burns from getting infected. One of the thrills of my life was when I went to do the dressings on some child that had been brought in by an older child. And I put my mask and gown and gloves on and said to the older child "what am I putting this over my* face for?" She said "so you won't blow bad germs on the burn". I'd got it made! They'd got the idea! This was a new idea.

J:~ So, you must have seen a lot of people then when they were really in a bad way, if they didn't know how to take care.

M:~ Well, they didn't know any better! So they were being damned as dirty Indians! But, they didn't have enough rags to cover their wounds! They got tuberculous bones that were leaking, leaking for years.

J:~ It must have been fascinating as a doctor to see that.

M:~ Yes, to explain to them why, if you had three or four children in bed together and one of them was coughing and coughing, that what they were coughing out was a sort of form of germs that the other children were breathing in and that were going to get into their chests and do the same sort of damage. And of course this is where Emma MacDonald was so useful 'cause she could put it into Cree that they could understand.

J:~ So, some sort of concept for the invisible that we dealt with scientifically but that they would have to deal with some other way.

M:~ Yes, absolutely. I mean, they knew all about the visible pests but nothing at all, no idea at all, about the invisible ones that were all around them. And maybe they should have put two and two together but they just didn't and it was a funny life, really. And, as I say, I was treating them all very vigorously with penicillin when they got strep throat and of course I did my own lab work, didn't get paid for it. I wasn't officially qualified to do the lab work but the people who taught me medicine in the '20s didn't know that you weren't supposed to be able to stain the slide and identify streptococci or TB or whatever. So.

J:~ So you were your own little medical clinic here.

M:~ Well, I mean, it was very much simpler to take a swab, stain it while you were finishing checking the patient over. You could say this is or is not gonorrhea or strep or TB. The TB took longer to stain but I used to have, I used to have three timers going. One was for the bread that was in the oven upstairs, one of them was for the TB film that was in the tank and the other one was for some blood test or other. You had to time the different stains, you know, how long you left them on. But it would have been so stupid to have waited for a swab report to come back from the city. Now you need to know what group of strep you're dealing with. But in those days we didn't even know that there was any strep.

J:~ And penicillin was shotgun.

M:~ *Penicillin was wonderful! We ended up with no badly damaged hearts but with one that was a mitral stenosis which you could hear and with one whose ... Where did I meet her? I met her a number of years ago. Oh I don't...you remember what the heart sounded like but you don't remember their name. You remember where they lived... (laugh).*

J:~ (Laugh). It's like remembering the book that has the red cover.

M:~ *Yes, quite. I mean, my memory is quite patchy anyway. But when you remember that to get to the house you had to make a wide half circle to get away from the dog that was tied up, and you remember the child and you remember the bed and you remember what her heart sounded like. And you remember how you had to explain over and over again that this child had to stay in bed because her heart was damaged but it was going to heal if she didn't run round. It took so long to explain!*

J:~ Yes, I'm sure that was very difficult.

M:~ *Just across the river, you see, was the other bunch of over crowded houses with large families of children. And at that time we had, I think, five families with more than, there were 12 living children. I was sort of cocky about the way these children were surviving pneumonia or whatever ailed them and then realizing that their fathers couldn't catch enough food for the family. Wondering if I was doing more harm than good.*

J:~ So, that then brings you to the question of birth control which you'd have had to address.

M:~ *Which of course was another problem! When birth control came in 1960ish, around '60, that was when the price came down. Before that there were one or two school teachers who could afford the pill but you couldn't expect a poor native to. I think they were $11 per month for the first year or two and then they came down. There was enough competition amongst different drug outfits that the price came down to $2 a month wholesale. So, if I got batches of them and allowed the women to get them for $2 a month then they had to come and get them. This wasn't a question of giving a prescription because we couldn't have afforded it, but if they wanted to go on restricting their families they'd got to come over once a month and get another supply of pills. The idea was to prevent them from giving unmarried* teenagers the pill. And also to make them deliberately decide that they were not going to have another child for a year until they got these babies out of diapers, you know.

J:~ It would be a big commitment for them, too, wouldn't it? I mean in terms of their lifestyle, a pill you had to take every day and sort of at the same time.

M:~ *Oh yes. The woman who, by the Grace of God, is still alive but the woman who decided that since her husband was in the bush she obviously couldn't get pregnant and didn't need to take the pill. And he, when he went over his trap line, got more furs than he expected so he came home unexpectedly so she madly started on the pill, went on through the first three months of pregnancy, three months, four months, and it's her daughter who is the mother of four school children who came over and cleaned house the last time my house was dusted.*

J:~ So it was, there was...

M:~ *No damage was done.*

J:~ No damage but there could have been.

M:~ *If it had been a male fetus, would it have been a homosexual? Or would there have been some kind of an abnormality? Getting all of this extra estrogen through early pregnancy, it might have determined that the fetus would be female or it might have determined that a male fetus would be badly damaged or would it? Who's to know? I don't. She was such an intelligent woman and she said, "well he was gone so I knew I couldn't get pregnant" and she didn't expect him back for a month or so.*

J:~ So she thought she had time. But there is a question here of people who are living a life that has a different type of regulation than ours does, having to take that pill everyday. And I wonder if this was also a problem with tuberculosis. When they started to bring in the treatments for TB, did you have people on those medications?

M:~ *Oh God, did I ever!*

J:~ Was there a problem of getting them to take them regularly?

M:~ *You had to explain over and over again. You had to let them look down the microscope and see these stained tuberculous bacteria stained a nice, bright red. And I'm sure some of them have still got the idea of these sort of red no-see-ums swimming around.*

J:~ Gee, that's what I always thought, too!

M:~ *Anyway. (laughs) Well, if you let them look down the microscope, at first they couldn't see anything and then they began to sort of focus their eyes. And they became absolutely fascinated! And then I had a hand centrifuge for a while before we got power and the kids were allowed – and of course the grandchildren, grandma's helicopter was lots of fun – and they would turn this thing vigorously and you would explain and show them of course the little bead of pus at the bottom and this was to get the germs all swung out. So then you could get the germs under the microscope and show them and they were fascinated.*

J:~ So your lab work was not only you doing lab work, it was part of the education.

M:~ *The lab work was hysterical, really. I mean it was quite funny. And then of course when homemade pregnancy tests came in, I was doing the pregnancy test but then showing them what I was doing and telling them why I was doing it and trying to get the idea into their heads that as soon as they got pregnant, things started to change in their bodies. Their breasts started to develop so they would be making milk because it would take quite a long time to build up enough milk tissues. And I used to let them listen to the fetal heart so they'd know what I was looking for. And they were fascinated.*

J:~ So it was …

M:~ *So … not medicine as ordinarily practiced.*

J:~ It was very human medicine.

M:~ *Very funny. But, as I say, Emma was a tower of strength. Because she would see things from their point of view as well as mine and she could explain things to them.*

J:~ So it was very important. You were already translating sort of hard medicine into a much more personal medicine and then she's taking that and translating that to the Cree.

M:~ *Translating that to something they would understand. Her Cree was better than their Cree because they were illiterate in their own language or limited in their vocabulary in their own language and she would be sort of translating to them. Like the man from Carcajou who had a discharging ear and it was explained to me that the bad milk was coming out. And it did smell like bad milk! To try and put that into Cree and try to explain that sticking a needle in his rear end is going to do any good to the bad milk that is coming out of his ear!*

J:~ It also indicates that he had an interesting idea of his own anatomy inside anyway, you know, to think that.

M:~ *No, no. But when I explained to some of the Ukrainian population that their insides were almost exactly like the pigs. Next time you butcher you go and look at the kidneys and see where they are, and see where the tubes are and this is where if you've got a terrible pain it can be a tiny little stone that's going down that tube and it will stop paining when it gets into the bladder but you must save all the urine you pass so we can see if the stone has passed. And so, you know, this gave them quite an interest in pig butchering, to see the heart and the lungs and the kidneys and everything.*

J:~ But they hadn't made the connection to themselves.

M:~ *They hadn't. They hadn't the least idea. I had a little scale model skeleton that stood on my desk and then I decided that I'd better to keep it in the drawer because the kids always wanted to play with it because you could bend its arms and legs and things and make it walk.*

J:~ Well, it would keep the kids entertained!

M:~ *Well, it was quite but it was a rather expensive little toy! But it was very good to be able to explain to them exactly what bone they had broken and why you had to do this and such. Particularly ankles. If you could explain why you put a bandage on in a certain direction, why you must build up the one side or the other of the shoe.*

J:~ This is a very different approach to medicine as even I have had it practiced on me which is that, you know, you're not allowed to see your chart, sometimes in the hospital.

M:~ *Yes, but I mean when you're starting from scratch you can't get people to do what they're told unless they know why. I mean otherwise it's mumbo jumbo and as I say, if I wanted to put a mask on that was my peculiar idea but they finally got the idea why I was doing it and why I was putting gloves on.*

J:~ So you didn't necessarily have the authority that a doctor would have in, in your own society at the time.

M:~ *Oh no!*

J:~ I mean, you do what the doctor says because the doctor is a doctor.

M:~ *Oh yes, I know, but they would never have! So you put a cast on somebody's broken arm or something and they went off 50 miles*

*into the bush to Rainbow Lake or wherever they came from, with
instructions, "if this gives a lot of pain, you'll have to come back in.
You probably better stay with so and so at the Paddle for a week or
two until I'm sure". But if it was something that I was reasonably sure
that I had got into good position and wouldn't have any trouble, so
they shouldn't have any pain with this, I'd tell them to go. "But don't
let them fight with it!"*

J:~ (laughs). It's true! It would make a wonderful club.

M:~ *And, I mean, some of them would come back with a cast positively in
rags with the fracture firmly healed.*

J:~ I guess the only way that you could earn their respect and
attention was by simply doing the job. I mean, you were being
successful.

M:~ *Yes and I mean, if you, if you got them understanding what you were
doing, it made such a difference. I mean, a patient's cooperation counts
for an awful lot even when you're dealing with a civilized population
and these were a lot of new ideas for people, but very interesting.*

J:~ And you never worried about anybody becoming a
hypochondriac after you'd given them the idea?

M:~ *No, and I never worried about anybody suing me. They knew I
hadn't got any more money than they'd got.*

J:~ So, there was no point.

M:~ *There was only ever one patient who was hostile and I couldn't blame
him. I mean, he was worried about his kid. But I don't know. It's a
weird way of practicing medicine. I mean that's why — that's one of
the papers that I threw away, or did I throw it away? It was a report
to Women's Medical Federation questioning ... now I've seen that
within the last week but I really don't know if it's still there or thrown
away. They wanted a whole lot of questions about how many hours a
day or a week or how many patients I saw and all the rest of it, you
know. Well I didn't know from one day to the next whether I was
going to see any patients or a dozen. And if they were Mennonites
they tended to bring in the uncles and aunts and cousins who might
as well get their teeth pulled at the same time.*

*And of course if grandma was going to die, it was a good idea
to put her on a load of grain when they came over. This was their
nearest elevator, so they would bring grandma a hundred miles on a
load of grain and would bring her up here on the load of grain and*

unload her here, then they'd go back and unload the grain and come back and pick up grandma. And Frank was fit to be tied because they were bringing heavily loaded trucks. There being no weigh scales, they'd put every last kernel which you could put onto a truck and they came up our dirt road when it was muddy, making ruts six inches deep. What could I do about it?

Grandma sometimes had, some of them had pathology that would curl your hair. I mean, there was one woman whose osteoporosis was so bad that her chin was making a dent in her breast bone and she hadn't been able to raise her head for years but she sat there in a chair in the kitchen knitting like a machine. So, a useful member of the community but she was probably going to die soon and I could give a death certificate if I'd seen her, but if I didn't know her, what were they going to do, you see? All Hell would break out if they buried her without having a death certificate.

[pause while tape is turned over]

M:~ *They needed a death certificate because they had to have a burial permit to bury the person in the graveyard. In the early days, they didn't need any permit, they just buried them. They buried them where they died very often. It's God's way. The Metis people weren't going to lug a body from here to the graveyard. The graveyard here had a lot of the smallpox deaths. They died right in the village and were buried in the graveyard.*

J:~ So, you were actually in a lot of ways, you were also doing a lot of the record-keeping for the community. I know you did check-ups for men who were going to war.

M:~ *Well, yes, I was the nearest doctor so I did a lot.*

J:~ I remember you also had a story about trying to find, get old age pension for Mrs. Bottle.

M:~ *Bottle, of course, is Chalifoux. They are Chalifoux but the name that they had sounded like "la bouteille" so when the French priests or fur traders came to the area North of Edmonton, North of Fort Edmonton, Grouard and so on, La Bouteille sounded to them like "the bottle," so that's what they called them. They couldn't tell the Indians apart anyway, but this particular tribe was, was Bottles. They* were all being called Bottles when I came to Keg River until when the family allowances were going to be paid, we had to get them all checked with the priest or the missionaries, you see, to find out how their names were really spelt and where possible, to find out the ages of them if they'd been baptized.

J:~ Have they kept the name Bottle?

M:~ No, but I was meeting this woman in the hospital the other day when I was waiting to go in and get my blood test done and she said, "you know, I don't know if you remember me." And I said, "you're Peter Bottle's daughter, aren't you?" And thought afterwards, you know, too late, that this probably was a deadly insult. Peter had moved to Edmonton with his family. It was funny. Now she said she hadn't seen me since her daughter was born and her daughter's youngest daughter was now 25. And I thought that puts that back into perspective! Oh dear.

Oh, she flung her arms around me and kissed me with genuine affection and I hadn't seen her since the '30s. So here is a woman whose youngest granddaughter's 25 but I still count because I brought her daughter into the world successfully.

J:~ So there's a real, a real connection here.

M:~ And yet most of the women, when I came here, had been having their babies without trouble. It was when Frank's wife was delivered with the aid of the next door Metis woman because Frank was down at the river waiting for the doctor to arrive.

J:~ What happened in her case?

M:~ She had a retained placenta.

J:~ Yes, I know that but I've also seen a picture of her supposedly going out to hospital. The placenta was retained and then she got very ill. She died, what, a few days later?

M:~ She developed what we used to call post-partum insanity and died but it was a lot of people in those days were dying of post-partum insanity.

J:~ And it was just infection?

M:~ It was a uterine infection, an acute and severe infection. I don't know now, but under English law from way back, if a woman murdered her baby within 10 days of birth, she couldn't be charged because she was considered to be insane for that length of time. And it wasn't an uncommon thing while I was doing obstetrics.

J:~ This is what they generally call puerperal fever?

M:~ No, not necessarily. They go insane without having enough fever that you'd know they were dying of an infection. But they died just the same, most of them.

All Frank's efforts to get her out ... it was so idiotic, you see, because she'd been out while she was pregnant and could perfectly well could have stayed with her parents. They had this magnificent house on the edge of Red Deer Lake and her previous two children had been born without any trouble with Dr. Brander looking after her. If the third child, I don't know, there's no way of knowing whether the psychological effect of having this baby born without her husband or a doctor, with an Indian woman she probably couldn't talk to...I don't know how much grief she picked up. I never dared to ask.

But this may have had something to do with the retained placenta and the long delay in getting Wop May to fly in and fly her out. She might well have had...oh I don't know. I don't know.

J:~ It's the sort of thing that when the accident, when it goes wrong, it can really go wrong.

M:~ Oh quite.

Quite a number of native patients did go wrong after I came in, which I thought was very odd because I had inquired, via Emma MacDonald, of course, for any account of women developing puerperal insanity amongst other things, but also obstructed labor. I was particularly anxious to know about how many women had died in childbirth, unable to deliver. Because this is what I had been seeing so much of in England.

J:~ Oh, the rachitic pelvis...

M:~ The pelvis, the woman with the soft bones of rickets. When she's quite small, sitting, the pelvis flattens, so you've got a woman who's got perfectly normal, good width of hips...

J:~ But can't...

M:~ But God help you if you don't check! I mean, a vital part of pre-natal care was to make sure that she hadn't got a flat pelvis because, if she had, she would die undelivered unless you either did a caesarean section or could produce premature labor while the head was still small enough and soft enough to go through. So, we were inducing labor in women who were seven months pregnant with all the risk to a premature baby whose head had been squeezed through a narrowed pelvis.

J:~ And this was not a problem?

M:~ *Of course it was a problem! You try to put forceps on in a narrow pelvis!*

J:~ No, I was thinking this was not a problem here when you came.

M:~ *No, again, this was what was so weird, you see, because here were people living, I was going to say, in almost total darkness for part of the year, for a couple of months through the winter. They weren't getting enough sunlight to produce enough vitamin D to prevent them getting rickets. And I couldn't see why they didn't get rickets which is when I wrote a paper for, ... oh, the devil ... I don't know where that is...*

J:~ It's probably one of the ones you threw out.

M:~ *This is why I say, for heavens sake, keep the rabies papers because, for all I know, I might need them though it seems extraordinarily unlikely. I mean, I probably will never have as good an audience as you again but now I've talked through a straight three days. I'll read them to a tape recorder.*

J:~ That said, they didn't seem to...

M:~ *They didn't have rickets, period. And their babies ought to have had rickets.*

J:~ And what were they eating that they would not have?

M:~ *They were wholly breastfed. This was before pablum and stuff was available so they fed their babies breast milk until they were big enough to chew on a muskrat leg or chew on a bit of half chewed meat. Rather like a pigeon feeding its young.*

J:~ But their own vitamin D levels must have been good enough then to hand on to these babies, right?

M:~ *Why their babies didn't need as much vitamin D as other babies, God only knows. But it's something to do with the amount of carbohydrate that babies were being fed as they were being weaned. They, white people, were supplementing breast milk earlier and earlier. They were gradually getting them to consider that the right time to start a baby on a varied diet was when they were six weeks old, at which I screamed loudly that the matured kidneys couldn't cope with the...*

I can't remember where that...I can't remember where the devil I was writing to... It couldn't have been the British Medical Journal but I think it was, either that... It was probably the Medical Women's Federation because the...I mean, here was a population that was, had not had rickets or if they'd had rickets it had left them with no damage to their pelvis. As I say, it was of my mumbo jumbo to make sure that I wasn't going to get stuck with a woman with a flat pelvis. And I never saw one!

J:~ And their babies weren't significantly smaller or anything?

M:~ *No! Their babies were significantly larger! They were a very large number of over-large babies, over-large by my standards.*

   I've got to move my leg, or else!

J:~ (laughs) I'm interested in the lab work that you were doing. Where did you, I mean, you must have had to cadge money for equipment and for dyes.

M:~ *Well, I had a microscope and I had a centrifuge.*

J:~ And you brought these with you?

M:~ *No. I bought the microscope with some money that I had got for…I don't remember what I got it for! It must have been either Workmen's Compensation or a coroner's inquest or something. Some cash money that I had enough.*

   I gave Penny my microscope not realizing that it would become an obsolete instrument in a very short time. But she was the only one of my grandchildren that would have had any use for it. So I gave it to her. I don't know whether she's still got it. I haven't the least idea. I shouldn't think so. I mean after you've been brought up with an electron microscope! But I've got, still got in the cupboard upstairs the microscope that I brought out when I came out from England, which was an exceedingly primitive thing compared with the one that I bought later. It didn't even have sub-stage lighting. You had to arrange the thing and arrange the mirrors to get the light through it. I gave it to the grandchildren and after they grew up and left home, Anne tried to clear the clutter out of her cupboards – cleared it into mine – and I had forgotten that it was there until I saw it the other day.

   But the grandchildren grew up seeing the circulation in a tadpole's tail or the circulation in water fleas!

J:~ But none of them went into medicine.

M:~ *Penny went into laboratory science…which of course is the vital part of modern medicine.*

J:~ It's the stuff you were doing.

M:~ *To tell you the answer! Penny for a while was matching blood in the U of A for kidney transplants and then she was in Whitehorse. She* was doing lab work in Peace River for a while and that's when I first got to look through a really good microscope.

J:~ Were you surprised of what you could see?

M:~ *Oh, it was marvelous to see. And of course it's got a lot of the gadgets. I mean, you no longer counted blood cells patiently, square little square by little square and added them all up.*

J:~ What do you do? Push a button and the computer tells you?

M:~ *Now the computer tells you the answer. And you assume that the computer can't be, isn't going to make any mistakes. It's marvelous. But of course lab work has become infinitely complicated and is giving us, giving us the answers to so many things. You can't practice medicine without a lab, which is one of the reasons you've got difficulties getting doctors to outlying places.*

J:~ So the sort of things that you did is just…?

M:~ *Well, the sort of thing that I did is so primitive as to be almost interesting as a genuine antique. But, I mean, I learned to use leeches when I was a medical student. I told somebody the other day and they said that leeches are now being used again.*

J:~ They're coming back, yes.

M:~ *I mean if they won't latch on, you get some warm milk and stir a little sugar into it and break the skin and the leech will then bite. Why, I don't know, because I mean sugared water, sugared milk seems to be very odd for a leech, but…*

This was one of the odd jobs you learned. They're very useful, very useful. And somebody, whoever was talking about it, it may have been on the radio that they made them talk about it, was for black eyes to get the blood away. A leech will extract a lot of this blood which otherwise takes weeks to turn yellow and green and finally fade.

J:~ So, there's all this stuff that you were doing…

M:~ *The blood counts that I was doing I had been taught to do and it would have been silly not to do them*

J:~ But you were subsidizing a lot of this work. You were not only not getting paid, you were actually putting money into it.

M:~ *Oh yes, quite. Any money that I could bum.*

I mean, people would send me money for birthday presents and things instead of giving me books, knowing full well that I was going to spend it on some gadgetry or something. And it was an expensive hobby but it wasn't any more expensive than if I'd been an expert photographer or something.

J:~ You know this sounds like immense self-sacrifice, you know, that you would be taking money and putting it into other people.

M:~ *It wasn't self-sacrifice because I was getting such a bang out of it.*

J:~ So you were having fun…

M:~ *I was having an extraordinarily interesting life! But if I hadn't been able to do the lab work, it would have been even more by guess and by God than it was! And, I don't know, it was an enjoyable life. I mean, if I had it to do all over again, I might well not have come to Canada in the first place. If I'd gone to Calcutta, the heat probably would have killed me. Sally Currier was one who did go. She got a degree a year ahead of me, anyway. She had gorgeous red hair. She was an extraordinarily good looking woman and for some reason she wanted to go to Calcutta. I've forgotten what she was going to do, whether she was going to teach or lecture or something. But she got cholera and narrowly missed dying and lost all her hair and came back to England. I might well have shared the same fate if I had been able to get the job with her.*

J:~ That you originally were going to do.

M:~ *That I originally thought, "how interesting." This was part of the Student Christian Movement. We used to have interesting people come and talk to us about the third world. The only one I remember is Sun Yat Sen's widow.*

J:~ So, this was the idea of medical missions.

M:~ *More or less. And you would get more obstetrics in India than anywhere else, more complicated obstetrics in India.*

J:~ So you also could train yourself at the same time.

M:~ *The men not able to, not being allowed to, look at a lot of these women. They were dying undelivered or dying of hemorrhage or whatever. So you would be doing a good thing by going there, but also it was a place to get almost unlimited obstetric experience at great speed. A year or two of that and you'd see more complications than you'd see in a whole working lifetime in England. Though, of course, we also saw lots, the rachitic flat pelvises being one of the things that we saw a lot of. And, of course, the hospital that I was working in, the maternity hospital, was taking in all abnormal cases from about a million of a population. This was in the days before blood transfusions*

were very expert and before anesthetics were very expert, and when
a very large number of the poor had had rickets in varying degrees
as infants, so that they showed up with pelves that were deformed or
narrowed, flattened. The conditions in the slums of Birmingham were
very much worse than in the slums of Keg River. I mean, these houses
were much better than a lot of the houses I had done my training in.
After you'd observed some cases in hospital, you then delivered some
under the supervision of the midwives and you then went out on the
district. And you were called out from the hospital to go and deliver
babies in the most appalling of slum conditions.

J:~ So, for all the things you've said about how bad the conditions
were here for delivery, sometimes…

M:~ *They were nothing like as bad as some of the slums in England.*

J:~ That's interesting.

M:~ *I mean, the hospital black bag was your sort of passport to safety in*
places where the police wouldn't go in except in twos.

J:~ So, they weren't going to mess around with somebody who was
coming in to help.

M:~ *The man who came or the boy who came to get you came to this*
particular door in the back of the hospital where the people who were
on district had a whole sort of wing that had our bedrooms and a
living room and sort of an entrance way with the bathrooms. When
you came in from the district, you stripped every last stitch of clothing
off and washed and put clean clothes on before you went into the rest
of the thing because the bugs and so on were dreadful and in those
day we had to be so careful we didn't carry any streptococci or what
have you. There was no penicillin, no sulfa drugs. You either were
clean or else!

If you ran into problems, you would get the senior medical officer
to help you. That was where I was so lucky. I got a second go as senior
because of an absolute tragedy. I can't think of her name. Greenough!
She took over after I left that position and she admitted to hospital
a failed forceps, a woman who was being brought in from a doctor
who had failed to deliver with forceps, a difficult delivery who was
admitted to the hospital. I forget how long she had been in labor. I
forget the details but, at any rate, the man who took this woman up in
the lift, the nurses in the operating room and Greenough all got acute
strep infections. The patient died and so did the three women in the

same ward who were never touched by her. I mean, the atmosphere must have been virulent!

But Greenough had got a streptococcal heart infection which put an end to her obstetric career. She ended up as a well-known psychiatrist! There was something or other in her name in one of the medical journals, and I thought, "well, by God, you know, you've had a whole lot easier life than you would have had if you'd not happened to admit that particular strep infection!"

But, then, you see, they closed off part of the hospital. Everything, everything had to be washed down with Lysol, the walls and ceilings and everything. One of the best of the operating room sisters was down with strep! This was what I went back into for my second batch as senior. They had to have somebody who had been the junior before being the senior and I'd been the senior and therefore the obvious person. I had started doing anaesthetics over at the Queen's hospital and all of a sudden I went back to the hospital that I had enjoyed so much!

Joe Green by that time was on the district and I'd have married him if he'd invited me but he didn't. He went to Nigeria instead. We kept up a conversation until I got married. He wrote me a lot of letters about his obstetrics in Nigeria and the way that they'd always destroyed children if they were twins because this was so unlucky so that he never got in on the twin delivery if they knew there was going to be twins. Or suspected they were going to be twins. He was very interesting, Joe. A rattling good surgeon.

J:~ And did he stay?

M:~ I don't know. I lost track of him after I got married. I mean, I wrote and told him that I was getting married. And he sent me a wedding present. It's still upstairs, a box with inlaid very fine leather work. It's my button box.

J:~ (laughs)

M:~ But I know that he was, I knew when he died. Somebody wrote and said "oh, did you know that Joe Green developed diabetes and died?" and that's all I know.

He was a good friend. A very nice fellow. I don't know that I thought of him as a potential mate, but certainly we were very good friends. But it would have never have struck me that, in the interns' quarters, his bedroom being next to mine that he would come to visit me or that I would go to visit him. It wouldn't have struck us! It simply wasn't done in those days! You know, that way of thinking. In other words, we were much less highly sexed than people who have grown up since the sexual freedom of the '60s and '70s. It simply didn't exist.

J:~ So, it wasn't part of the culture.

M:~ *It wasn't part of the culture. It wasn't something…I mean, you didn't eye every man as a potential bedfellow. But Joe taught me to drive a car and I did a locum for his brother one time out in the country. This was the way that general practice should be done, with a car and chauffeur. When they called you out in the middle of the night to go to a delivery, you didn't have and try to start a car in the cold night or anything. You were ushered into the car as though you were a duchess or something. When you got to the patient, the patient's midwife had everything all ready and the patient was in advanced labor and you didn't have to do a damn thing and you got paid for it! Joe's brother was a very nice fellow, too.*

J:~ You used to get picked up at Battle River Prairie with a sleigh and a horse!

M:~ *I was saying to someone about his raising mules that some of the people in Battle River had mules in the good old days.*

We should go to the Senior Citizens lodge and see if Jenny Asmussen's in. She was Jenny Schamehorn.

J:~ Oh, I was going to ask you about the Schamehorns because they show up all through your letters.

M:~ *Most are dead now.*

J:~ And Asmussen, too, is that…

M:~ *Jenny married Asmussen after I left Battle River.*

J:~ So, this is one of the guys who was on the committee who was in charge of your well-being?

M:~ *Well, no, it was his brother that she married and he just died of cancer of the lung recently and she's got into the Lodge.*

J:~ Where is this? At Manning?

M:~ *At Manning, yes.*

J:~ Why don't we…

M:~ *We should go and visit her.*

> [And with that, we hopped into the car and drove a hundred kilometers to the Lodge!]

Second Interview
19/04/94

J:~ Interviewing Mary Percy Jackson. It's the 19th of April in Keg River. This is the second interview. All right, Doctor Jackson, could you tell me about the rabies epidemic that was here in the 1950s.

M:~ *The rabies. There'd always been rabies in the Northwest Territories, in the Arctic. They would get rabies occasionally in the Eskimo sleigh dogs but it started moving south, back in the early 1950s, and when it reached Fort Vermilion, the two doctors – Kratz, Hannah and Julius – were practicing there. They had come to Canada from Israel where they had seen rabies and had treated it by the Pasteur method, making their own vaccine.*

When they saw rabies in Fort Vermilion, they realized that people wouldn't know what was the matter with the animals. They wrote to the provincial government and the Dominion government and were written off as being Germans who didn't know what they were talking about. They were nothing like as fluent in English as they subsequently became and were described as those crazy Germans. Nobody paid any attention, so they came over to Keg River one day – 120 miles of gravel road – to tell me about it. They knew that I was going to see rabies and probably wouldn't recognize it. There hadn't been any rabies in England for many many years because of the very strict quarantine to keep rabies out. If you decide to move to England and take your dog with you, your dog goes into quarantine for six months.

And so they came to warn me to tell me about rabies and how animals looked when they were rabid and so on and to see if I would write to the government. Maybe they'd pay some attention to me! And so they went away again and we were having supper and old Octave Ducharme was there and we were talking about what the Kratzes had said. Octave said, "that sickness is here already. I heard the foxes talking across the river and there's something wrong with them."

Within two or three days after that, everybody was seeing rabid animals. There was a very high population of wild animals in this part of the world. There always had been but it had been increased when the big forest fire went through in 1950. So many animals running ahead of the fire had stopped in the Keg River to Fort Vermilion area. We'd always had lots of animals around, that's why it was such good trapping and hunting country.

When an animal's rabid, it may eventually become unconscious and die. It's what they call dumb rabies. A percentage of animals will develop what's called furious rabies and they run biting everything they come to. Anything that moves they will go for. They become exceedingly dangerous and they can run for days without food, biting at everything.

It's the bite of the furious rabies animal that spreads the disease. With our heavy fox, coyote, wolf population, we had a record number of animals who, if rabid, were exceedingly dangerous. If they had furious rabies, they could run for a hundred miles biting any animal, including people. The incubation period in a person who's been bitten varies with where they've been bitten. The more nerves there are, the faster the virus spreads up the nerves to the brain. Bites on the face and hands are particularly dangerous and other bites may take literally months before the rabies develops.

If you're going to treat rabies, you've got to do so before the person becomes rabid. You've got to start in as quickly as possible to give them an attenuated vaccine, gradually increasing the dose every day for 14 days. That's not so nowadays, but that's what it used to be in the 1950s. And the person who'd been bitten might or might not be going to develop rabies but you couldn't wait and see because, if you did, if they got rabies, it had a 100% mortality. If you debated too long, you might be going to give the vaccine to somebody who was already beyond hope: the virus was traveling to the brain and was going to kill them before you'd built up enough immunity from the vaccine doses. And, since the vaccine could on occasion – perhaps one in a thousand or so – kill a patient and you didn't know whether the patient was going to get rabies from the bite or not, it was critically important to get the brain of the animal out to the provincial lab in Lethbridge for them to look for Negri bodies so that they could tell you, yes, this animal is rabid.

That way, you knew that it was justifiable to go ahead and immunize because at least you knew that they might have gotten rabies from the bite. But if they were bitten and you didn't get the head, you had absolutely no proof that the animal that had bitten them was rabid. Of course, with rabies so prevalent, you had to assume that it was a rabid animal. It was a very tricky situation really. When we had a lot of little pigs bitten here, some of them were only scratched, but they developed rabies just the same and you sort of felt that if a scratch that hardly drew blood, a scratch by the teeth of a rabid fox, on a pig's hide, then a scratch or a little more than a scratch on a human might also give rabies. It didn't have to be deep bite that hadn't been cleaned out properly, it could be contamination of hands that had got bits of skin knocked off them.

When people were bitten by mice who had never been bitten by mice before, particularly people who were sleeping and who were wakened by a mouse biting on the face or hands, it was very tricky. When we had a lot of cattle die here, there were thousands of dead mice at the bottom of their straw stack. We assumed that the animals got the rabies from mouse bites because their owner had never seen any fox attacking them, the animals had never shown any sign of bites and there had never been any blood on the snow or anything. But, the whole herd of cattle died of unmistakable rabies and so when people were bitten on the face, it seemed safer to vaccinate them against rabies. There was no mouse brain to check for Negri bodies because when people were bitten, they sort of instinctually threw off the mouse and the mouse wasn't caught. So you were just hoping…mice bites are quite shallow but quite recognizable bites. If you get a bite there on your face, it isn't very far for the virus to travel to the brain. You can't spend too long hesitating before starting to vaccinate them. Then the expert in Ottawa said that mice didn't spread rabies, to which the farmers in Keg River said, "like hell!" Well, I mean, if you had pigs shut up in a barn and no fox got into them and they died of rabies nonetheless, mice were the probable answer.

J:~ But if bats spread rabies…

M:~ We didn't have bats around.

J:~ But it is recognized that bats spread it so you'd think that other rodents would be suspect.

M:~ It is recognized that bats spread rabies but bats are supposed to be the only warm blooded animal that can get rabies and go on living. All other animals that are infected, including man, will die of the rabies. I mean it's 100% fatality rate.

J:~ Ah, so bats can *carry* it then.

M:~ *Bats in the northern United States that were infected were supposed to be the source of infection for some of the cattle and then they said that the bats in Ontario, some of them, had rabies. Very difficult, awfully difficult to prove whether an animal has rabies or not. You had to get the brain to the lab – and Alberta had only this one lab, in Lethbridge – where they could stain it and look for Negri bodies. Of course, you were also dependent on the skills of the lab technicians and pathologists to stain them properly and recognize them when they saw them.*

J:~ You were doing a lot of your own lab work. Why didn't you do the rabies?

M:~ *I wasn't looking for Negri bodies!*

J:~ So, that would have been too, too hard.

M:~ *It would have been completely beyond me! You have to make very fine sections of the brain to stain them to look for them, you see. And you may have stained the wrong bit of, the wrong section of brain, and not seen any Negri bodies whereas if you had looked at a different section you might have seen them. So that if you sent a head out and they didn't find any Negri bodies, they always covered all angles by saying that Negri bodies were not seen but that they had inoculated mice. And then you had to wait to see if the mice would die of rabies and that was wasting time from the point of view of the person who had been bitten. You wanted to know! If you saw Negri bodies, at least you knew you were fighting something that was there. If they didn't find any Negri bodies and said that they would inoculate mice, you had to wait through the time in which you could prevent rabies in the person if you vaccinated them. And if you got a positive result a month after you'd sent the head out, the patient was probably beyond all hope, going to die of rabies.*

J:~ So, you got interesting statistics, but a dead person.

M:~ *Oh, it was, it was something of a nightmare because the rabid animals were all over the place. There wasn't a household in the community that didn't have some rabid animal trying to get in through the screen windows or trying to get in somehow. Annie Michalchuk was shaking her floor mop outside the door when a fox jumped and latched onto it. She threw the mop outside and shut the door.*

J:~ So, people were under siege.

M:~ *People were. We never went out of the house to go to the barn or wherever without a club or a .22 or something. And a hired man carrying a .22 shot our big yellow barn tom cat just as it was going for Frank. The rabid animal is vicious beyond anything that any normal animal is. I know Dan, the hired man, was really quite shaken. He said, you know, that thing looked like a tiger. We carried flashlights at night if we had to go out after dark, which we avoided doing. My grandson was living with me to go to school at Keg River because there wasn't a school at Naylor Hills yet. He could have walked to school in the ordinary way but not with rabid animals all around every corner. There were times when you could go upstairs and look out of one window and you would never fail to see a rabid animal in one of the fields around the house. So, I used to take Ronnie down to school on the tractor quite often.*

J:~ That's a slow way to get to school!

M:~ *Well, yes. It didn't take that long, but the teachers were afraid to let the kids play outside.*

J:~ How long did this go on? Is this just for that season?

M:~ *This is for all of 1952, I think it was. Rabies reached us in the fall and all through that fall and winter and the next spring, summer. I think the rabies was starting to die down in '53. That was the year that we got the Master Farmer Award and by the time that the sort of experts were coming up and studying us, things were dying down. This is back in 1953 and at that time the rabies was dying down largely because most of the animals were dead.*

J:~ So it wasn't just that finally somebody got the idea and had a concerted poisoning campaign.

M:~ *You couldn't poison the animal that was rabid because a rabid animal can't eat or drink. What we were trying to do was to wipe out the animals who were possibly incubating or the animals that might become rabid. It was sort of a scorched earth policy to try to persuade the government to kill out all the animals so that there wouldn't be enough to carry an epidemic. So that when an animal was running with furious rabies, it wouldn't find another animal to bite. But there were odd cases turning up, I think, until '55, but not very many. They had done a fairly massive poisoning campaign in about 1953, I think. And they didn't really start it with any enthusiasm until they had a rabid dog killed in Edmonton.*

J:~ So it had gotten that far south.

M:~ *It had got that far south. We saw it moving steadily south. I mean it was much worse at Fort Vermilion than it was at Keg River. After the Kratzes came, it got rapidly worse in Keg River. And then it was showing up all the way down through the Peace River Country. There are some maps in those Within Our Borders magazines that you've got in that a bunch that I think shows the sort of line where the movement stopped.*

It was moving much faster than we had thought it would spread, judging by the time it had taken to move down and out of the North West Territories to Fort Vermilion. Then there was so much greater number of animals to carry the infection because of the density of the animal population. It got particularly foxes, coyotes, wolves, lynx, bears, cattle, sheep, hogs, mice. Frank built a wire fence all round the big yard there, you know, with the sort of 6-inch square – and he would see foxes trying to get in. They'd put one paw through one hole and another paw through another hole. They hadn't got enough sense to try to get through one hole. And then we had animals die. We had kittens die of rabies that had been born in the house and never been out of the house. We were fairly sure that the old cat had been bringing in mice to feed them and that the mice had rabies. The cat had been immunized. We immunized all the cats and dogs that we could get hold. The government provided the vaccine but some of the animals – some of the dogs that had been vaccinated and re-vaccinated, in other words done in 1952 and done in 1953, still developed rabies. It was a long way from being 100%.

J:~ And did it have a high mortality rate then, too, among the animals? I know the rabies vaccine is very dangerous to give people.

M:~ *Well, I was going to say, if the animal died you didn't know whether you had killed it with vaccine or whether you had failed to get in ahead of the rabies. The number of animals that were dying was absolutely heart breaking. And it practically ruined some of the farmers. They shipped their animals whether they were finished and ready for slaughter or not. It was better to get them out of here because you couldn't protect them. As I say, Frank managed to protect his and still had brood sows go down with rabies in the barn and they'd been in the barn, they'd never been outside. We knew that* they hadn't been attacked by foxes or coyotes. The presumption was that it was mice because of the heads we sent out. I mean, they saw the Negri bodies. Of course, you're totally dependent on the skill of the lab technicians and the pathologist. If he says it's rabies, it's rabies but they must have been getting almost cross-eyed down there trying to do all the animal heads that went in.

Then, the government told us that they knew there was rabies in the country and they didn't want any heads of any animals sent out unless there was some person involved. If the person had been bitten by a dog, then for heaven sakes get the head out with all speed, kept iced down, because they would then look for Negri bodies, so that you'd know whether the animal that had bitten them was rabid. This means that the vast majority of diseased animals went unreported. The thousands of animals that were dying of rabies were a major epidemic for those of us who were living with it but the Department of Agriculture could truthfully say that there had only been 10 cases of proven rabies or something, whereas we might have seen 200 die that week. But the only heads we'd sent out were the heads of animals who had bitten somebody and we wanted to be sure whether it was rabies or not.

J:~ What about the people? Did you have any deaths of normal people?

M:~ No, we didn't. As I say, I never know whether what I did was what saved them or if they wouldn't have gotten rabies anyway. whether I was giving them much more risk from the vaccine than they were at from the rabies. You couldn't tell because you couldn't very often get the head from here – iced down nonetheless, packed in ice and sawdust in a five-gallon pail – to Lethbridge to get it down there before the brain liquefied. It was sort of nip and tuck, particularly with our transportation. I mean right now you can get from here to Lethbridge in a day but you couldn't then… and it was quite glorified guess work, the whole thing. But some of the people had extremely narrow escapes. Some of the people we knew at Fort Vermilion really were very lucky that they weren't killed by rabid animals. And some of the people traveling on the old gravelled highway, the MacKenzie Highway, were attacked by rabid animals. I mean, the animals would attack the vehicles.

J:~ Would they bite and then leave?

M:~ *They'd bite and go round and round. I mean if you jumped in your car to escape them, they wouldn't let you get out of the car.*

M:~ *One man was changing a tire on his pickup or something and a lynx came out of the bush and went for him. He jumped into the pickup and the animal kept him there for hours until somebody came along and shot it. We all carried guns.*

J:~ So they must have had massive strength, in spite of the fact of not being able to eat and not being able to drink and being very ill.

M:~ *Oh quite. And what was so extraordinary was that the length of time that they could go on traveling after they got rabies was greater than it would have been if they were in good health.*

J:~ So it's adrenaline that they're...?

M:~ *They're sort of de-cerebrate, When Harry Bowe shot Nick Tomilo's big black steer, he shot it three times in the head at point blank range before it went down and he was using a 30/30 rifle. And, I mean, we were only a few feet from the animal. The animal was trying to knock the fence down to get at us. And Harry hit it the first time and it practically only shook its head and went on. Really frightening, very frightening.*

    The population was scared to death for their children. One of the little boys saw a fox in the yard, you know, and was calling kitty, kitty, kitty. It was such a pretty little animal. And luckily his older sister saw him or he might have got bitten. But they say with dumb rabies... Our dog died of dumb rabies. Just lay down and curled up and died.

J:~ And that was the majority of the animals?

M:~ *This was the majority of the animals. There were dead animals all over the place but it was the ones with the furious rabies that we were at risk from.*

J:~ What about disposal of all the bodies?

M:~ *The disposal of the animals that died of rabies was a problem too in the middle of the winter. They tried to burn them up, the idea being of course that if a wolf or a coyote or something ate our animals dead of rabies it might get infected. But the virus seemed to localize in the brain.*

J:~ So it's only passed through saliva then?

M:~ *The saliva, and the virus travels in the nerves. And another of the tricky things is that the incubation period is so variable. They give you statistics as to how long it's going to take after somebody's bitten* before they develop the disease. But, of course, when you've got as much rabies as we had around, you didn't know for sure when the bite was. The animal might have been bitten by a mouse before that, or by a mouse after that. So, you've got animals – dogs, cats – developing rabies and you were sure that they hadn't been bitten recently but you weren't looking for mouse bites. I mean, you would have known if they had been torn up badly by a rabid wolf.

J:~ What about compensation for all the loss?

M:~ Oh, there wasn't any compensation. The government provided the vaccine. We didn't have to pay for that.

J:~ How much vaccine did you use? You vaccinated all the sled dogs at one point.

M:~ I was going to say, they were supposed to vaccinate all the sleigh dogs but they didn't come until most of the trappers were gone to the bush. So Frank and I did it. And if that wasn't a three-ring circus! Believe you me, sleigh dogs are not very tame animals! Not just tame dogs anyway and before I could stick a needle into them, Frank would have to tie a strap around their mouths, you know, and then try and control them and they didn't like it at all. But we got most of them done. And then, as I say, some of them that had been vaccinated and re-vaccinated developed rabies. And that, without having been extensively bitten.

J:~ It must have been a very virulent stream of rabies, then.

M:~ It was very worrying. One dog was badly bitten on the face by a rabid fox and the fox would not let go.

[pause while tape is turned over]

M:~ The man beat the fox off, and the dog had been vaccinated but the instructions were that, when any animal had been bitten, it must be shut up – fed and watered – but shut up in a building from which it couldn't escape. That way, if it was going to develop rabies, it would do so safely for the rest of the family. Providing that it was fed and watered by somebody who realized that it might have become furious rabies over night and providing that the children couldn't get into the building to play with the dog. Oh, there were so darn many ifs and buts.

J:~ It must have been heartbreaking for some people to destroy not only the animals that were their livelihood, but there must have been pets, too.

M:~ *Oh quite. The Michalchuks lost their little pony that used to drive them to school every day. And, I mean, here were people who were fully aware of the dangers of rabies. The boys went out to harness up the horse in the morning to go to school and one boy went back into the house and told his mother that he couldn't get the horse to, I've forgotten, to get up or something. Annie went out and went to pull the horse up and realized that the animal had rabies and they got it out of the barn and it wandered around in the pasture for a while and then died. It wasn't furious rabies but it left the kids without a horse to take them to school and they lived three and a half miles away from the school and this little pony was the dear friend of the kids as well as a useful little animal. A nice little animal.*

The Hudson Bay man's pony, his son's pony… Raymond tried to get him to get up, tried to get a bit into the mouth and got the skin scraped off his knuckles on the horse's teeth and that was rabies. And Johnny Vos was feeling around a heifer's mouth because she didn't seem to be able to eat properly. He thought maybe she got a bit of a rosebush stuck under her tongue or something and the next day this was obvious rabies. There were so many cases that people figured that the only thing to do was to get rid of the animals. They'd ship them and they'd be getting a little money for them, even though it was nothing like they would have done if they'd been able to finish them properly.

J:~ How long did it take the wild animal population to come back?

M:~ *Well, the foxes, it's just been about the last three years. Wild foxes have been seen again but nothing like the density there was in the 1930s and '40s when you expected to see foxes and coyotes and skunks quite frequently. I mean, you see them occasionally now, but only occasionally. I had a big cross fox run through the yard here six months ago maybe. And for a second I didn't know what it was. It had been so long since I'd seen the cross fox running.*

J:~ Cross fox, is that C-R-O-S-S fox?

M:~ *Yes. They're the ones which are neither silver nor red. They have a dark sort of cross on their backs. I've got one upstairs I think, still. Frank gave me one.*

J:~ The devastation of the epidemic was really among animals, then, and people who were trying to live here who lost so much stock.

M:~ *How many animals – that'll be somewhere in the letters that you've got – were lost to the epidemic? Counting the animals who were disposed of, it ran into the thousands. But as far as animals that were actually killed by rabid animals, I don't know. Maybe 600 or a thousand in Fort Vermilion all the way to to Keg River and the Battle River district.*

J:~ People must have been very angry at what they saw as government inaction.

M:~ *People figured that something should be done about it but the problem was to know what to do. My theory was that, if you could reduce the population of wild animals ahead of the epidemic, so that when a fox had furious rabies it wouldn't find half a dozen other foxes to bite or half a dozen other animals to bite. That way you could stop the spread of the epidemic. But, that if you all did was wait for it go away you were going to lose just as many animals as if you had poisoned them. Domestic animals would be at infinitely greater risk than if you tried to reduce the exposure by reducing the number of particularly foxes, coyotes, wolves and lynx. But it was a … it's a problem that Ontario is facing right now. What are you going to do to protect animals against rabid animals?*

J:~ When did this later epidemic in Ontario start?

M:~ *I don't remember. Say in the 60s or 70s, quite a long time ago but they're still fighting it. You'd be able to get the statistics from the agriculture department. How many animals – it was in the newspaper not long ago, one of the farm papers, within the last few months – of how many heads had been examined in Lethbridge, how many tame animals and how many wild animals. They had one positive head in Alberta and it was assumed to have been from a Saskatchewan skunk that had brought in rabies to Southern Alberta. They're doing their best to avoid letting any sort of skunks in. But presumably the local epidemic in Southern Saskatchewan is dying out for lack of any more animals to bite.*

J:~ Did the government then call on the expertise of people in this area when they were dealing with the Ontario epidemic?

M:~ *Oh, there were some fellows came here and wanted to know all about the epidemic here and what we'd done, what we thought ought to be* done, what wild animals were the ones that were most dangerous. But they've still got lots of foxes and skunks in Ontario and still spreading rabies. We didn't have bats and how much the bats are to blame for the Ontario epidemic, I don't know. Certainly they've been losing a lot of animals year after year. A lot of farm animals, I mean, are being killed by rabies. How many people have been exposed, I don't know. But those people who have had to be vaccinated it's quite expensive and, of course, for the lab workers who study the heads of the animals that are sent in looking for rabies. These are highly skilled and hopefully reasonably well paid individuals. I mean, the amount of money that it is costing Ontario to pay every farmer for the cows or horses that are killed by rabies, it must be mounting up considerably. Whether they could have done anything when they first realized they'd got it, whether they could have done as they did in Alberta and kill everything in sight in the way of wild animals, I don't know. It was one alternative. You could either do nothing and wait till it died out or you could kill the animals before they got the rabies but to prevent the rabies spreading. It was a decision that was very difficult to make.

J :~ And that's what was done? Did they put a bounty on animals here?

M :~ No, they didn't put a bounty on them, which made us absolutely furious! Here were trappers who were quite capable of going to the bush and destroying animals and being paid for it! Wolves were particularly dangerous because a wolf can run 200 miles while it's rabid. Also, they think again … it's still very difficult to prove… The trappers were going to the bush and were trapping fur-bearing animals because this was their job. This was what they did. This was their livelihood. The government figured they shouldn't go into the bush at all and there were risks of being bitten by rabid animals. But they would have been the most competent individuals to put out poison and to kill animals. They would have happily killed the wolves if they'd been given a $10 bounty or something. And they needn't have handled the corpse and endangered themselves. They could have whacked off a tail to produce for the bounty or something. But, anyway, they did put out poisoned baits. I don't know how many. You could probably find that. The Department of Agriculture would probably have the records of how many thousand baits they put out.

J:~ Did they drop these from planes or how did they do this?

M:~ *No, they had people who put them out where the animals would be expected to find them. This again, I mean, they'd got to be skilled hunters and trappers. You didn't just throw them out around. They were, I believe, strychnine embedded in meat and put into little paper cups covered with tallow or something, so that in theory only the predator animals would take these baits. How many we killed and how many the rabies killed nobody will ever know. But it certainly ran into the thousands and thousands. And it is sort of heartbreaking to think of killing them deliberately. It was equally heartbreaking to see them dying slowly of a miserable disease like rabies. It is difficult to think of any more painful, miserable death.*

J:~ Even dumb rabies?

M:~ *Even the dumb rabies is bad enough.*

J:~ It's painful? Is it painful or is it just…? I mean, I guess you don't know.

M:~ *They lay down, they lay down and died. It took a day or two to die, I think. We, I mean, the farmers who knew their animals as individuals… to have to see them die of rabies was intolerable and the only way they could protect them was to send them to slaughter. Oh, it set farming in this district back by 20 years.*

J:~ In terms of establishing herds?

M:~ *These people had herds that were shipped. I mean, the bulls and the cows and heifers and the calves, everything. If you couldn't protect them, it was better to send them for slaughter or to be sold.*

J:~ So, you'd wipe out your entire breeding population.

M:~ *You wiped it out. So, you left the district with not even any milk cows and kids' ponies and so on. Several of them went rabid and they… there was some feeling of…that the government ought to have done something.*

J:~ Yes.

M:~ *This is the typical attitude, of course, but the point was, that if you were going to trap animals for your livelihood, the animals were supposed to belong to the government. You had to pay so much for your trapper's license and they would say whether this year beaver was closed or not and so on. They argued, "this is all Crown land. These are all government animals. They are killing our stock. You* ought to do something about it," which the government didn't! They are doing it in Ontario, paying them something.

J:~ So, it's interesting to think about whether it's just a risk of farming, like bad weather, that occasionally you may get rabies or whether it is the responsibility of a larger unit.

M:~ *They, the government, I think, was treating it as an act of God. We of course felt that while it was in the Northwest Territories would have been the time to try and stop it because the density of the animal population was so much lower. I think they had about seven years that they could have done something about it before it ever got to Alberta and the ranching and farming.*

J:~ So, it was just considered remote and there were so few people in the area, they didn't bother with the Territories.

M:~ *Whether there was an Eskimo death rate from rabies, I don't know. Certainly they knew rabies. It was a hazard that dogs might get bitten, the sleigh dogs might go rabid but whether those rabid sleigh dogs bit the children or not, I don't know. Or whether, even if the children had been bitten, it would have been recognized as rabies when they did, I don't know.*

J:~ So, this is again, this is the real frontier in terms of rabies. This is the first farming area that it hits and it's only when it begins to steamroll farther south that it is taken seriously.

M:~ *Fort Vermilion of course got hit particularly hard because they didn't know – it was the Kratzes crying the alarm – they didn't know rabies, you see. And one fellow – I've forgotten who it was – he fought off a rabid wolf, backing up all the way to the house. He had a pitchfork. This was all that he had to keep this animal at bay with. And another fellow ran up his wood pile to escape…I think it was a rabid wolf, but I wouldn't swear to that. Anyway, he yelled to his wife to get the gun and shoot the animal. It got the man's gumboot and pulled it off his foot, as the man got up the woodpile. That was how close he was being chased by this rabid animal and as the wolf bit and pulled the boot off his foot, his wife came out and shot the animal.*

We lived looking over our shoulders really for the first winter. It was really terrifying. You didn't dare to let the children play outside because you couldn't protect them from rabid animals. You didn't know if there were any rabid animals around but you'd see so many of them! The children managed to get to school all right but a lot of them, their parents were taking them.

J:~ So, it just fundamentally changed your, your approach to life.

M:~ It, absolutely, it altered life completely! Nowadays, there is nothing like as much risk because I don't think anywhere in Alberta there's anything like the density of wild animals that we had here. And the Forestry men, the Fish and Wildlife men are all being immunized. I think they were for a while. I haven't talked to any of them lately. And the treatment now is only 5 shots and with a very much less dangerous vaccine. I don't think there is any death rate from the present vaccine. And the diagnosis of rabies is very much modernized. They can give you the answer right away, practically.

J:~ It's an interesting example of what may have been a natural way of killing off overpopulation of wild animals. It is only perceived as a problem once you've got people in the area that you're going to affect. I mean, obviously in the Northwest Territories they would let it just go if there was no perceived damage to humans.

M:~ Well, of course. And this was complicated by the fact that the people were illiterate. They knew nothing of rabies. They couldn't read the story of Pasteur and the rabid wolf, which is more or less one of the things we were brought up on.

J:~ Yes, the classic story.

M:~ The nun stuck her hand down the throat of the wolf and saved the children. And, I mean, until I'd actually seen rabies I never realized why Pasteur would have started on a fairly rare disease. Now, if you'd seen it, you could see that it was very spectacular. Of course, his method of treatment or prevention was really sort of glorified guesswork. It was extraordinarily lucky that it worked. It might just as easily not have worked, but that was the method by which they were making vaccine for many many years.

J:~ Were you functioning as basically the public health officer at the point, unofficial?

M:~ Unofficial, strictly unofficial!

J:~ And unpaid.

M:~ And unpaid. But then, a lot of the jobs that I was doing were not exactly general practice. Certainly inoculating sleigh dogs was beyond the call of duty. On the other hand, if these dogs went rabid and developed furious rabies, they were a terrible danger to the people in the village. It was a good idea to try and prevent rabies. They are still talking bout vaccinating all domestic cats and dogs against rabies. This is why I've got to take my little dog, Sam, down. I think she's due for a rabies shot. They do them I think every three years.

J:~ My cat in Calgary has to have her rabies shot.

M:~ Well, it's a very good idea to the extent that it does protect most animals. You are unlikely to have your dog go rabid overnight and bite your child's face the next morning.

J:~ It also removes the threat of a growing epidemic, right? That's the same argument they use for why you should have your child vaccinated against whooping cough or all these other things that nobody gets any more, theoretically.

M:~ The fact that you have immunized the cats and dogs is of no protection in an area where cats and dogs are a minimal number of animals and there are thousands of foxes and coyotes and lots of others!

I showed you, did I, the fur list that I had written out for the book? This was the yield in the 20s. They weren't wiping out everything that they met. This was a sustainable yield, until there was enough competition by fur traders and prices, of course, went down so desperately during the Depression. They had to kill more foxes because of the need to have money to buy food or clothes or whatever. And ammunition. You had to kill more animals if the price of a fox went down from $100 to $25, you'd got to kill three more.

But there was a very dense population. We used to when we were riding…we were going to ride the saddle horse from here to Carcajou, which is a long day's ride, just about 40 miles, you see. And there'd be a skunk with a row of little skunks walking behind it and they'd walk deadly slowly about a mile an hour and no way would they get off the road and no way would you attempt to pass them. And so, you'd sort of amble down the road wondering if they were going to be a mile or two miles before they would get off onto their trail. What business had the on your trail instead of their own? But they were so pretty! The little skunks were most attractive little creatures.

And, of course, when Anne was a kid – she was around two years old – she was playing hide and seek with Louis and they were around the pond and she called out, "I see you! I see you!" But what was sticking around the corner of barn wasn't Louis but a silver fox and, *you know, this was a great joke that she had mistaken her fair-haired brother for a fox!*

J:~ So, you really had a variety of jobs. I mean, your medical practice was almost beyond belief! You were doctoring, you were birthing, you were doing lab work, you were the vet, you were a public health officer to some extent, you set up your own hospital.

M:~ *Well, it wasn't a hospital. It was a place for people to go*

J:~ Yes, the outpost.

M:~ *But it was a very useful place for a number of years. It was a solution to an impossible situation. There were so many people I couldn't have ridden out and back to. It just wasn't, there weren't enough hours in the day.*

J:~ Well, I should think not, with all the things you were doing!

M:~ *Well, I mean, if they moved in, they were only a quarter of a mile away and I could get back and forth twice a day and all.*

J:~ And these were mostly pregnancies that you had there? I know you had at least one sick child that you used penicillin on.

M:~ *Old people with pneumonia and people that had injuries of one kind or another. It was some place they could stay for a night or two until we got organized to get them back home or to make sure that they were doing all right.*

J:~ Were you also doing the nursing then to some extent?

M:~ *Well, mostly their relatives stayed and cared for them.*

J:~ So, they brought family with them.

M:~ *Everybody moved in, 'cause they were all used to moving around as families anyway. It was perfectly simple to pick up the wife and kids and move in when anyone was hurt or something. It was very useful. They split their own wood. They got their own water from the river. They brought their own food. It was simply their own house for the time being and I could go down and dress the child with scalds or whatever.*

J:~ Whereabouts was it located?

M:~ *Well, just over a quarter of a mile from here. It was the old Revillon Brothers Trading Post. There had been Revllion's and Frank's and the Hudson Bay posts and the village around. The houses were all far enough apart that they weren't in each other's hair too badly.*

J:~ And the village is now gone.

M:~ *The village is now gone.*

J:~ And where was that? Was it on, right on the main street?

M:~ *It's right where you were, with the little church and the library and the community hall. It was on part of a quarter section that was set aside for Indian/Metis settlement and the houses were along the river. They were little log houses with sod roofs that had grown up to weeds, so they were almost invisible.*

J:~ Are there any remains left of them now?

M:~ *I don't think so. I think somebody said the other day that someone was still living there, but no, it's all gone.*

[pause while tape is turned over]

J:~ At the same time you're handling this unusual medical practice, you were...you described yourself the other day as a farm wife.

M:~ *Well, I was a farm wife!*

J:~ So, there was the threshing crews and your own gardening and... how did you find time? You said just a minute ago there weren't enough hours in the day. I'm surprised you had as many hours as you did.

M:~ *Oh, I managed all right. Of course, I had two stepsons who were very competent and I had a husband who was a super expert at most things and then I had two children who were busy.*

J:~ And the family must all have supported what you were doing or considered your work important.

M:~ *Oh, I was going to say, they didn't think anything about it. I mean, this is what I did and that's what they did. From the time they were big enough to stagger into the house with one stick of wood at a time, they filled the wood box. And the boys used to go and hunt prairie chickens and geese and ducks and get fish out of the river, help with the gardening and help with the cooking when I had to leave and go off some place in a hurry.*

J:~ Yes, you mentioned that the children learned to work when they were very young.

M:~ *The children learned to cook very young and Louis became an exceedingly good cook and Anne and Bob both became very good cooks partly, because of my sort of rushing off periodically leaving them to go on with whatever I'd been cooking, or to cope.*

J:~ So, you'd have to go off in an emergency situation and the family was left to shift for itself.

M:~ *Oh yes. And some of the emergencies were so far away that... I mean, I'd go down to Carcajou for a few days, leaving the family. They'd got to be able to cook and they enjoyed cooking and both of them have become absolutely first rate cooks by any standards.*

J:~ So, it all fit in. Your lifestyle is very much of a whole, it was very whole.

M:~ *It was absolutely... As I say, you'd get up in the morning and you never knew where you were even going to be by night! People would come for you and the children said you could tell how much of an emergency it was by how fast they were riding. If they were coming in to get you to something that was really desperate, they were coming at a full gallop. And really, I hardly had any false alarms. Most of them, when they figured that they had something they needed a doctor for....
It was sufficiently difficult to get a doctor. I mean they either had to ride in to get me or they had to bring the patient over. So there weren't any, there weren't many false alarms, most of them were true ills, all right. They figured it was an emergency. I didn't have to think well, what a waste of time.*

J:~ This fits in with your comment to me once that you got to do more real medicine here than you would have gotten to do if you had stayed in England.

M:~ *Well, nobody came to see the doctor to see if they were fit to go jogging or whatever! Very few of them brought in well babies to see if the babies were well. What they brought in were sick babies because they knew they were sick. But I managed to get them once a year. I would round up the year's crop of babies and vaccinate them, against diphtheria, pertussis and tetanus – DPT in those days – and vaccinate them against smallpox.*

But the reason that I got to vaccinate the kids is because they'd had an epidemic of smallpox here in 1922, 21 or 22, some argument as to the date. They had seen a large number of people die of smallpox. Well, I was able to explain to them that if I gave them one little spot of smallpox then they would have had it and they wouldn't get it. At least they got something to show! If I gave them smallpox vaccine, they developed this little smallpox pustule. But if you gave them a shot to protect the child against whooping cough or diphtheria or whatever you

stuck a needle in and the baby screamed bloody murder and the baby
probably was fussy all night and you hadn't got anything to show for it!

But Sarah Martineau of the Paddle had seen a diphtheria
epidemic before they moved to Paddle Prairie and she was able
to explain to people what diphtheria was like and why it was well
worthwhile having the babies immunized. And that wouldn't have
convinced them half as much as when the whooping cough vaccine
came in. They'd seen every time there was whooping cough always
one or two children died and one of them who narrowly missed dying
was my little son. He started whooping on his first birthday and he'd
been just sort of starting to walk. He was eighteen months old before
he walked. It had put him right flat back. He couldn't even sit up in
bed. He was desperately ill for a while. He'd just sort of regained from
being a premature baby to being a normal size and a normal child
and then he got hit with whooping cough. A number of children had
died of whooping cough.

J:~ So, that was important in terms of making them think that the
doctor's mumbo jumbo made some sense.

M:~ Well, if you could promise that if they had the child vaccinated it
wouldn't get whooping cough and when they saw that it didn't get
whooping cough, this was quite convincing! The tragedy was, of
course, that we couldn't get the Mennonite population to accept
any vaccination against particularly tragic polio here – because
they considered that was God's will. It was particularly difficult. A
group of them who left – Old Colony Mennonites who left and
went to Bolivia – came back, a number of them came back, without
the children that they'd taken because they'd run into an epidemic
of diphtheria in Bolivia. The only children who survived were the
children who had been vaccinated in Fort Vermilion. This was
kind of a convincing demonstration. Very tragic but we had done
our best. And even the Kratzes, who were German speaking and
could communicate with these people, hadn't managed to get them
persuaded to be vaccinated against polio.

J:~ Did they become a dangerous locus of disease then for other
people or did they pretty much stay within their community?

M:~ No. I was going to say they stayed within their own community. They
had a disastrous polio epidemic. I've forgotten how many children
died but I mean it was a particularly virulent outbreak.

J:~ So, this was after the Salk vaccine was available that they had the epidemic.

M:~ *Yes, in the 50s.*

J:~ Well, I know when the Salk vaccine came in. I was a Polio Pioneer, so I was one of the many school children it was tested on. So, that was the 1950s.

M:~ *I should think it was the early 50s. Of course, that revolutionized medicine, too. You didn't spend all summer wondering about a child with fever and a vague illness and wondering was it going to turn out to be polio.*

The Mennonite people were particularly difficult to persuade. And a lot of the old Indian grandmothers couldn't see the point of sticking a needle into a healthy baby. But they got the idea after a while. I mean the dramatic drop in the number of children who got whooping cough within a few years made it quite obvious that it was the kids who'd had the shots didn't get it.

J:~ How much were people paying you for a house call of 40 miles or more, 80 miles round trip?

M:~ *A lot of them didn't have any money to pay with but they gave me what they had. The Mennonites in Carcajou made some of these perfectly beautiful, light as a feather quilts made out of their own sheep's wool. I tried to resurrect one wool comforter. You know, you wash them and you have to do them with carding things again.*

J:~ Yes.

M:~ *Makes my shoulders ache to think about it. I had no idea how difficult it was going to be. When I took a whole quilt apart and imagined it was going to take two or three evenings, you know. I think it took me a month before I got the quilt reconstituted!*

J:~ So, in a lot of ways what you had was a barter sort of situation, often.

M:~ *It wasn't a question of barter. I gave them what I had to give them and they gave me what they had to give me. I mean somebody would bring me a bucket of wild strawberries and I knew how long it had taken to pick those wild strawberries and I was very grateful. I might have treated the baby for pneumonia in the winter but they didn't have any money to pay me but come summertime, they brought me a present.*

J:~ So people tried…

M:~ *They gave me moose meat,*

J:~ And so it was really very much for everybody in the community giving what they had to give and what you had to give was outside medical knowledge.

M:~ *Yes, it was the Indian way of what you had, you shared. So, if your moccasins were worn out, somebody would make a pair for you. And beautiful moccasins they were! And it wasn't thought of as payment or barter. It was a present. And it was treated with gratitude.*

J:~ So, your doctoring them also would have been viewed as a present

M:~ *Yes, this was something that I could do...*

J:~ ... you had it to give...

M:~ *... and therefore should do. If they had the money to pay for the medicines, how nice!*

J:~ But you were also cadging money from the Fellowship of the Maple Leaf for medicines.

M:~ *Oh, absolutely! And my parents and uncles and aunts sent me money for Christmas or birthday presents and so on. Very handy.*

J:~ So, that's a lot of what you really were. You were a real connection with the outside world on a lot of levels. I mean you were also in the rabies epidemic you were writing and complaining, generally.

M:~ *As loudly as I knew how!*

J:~ So that's another part of your job in the community.

M:~ *So was Frank, of course, particularly when it came to the rabies epidemic. I typed his letters for him and diluted his language a bit on occasion because telling the government officials what you thought of them did no good. You might as well be as tactful as possible. We wrote to Solon Low and we wrote to Floyd Gilliland and we wrote to the provincial Minister of Agriculture or whatever he was. We wrote to the federal health of animals people. We wrote to local vets and Frank wrote to cattle ranchers that he knew, warning them of what was coming and what it looked like and to watch out, for God's sake, watch out for foxes that were acting strangely. Any animal that was acting strangely was rabies until you proved it wasn't and, for Heaven sakes, be careful with the kids! Don't let them out of your sight because the rabid animal who comes out of the bush is going to bite anything that moves if it's got furious rabies.*

J:~ So there's all that part of what you were doing, as well, which is the connection of somebody who knows who to complain to at least, I would think.

M:~ *Well, yes. And using Frank's old typewriter, which was a genuine antique. Why on earth he gave it away! Well, of course, we didn't' think about it as being potentially valuable.*

J:~ Oh, I'm sure.

M:~ *But that was the typewriter that Frank got that was before the standard keyboard. And I had never learned to type, then learnt on this machine and of course had never been a good typewriter on the standard machine because I never learned to … fingers didn't go in the right place.*

J:~ Everything's in the wrong place.

M:~ *I'd type with a lot of mistakes but Frank used to tell me what he wanted said and I would put down what I thought.*

J:~ You would translate into acceptable language,

M:~ *Yes, absolutely.*

J:~ I wanted to ask you… I warned you of this. It's terrible when somebody says what was your favorite or what was the best, but I was just wondering if you could talk for a couple of minutes about your most interesting cases. We talked about one yesterday, the woman with the leaky heart valve.

M:~ *It was so interesting getting the odd case like the woman whose budgie got psittacosis. I mean, she and her sister bought budgies in Grande Prairie when they were there. They were such pretty birds. So she brought this pretty bird home to Keg River. I didn't know anything about it but I did a house call because she had, because she was very sick. And she had a weird pneumonia and she also had, which she hadn't had on previous house calls, she had this budgie. And I said, "oh when did you get the bird?" And she said, "we got them in Grande Prairie when we were out there." She said her sister's bird had died. And I put two and two together and made six very promptly, you see, and I got the … I can't think of his name now. Heaven knows. I knew him well enough. He was the sanitary inspector from Peace River Health Unit. He was also the mayor of Peace River and a good friend. Anyway, he came up and removed the budgie which had psittacosis and so did my patient. And when you know the diagnosis it's all right, it's easy enough to find the right treatment, you see.*

I mean, what an odd sort of disease to get in Northern Alberta in an isolated place like Keg River.

J:~ Which would have to do with increasing prosperity, being able to bring in those types of birds.

M:~ *Oh quite, but I would never have guessed from her chest that she'd got psittacosis.*

J:~ It was the budgie that made you suspicious.

M:~ *All I did was put two and two together. This had to be, this absolutely had to be that this animal, this creature, was spreading psittacosis.*

J:~ What date approximately? What year?

M:~ *I don't know. Twenty years ago, I suppose. I don't know. They've left the country now though Anne said she'd seen her not so long ago. I didn't even know they were in the North anymore.*

J:~ So, that was one.

M:~ *And then there was the woman at Paddle Prairie who got tularemia, the rabbit fever. Which I missed completely. She got these great big swollen glands and the nurse – I've forgotten how the nurse who was the government health nurse at Fort Vermilion happened to be in Paddle Prairie – happened to see this woman on her way to come and visit me. She suggested that this was tularemia, which I had never seen and knew nothing about it. But this was the answer to that one.*

J:~ Where would you get tularemia from

M:~ *Rabbit fever. Some of the people were…some of the patients died…oh, give me the Merck! I don't know if tularemia would be in here but it should be. I haven't thought about it for years.*

J:~ Would they get it from just working with the rabbits?

M:~ *Presumably, it was be an infection in her hands, via her hands, I mean. But what I would have thought that she had, I don't know.*

[tape turned off while Merck is consulted]

J:~ You're saying this is another rare disease.

M:~ *Tularemia was mercifully a rare disease in the country but this woman got it. And thanks to the nurse who spotted and told me what she thought it was! So, the woman recovered!*

J:~ You said the other day that you made a point of – when you sent somebody out -saying what you thought your diagnosis was. You said they could think you were an idiot or not.

M:~ *It made you read up whatever – hence the manual.* [Referring to the Merck] *Every edition as it came out I have bought, you see – which is nearly as up to date as anything I could get for reference.*

And if I was going to send a patient out and merely record what the
patient had in the way of symptoms and not say what I thought…
Well it made me…it kept me on my toes more or less because if I
sent them out and said what I thought what was the matter with
them and this was absolutely far out and crazy, they would know
that I was bushed!

J:~ (laughs). Well, they'd hardly recall you since nobody was paying
you up here anyway.

M:~ *Oh yes, quite. But when we had a case of pellagra, the woman
unfortunately died. She was a Metis woman from Paddle Prairie
and I figure I was sticking my neck right out when I sent her down to
Edmonton with a diagnosis of pellagra which, as far as I know, didn't
occur in Alberta. But this was pellagra as far I could figure.*

J:~ So, a deficiency disease.

M:~ *She died a day or two later, in Ponoka. They figured that this was
right enough, that the diagnosis was correct but since she was dead it
wasn't of any very great importance to anybody.*

*It's sad that she was dead because, if I had seen her before she tried
to commit suicide, I might have thought, this being pellagra, let's
try and treat it. And she might have recovered because people were
recovering in droves in the southern United States where they had, I
don't know, thousands of people in mental hospitals with pellagra.
There were lots of people dying of pellagra. I know the moment that
they knew what it was due to, they sort of emptied the hospitals and
you could reverse it almost over night. They were living on hominy
grits and salt pork, I think, was the diet, and it lacked this necessary …*

J:~ Is it B vitamin or a trace element?

M:~ *It's one of the B vitamins. It may be still in here.* [consults Merck] *I
don't think pellagra's disappeared in the world.*

[tape turned off while medical research ensues]

J:~ Repeat what you said about the leishmaniasis.

M:~ *Yes, the Mennonite fellow who got the Brazilian leishmaniasis which
very nearly killed him. He had presumably got it from his mother 22
years before and waited to bring it from Paraguay to La Crete before
he developed this very peculiar condition. His soft pallet was hard
and indurated and sort of fissured. And when I felt it, he'd already
been on penicillin tablets from the doctor at Fort Vermilion. He*

said he'd complained of a sore throat so he'd been given penicillin tablets and they'd done him no good and he was getting worse. And I thought that this was a malignancy but a man of 22 couldn't have a malignancy of his palette and uvula, or could he?

And it happened that the Cross cancer people send doctors up to Peace River periodically. They see a whole lot of cancer follow up cases. It saves them all going down to the city. And they had this clinic in Peace River and I got this man out in a tearing hurry because this would save him going all the way to Edmonton to go and see the expert and see if he thought it was cancer. And I thought he would probably do a biopsy or something. And anyway he took him on down to Edmonton and he said this was Brazilian leishmaniasis. It was certainly over a year before he went to Winnipeg to visit relatives there because he was going to die and they thought it might be connected with this ulcer on her leg that – why they'd even think about that – his mother had when they came to Winnipeg all this long, long time ago. This fellow had had this organism in his throat or whatever waiting all this time to develop in an outlying place like La Crete!

J:~ So it wasn't until somebody started thinking about it in the right way that you could even ask the right questions and do the right tests.

M:~ I had asked if he'd ever been out of Canada. And if he'd have said that he had been born in Paraguay, it still wouldn't have clicked that this could have anything to do with where he'd come from over 20 years ago. But he was 22 at the time, I think, and he'd been born in Paraguay and had been a toddler when he came to Canada and I mean he'd been a perfectly healthy individual until he developed this weird sore throat. Which, if I had happened to have looked it up in the skintext book there was even a picture of it, but I...

J:~ ... didn't think to look

M:~ You don't think about tropical diseases...

J:~ ... up here...

M:~ ... up here. But I have diligently asked all Mennonites since then if they've ever been out of Canada and, if so, where because there was one of them that had had malaria and had a monstrous enlargement of his spleen. You know, I'd never even dreamed of a spleen that size. Here was this man with this abdominal tumor and the answer was malaria.

Just one of those things but medicine is going to be easier when you can punch the symptoms into a computer and the computer will, in a few minutes, hand you a list of all the weird possibilities of all the weird diseases that might have occurred in any part of the world.

J:~ And then you can go looking.

M:~ *Well, then you can start knowing that this could be, oh, everything from leprosy upwards! No end of a help, I think. Maybe not as exciting but definitely quicker.*

J:~ I wanted to ask you one last question which is how did your practice change when health care came in and there was medical insurance to pay for people's treatment and tests.

M:~ *Oh, when insurance first started it was long before medicare, you know. In Alberta you could get, I've forgotten what we called it, some of the teachers had this insurance and so one got paid. This was very sensible medicare because they charged enough premiums to cover the costs of what had been paid out. If the ... when they paid the doctors they only paid them 75% of what the fee was. And if at the end of the year there was enough money in the kitty, the doctors would get the additional. But if there wasn't, the premiums went up the next year, but they always made the premiums balance with the expenditures. And it worked very nicely because it was run by doctors for doctors*

J:~ This is the end of the second interview. [We likely repaired for tea.]

In her tomato garden.

Checking out the apple tree.

Receiving the order of Canada, 1990.

~: Epilogue

Mary Evangeline Percy Jackson died 6 May 2000, a few months short of her 96th birthday. Only at the very end was she unable to live independently, albeit with care and attention provided by friends and neighbors. She had had to leave her home in Keg River in 1996 to be closer to medical care and, fittingly, moved back to Battle River Prairie, long since renamed Manning. Even then, she chose to take trips to Calgary and Edmonton, to speak in public and to receive well-deserved recognition.

She lies beside Frank in the little cemetery I walked out to visit on my first cold visit to Keg River. They share a tombstone and Anne was careful to fit on all her mother's letters of distinction: "M.B. CH.B. M.R.C.S. L.R.C.P. O.C. L.L. D." The warm day I visited, the poplars had just come to full leaf and were whispering in the breeze.

⁓ Index